In prai   Jp

"This is an excellent book to help navigate the often highly pressurised environment that those working in the advertising industry encounter. Tuning Up is frank and honest about these challenges but also provides invaluable tools and insights to help navigate the modern creative workplace whether your new into it or have been in it for many years like me. A timely book right for the moment and another essential read from David."

Pete Markey
CMO, Boots

"F****** BRILLIANT. Finally the 'pressure makes diamonds' approach in our industry can be put to bed thanks to the Meikle Matrix. It should be an absolute joy to be part of the creative industry, surrounded by the brightest, most eclectic and colourful minds in the land. And by removing the unnecessary stress and pressure, we can once again be proud to be a part of it."

Aimee Luther
Managing Director, The Liberty Guild.

"It took me thirty years to learn that stress is a really dumb proxy measure for personal productivity. Just because you feel like crap doesn't mean you're doing a good job. What took me three decades and a series of panic attacks to understand, David's book will teach you in a few hours."

Rory Sutherland
TED Speaker; Vice Chairman, Ogilvy UK

"This book is gold dust if (like me) you believe in the concept of freedom, and you have the confidence to believe that businesses perform better when they give people the autonomy to excel. I'm so happy that David has written this book and articulated the concept far better than I have ever done. The theory of responsibility & control is a great framework for success in unleashing the potential within teams, as well as client/agency relationships."

Jenny Biggam
Founder, the7stars

A good model offers explanatory power, helping you make sense of complex issues. A great model makes you feel as though you have discovered a secret view into how the world really works. Tuning Up delivers such a secret. It took me from "Holy sh*t!" to "Of course; it's so obvious now" in only a few pages. It is now the lens through which I look at client-agency relationships and the role of marketing procurement in particular.

Blair Enns, Author, The Win Without Pitching Manifesto &
Pricing Creativity: A Guide to Profit Beyond the Billable Hour

"For an industry that constantly seems to jam, Tuning Up is a brilliant handbook to get the best from its people. Tuning Up is simple but not simplistic, practical but not pedestrian, and a great read overall; one that can get people working and performing in sync and not playing on top of each other."

Antonis Kocheilas
Global CEO, Ogilvy Advertising

"Tuning Up is a fantastic handbook full of lively stories and helpful tips for anyone working in the advertising industry who manages people and cares about their wellbeing. David unpicks the relationship between responsibility and control and looks at what happens when the equilibrium is out of whack. The book explores the pressures faced by most individuals working in an ever-changing industry where the stakes are high, although as David quite rightly acknowledges, we're not saving lives. The book also examines the most common stress-inducing situations and suggests ways in which people can approach them with a different outlook to help maintain perspective and remain productive in their jobs. David's writing is engaging and lucid, and his advice is practical. This is a great read."

Dame Annette King, DBE
Chair, The Advertising Association

"Tuning Up is an important book. It tackles head one of the key reasons we lose talent from our industry, which is unnecessary stress. If everyone understood the brilliant Meikle Matrix and acted accordingly, our industry would fast become a better, more sustainable one to work in. So, please read it and pass it on."

Jamie Elliott,
CEO, The Gate

"In contrast to many business books that are just bloated blog posts, Tuning Up never outstays its welcome. The core concept is simple but profound, and David deftly illustrates it through a range of complementary perspectives. It's the kind of book you'd happily recommend, knowing that readers will apply the learnings for years to come."

Robin Bonn
Founder, Co:definery and Marketing Week columnist.

"With his customary light touch, David Meikle distils a huge amount of real professional experience in this book. He tames the elephant in the room of client-agency relationships."

David Abrahams,
Director, Brand Mediation; Author, Brand Risk.

Edited and designed by:
Softwood Self-Publishing - swspublishing.com

Published by:
Lishakill Publishing
The Oven
1 High Street
Banbury
OX15 4BZ

Enquiries: www.lishakillpublishing.com

ISBN: 978-1-7394637-1-7

For those from whom I have learned most -
my mother and father, and my brother.

Note from the author

Tuning Up's purpose is to help those in the marketing and advertising business improve their performance and reduce their stress. Although, make no mistake, it isn't always easy.

If you are reaching for this book because you are routinely stressed by work, as much as it's my intention for this book to help, don't rely on these pages for an immediate solution. If you're under intolerable stress see your doctor straight away.

In the UK you can also find more information and support from all the resources listed below. Use them, any of them would be glad to support you.

MIND
www.mind.org.uk
Mind offers information and advice to people with mental health problems and lobbies government and local authorities on their behalf.

National Advertising Benevolent Society
www.nabs.org.uk
NABS is the employee support organisation for the advertising and media industry. We work in an incredibly exciting profession. But it can also be an extremely challenging one. NABS understands that it's often hard to keep up in a business that's constantly evolving. So we're here to bring out the best in you. We always start with a simple question: how's work? The response though is rarely straightforward. You may be looking for career guidance. Or there could be a skills or knowledge gap we can help you fill. Then again, the issue might be of a very personal and complex nature. Whatever you're going through, NABS is here for you. And because we're a charity it won't cost you a thing.

The Campaign Against Living Miserably

www.thecalmzone.net

Campaign Against Living Miserably, or CALM, is a registered charity based in England. CALM run a free, confidential and anonymous helpline as well as a webchat service, offering help, advice and information to anyone who is struggling or in crisis.

The Samaritans

www.samaritans.org

Call 116123

The Samaritans is a registered charity in the United Kingdom and Ireland that focuses on providing assistance to individuals who are experiencing emotional difficulties – finding it hard to manage, or in danger of taking their own lives. They typically provide aid through their telephone helpline.

Mental Health First Aid England

mhfaengland.org

MHFA helps organisations improve the mental health of their employees. For 15 years, they have been initiating discussions about mental health in the workplace, and they recognize that becoming an effective MHFAider® necessitates ongoing education and support beyond the initial training.

tuning p

improving performance
and reducing stress in
advertising and marketing

David Meikle
Author of best seller *How to Buy a Gorilla*

Contents

Managing stress for ourselves.
In Part Three we look at the Meikle Matrix for individuals, how responsibility and control manifest differently for different roles and how we can Tune Up our relationships for improved productivity and personal wellbeing.

Introduction

"To be in hell is to drift; to be in heaven is to steer."

George Bernard Shaw, playwright and critic, 1856 - 1950

It is both ironic and tragic that the marketing and advertising industries, which both pride themselves and rely upon on their deep understanding of consumers' motivations and emotions, can also be so frequently ignorant of the motivations and emotions of their own people, which so affect their performance and therefore upon whom their businesses depend.

Marketing and advertising are well known to be tough businesses. High speed, high pressure, and high stakes, with dog-eat-dog cultures, where, paradoxically, experience is highly valued but age often counts against more experienced people.

At the start of my career in advertising I was also told it was an unavoidably stressful industry; I was told it would be difficult; I was told I would have to be able to move mountains to meet deadlines, sell ideas convincingly, handle difficult people, be persuasive to colleagues and clients, sometimes even lie – but, at the same time, be as infallible as the Pope and all the time be a 'people person' who could win others' confidence and trust. To be successful as account handlers or 'suits', as we used to be so unaffectionately known, we had to satisfy the greatest number of departmental stakeholders, across all departments, as well as our clients – and make money for the agency – all at the same time.

As my career progressed and I moved to bigger and better agencies, I'm glad to say that much of the sharp practice I had been warned about was limited to those companies that used them as coping strategies for their people's relative inexperience or ineptitude. However, pressure and stress were consistent themes as the stakes grew higher because the clients and budgets I managed also grew larger. People are different and they respond to pressure and stress differently. But there's an important distinction to be made between being busy, i.e., under pressure, and being stressed. And there is a fine line between having just the right amount of pressure (busyness) for us to perform optimally (be that too much or too little pressure for you specifically) and too much pressure tipping over into stress that can harm our mental and physical health and compromise or ruin our performance.

Thankfully, in more recent years, agencies and their clients have increased their investments in their people's mental health and general well-being at work, but much of the attention seems focused on managing the symptoms of stress rather than the cause. The purpose of this book is to address the latter, but not just for agencies; marketers can experience equally unbearable stress, too. What I've found from my experience in both roles and that of others is, far more often than not, the stress is caused because we're playing *out of tune*.

Throughout my career in advertising, I seemed to stumble into trouble-shooting roles more than most. So, by default rather than design, I found myself in positions that some would judge to be very high pressure and stressful. But in 2001, I happened across an insight about life and work that changed everything for me. It prevented the enormous pressure I was under from tipping over from unmanageable stress to illness. At the same time, it improved my performance and enabled me to contribute greater value at work. Since then, I have used it not just for myself and my performance, but I have also used it when managing and working with others. I used it for relationships with my clients during the rest of my agency career, when building a management team and running an agency, I've used it as a marketer, and now as a consultant – I use it both when operating with my own clients and when designing client and agency relationships for them. From this insight I developed a model: the Meikle Matrix (for those who are not from Scotland, Meikle is pronounced MEE-*kuhl*).

Although I didn't know it at the time, what felt like a heart attack was probably where this book began. Like many ideas, *Tuning Up* was inspired by the solution to a problem – necessity is the mother of invention; change comes from a crisis, etc. Rather than a physical condition, it transpired that I was suffering from a mental condition that manifested physiologically – it could be described as something like a near-permanent panic attack.

By way of explanation (and readers of my first book, *How to Buy a Gorilla*, will have to forgive me as I go over a little old ground for them), in 2001, I was working in advertising as a business director for Ogilvy & Mather in London on their newly-won global account for BP.

Within a year of starting my new position at Ogilvy London we had to launch a new BP retail offer, called BP Connect, both in the US and the UK. BP's global retail account was run from Ogilvy's Chicago office, close to BP's global retail head office. While I knew we needed to develop some TV ads to support the launch, somewhat out of the blue I was asked to go to Los Angeles with a small team from the UK to oversee the production of three new TV commercials to make sure they didn't look 'too American' for the British market. In February 2001, I duly went to LA to make the ads with three colleagues: a copywriter, Mark Cooper, a TV producer, Nicole, and an account coordinator, Felicity. None of us had seen any advertising ideas from our Chicago office, but we were told not to worry about it and we'd see their work when we got to LA. Mark and I were under the illusion that this was a supervisory role, which simply required us to stay in a nice hotel in LA and look at other people's work, casting our pearls of strategic and creative wisdom whenever required – a pretty good gig, really.

When we first saw the ads developed by our colleagues from Chicago our hearts sank like synchronised swimmers. As the saying goes, you can't polish a turd, but these we couldn't even roll in glitter. The style, the tone, the material was all totally wrong for the UK, and without some major intervention, the new campaign for the company formerly known as British Petroleum would have become a laughingstock to the British public and a source of huge embarrassment for the agency. We couldn't see how the ads could possibly work.

Mark and I were told the storyboards were already agreed and we needed to rewrite the scripts with new voiceovers to make them suitable for the UK (we would have the chance to approve casting, sets, cars, and so forth, later). After a long day of one rolling pre-production meeting, we returned to our hotel in Century City and started to work on the first script. Our ambition, and I confess we were aiming low given the available time and creative material, was to make the ad we had been given into something we considered 'unembarrassing'. It felt like both a reasonable and a realistic standard to which we could aspire.

But it was harder than we first thought. We worked late into the early hours, and the following day, bleary-eyed, I presented our adaptation of Chicago's script to my assembled group of colleagues from the UK and the US and the commercials director we would be working with, called Leslie Dektor, and his team in their offices.

Surprisingly, what Mark and I considered to be only unembarrassing was far better received by Leslie than we had anticipated – he loved the rework. He felt we had developed the story, the central character had much more personality, and we'd even injected a little humour. So, Leslie innocently asked our Chicago colleagues if *they* could adapt *their* script to be a little more like ours. Leslie's request did not go down well. But with the client flying in at any moment, it was difficult to deny, so off went their team to try to make their work as good as our 'unembarrassing' version.

To our horror, the next day we found the Chicago team had developed a whole new idea, which sent me and Mark straight back to the drawing-board. They had trashed their original script, and consequently our work along with it became collateral damage. Apparently, the storyboards weren't as fixed as we had been told. Once again, the Chicago team had something to shoot, but Mark and I had nothing. So, once again, we worked through the night (bear in mind this was the first of three scripts), with the clock ticking down to the start of the shoot the following week. In the meantime, locations, casting, sets, and wardrobe were all being approved – which was a painful enough process.

"You never know what is enough unless you know what is more than enough."

The Marriage of Heaven and Hell, William Blake 1757 - 1827

By the end of our first week in LA, I discovered I had a constant feeling of something like a ten-kilo weight pressing on my sternum and wondered if I might be about to have a heart attack. The weight was there from when I woke in the morning until I fell asleep at night and lasted the duration of the trip – about 6 weeks in total. And when I returned to London the feeling was still there. I gave up alcohol and coffee, visited a stress counsellor; I listened to her tapes and went to her sessions and still made no improvement. Increasingly worried about my condition, I asked to see a doctor by way of Ogilvy's HR department, and, after a little negotiation, HR arranged an appointment for me to see a private GP near Ogilvy's offices.

I met a young doctor, probably no older than me at the time – I was only 31. He was memorably calm, kind, and sympathetic. He smiled, sat me down, and simply asked me what the problem was.

Over the following 45 minutes I broke down into a wreck. I described my job, the shoot in LA, working through the night, presenting scripts to the client while on location, the weight on my chest, the stress tapes, giving up coffee and drink, everything. Throughout my story the doctor listened attentively, and finally he gave me a broad, comforting smile and sat back in his chair.

I remember thinking, *Am I about to be medicated so I can do my job? Should anybody have to be medicated to do their job?*

But instead, the doc said, "I think I know what your problem is."

Yeah-right ...for sure you do. said a sarcastic and ungrateful voice in my head.

"You have responsibility without control ..." said the doctor "... which is a clinical definition of stress."

He was right. I had responsibility for the BP retail account for the whole of Europe and I had been under the control of the Ogilvy Chicago office, limited by their talent and that talent's ability. Admittedly, they had responsibility for the BP retail business globally, but we hadn't had a conversation about responsibility in my territory when Chicago retained disproportionate control over the development of the creative work.

There's a negotiation technique described as taking a balcony view. Negotiators look beyond the substance of the negotiation to what's going on between the negotiators – how they're feeling and behaving.

The doctor had shown me the balcony view of my own circumstances, and once I'd seen it, I couldn't un-see it. In that moment in the doctor's little consultation room, I saw every relationship in my life, with friends, bosses, people reporting to me, my colleagues across the pond – I could see them all through this lens of responsibility and control.

And within a few short minutes of the doctor uttering those words, the weight lifted from my chest. It was completely gone. As if by magic.

I have told this story many times, in speeches, presentations, and in training sessions, and – unfailingly – this story and the Meikle Matrix model I developed as a result of it, has connected with my audiences and training delegates the most.

The Ogilvy network had rushed into solving problems and making ads and generally doing stuff, without *Tuning Up* first. Admittedly, this was in response to a very demanding client that had been instructed to work exclusively with Ogilvy – worldwide – before the agency had a chance to manage a migration of the BP account properly.

But in that moment, simply by consciously recognising where both responsibility and control lay for the work I was doing, I immediately had an understanding so profound that the stress disappeared completely. From then on, at the first sign of stress, I was able to manage it far better. First by recognising what was going on – that something was out of tune – and then by discussing what I was supposed to do or not do, achieve or not achieve, based on the degree of control I had and whether it was compatible with the responsibility I was taking or being given. I *Tuned Up*.

Times come in our lives when we cannot avoid huge responsibility and we cannot change the small amount of control we have – but just by consciously recognising it I found I could reduce my stress level, simply by understanding its cause. The next step was to understand how to improve things.

Back in the doctor's surgery I realised I had two options: either assume greater control in my work such that it was consistent with my responsibility or make clear that I could not be responsible for the outcomes of my work if I did not have enough control over it. In such plain terms this might have seemed like an exercise in the blindingly obvious. But such is the nature of the work we do in advertising and marketing, and our emotional investment in it, the imbalanced apportionment of responsibility and control can be emergent. Often, we don't notice how stressful our situations have become until they either manifest in our poor mental and/or physical health, pass until the next time, or culminate in disaster.

Not a lot of good comes from that kind of work-related stress. We lose patience. We find it harder to listen. We find it more difficult to accommodate another point of view, idea, or perspective. Our relationships in and out of work suffer. And the work suffers.

Throughout my personal and professional lives I have been both fortunate and unfortunate enough to have had experiences at the extreme ends of these combined parameters of responsibility and control; some before, but most after this epiphany. Many of these extreme experiences came after my time on BP and during the four years I spent running Ogilvy's agency in Moscow during the BRIC boom period of extraordinary growth on the early 2000s. As a country of extremes, Russia provided many circumstances at the far ends of the scales of responsibility and control, so I can make no apology for the multiple references to my time there. (International relations were much happier and more civilised then than they have been in more recent years since the dreadful invasions of Ukraine.) But stories of extreme stress and its consequences are found in all walks of life, and as you'll see I've called on many others' stories than just my own. I hope you find them all as bizarre, entertaining, and ultimately useful as I have. However, many of my own felt anything but entertaining at the time.

Although I knew advertising could be a stressful career when I began, the nature of that stress and its impact was understated. Stress was considered an occupational hazard, something that just comes with the turf. But I don't believe it has to be.

So, whether you're wet-behind-the-ears or long-in-the-tooth in your career in advertising and/or marketing, I hope in this book I will have laid out and codified the benefit of my experience and my understanding of responsibility and control so that you can have a better path ahead. My hope is that it will either help you *Tune Up* your working relationships (maybe other kinds of relationships, too) and reduce the stresses of the demands made of you or – if things are going well – provide a lens through which you can help your life stay in tune and allow you to help others *Tune Up*.

It would be unforgivably arrogant of me not to recognise that I developed this thinking and wrote this book from my own perspective, which it is not one of neutrality. I have enjoyed my life and career from the privileged position of a white, middle class, relatively healthy male, with all the automatic opportunities, benefits, and access that combination allows. While I hope this book will help anybody who reads it, I wouldn't dare to assume to know how many times more difficult and stressful life is without some or all these privileges and how much more difficult taking control of it must be.

The Meikle Matrix, the model I developed from this insight, is an analytical tool. It helps us understand both where a relationship is and where it has been. But more importantly, it is also a tool for change that can help us to see what we need to do to make things better, which is every bit as much about getting the best out of relationships and improving performance as it is about surviving and changing relationships that are toxic or dangerous.

I first applied the Meikle Matrix in 2012 when The Post Office engaged me to assess their working relationship with their media agency, which was OMD at the time. My approach to the assessment involved multiple interviews, and part of those interviews was to present the Matrix as we will see it in the first chapter and ask the interviewees where they felt they were in it. Garrett O'Reilly, then the Account Director for the Post Office at OMD, without hesitation pointed to the bottom right-hand corner – responsibility without control – *Stress*. His team was overworked, under-resourced, and under-funded. It transpired that forty percent of the briefs OMD received from The Post Office were being worked up into plans by the agency and then cancelled by the client. Sisyphus meets marketing.

Returning to the Post Office to ask the same question, I expected to find their marketing team in the opposite quadrant – control without responsibility. Instead, and to my enormous surprise, the Post Office marketers indicated their position as the furthest possible tip of the bottom right corner – more stressed and more frustrated than their media agency. The root of the problem was the Post Office's product marketing department; the product marketers were using the efforts of both their marketing department and their agency to speculate as to whether they wanted to advertise at all with spare bits of budget here and there.

The result, for which I was naturally grateful, was a lot more consultancy. There was a lot of *Tuning Up* to do. Over the following four years, we redesigned the Post Office's internal marketing process according to a more balanced apportionment of responsibility and control, improving efficiency and productivity while simultaneously reducing stress. We put in place regular relationship assessments between them and their marketing services agencies to make sure they all stayed in tune. When the statutory review of their creative agency's contract came up, I managed the pitch process for The Post Office – all using the principles of the Meikle Matrix.

The added benefit of this exercise was that I had not anticipated how the Meikle Matrix would guide me as it did through levels beyond a two-party relationship. On reflection, it stands to reason that asking this "where are you?" question needn't stop when we get an answer from each side of one relationship and that it could implicate other relationships, too. It makes sense to me now that the consequence of responsibility and control when they are out of tune could cascade through organisations, creating multiple problems, with stress being transferred time and again until a point of completion or delivery. (If you're not sure what I mean about an end point, just spend a little time in an agency's production department.)

Since its first application, I have employed the principles of the Meikle Matrix in the management of all the pitches I run to find creative and media agencies, and I have measured my success both by my clients' satisfaction and that of the participating agencies, whether or not they were successful. It may seem odd to be endorsed by agencies that didn't win my pitches, but by and large, they have all appreciated pitch processes that allow them increasing control as their responsibility increases (i.e., their investment of time and money) and their chances of success improve at each stage of the selection processes.

I hope you find *Tuning Up* and the Meikle Matrix equally useful in any application you find most helpful.

How to use this book

Tuning Up is not intended to be a self-help book, though the ideas presented certainly improved my mental health and have helped many others. Nor is it intended to be a 'business book' per se – which I hope absolves me of the responsibility to include all the necessary references and empirical evidence for my ideas and hypotheses. I hope you will find the ideas sufficiently robust and self-evidently true. However, I wanted to write *Tuning Up* in an attempt to make things better in the challenging industries of marketing and advertising, and in life, to whatever degree you find useful.

Tuning Up is intended to benefit you, the reader, as an individual, rather than with the purpose of transforming your business or organisation (which may not be within your remit anyway). In the world of marketing and advertising, relationships and their interdependency are almost limitlessly complex, and this book would be three times as many pages if I exhaustively covered the ins and outs of every aspect of them.

Tuning Up is divided into three parts.

1. Part One describes the Meikle Matrix model, how it came about, its application, and its breadth and depth according to the variable definitions of responsibility and control.

2. Part Two looks at how marketing and agencies can get the best out of one another by using the Meikle Matrix, but also how the model can be applied to internal relationships between departments and stakeholders. The hunt for a new agency and new business pitches also have a chapter, because it can be one of the more stressful parts of life in advertising and marketing.

3. Finally, Part Three focuses on how the Meikle Matrix works for different levels of responsibility: as an individual, as a manager, and as a leader. Once you've read Part One and have a grasp of the model, feel free to read as much or as little of the rest as you wish, although there is some cross-referencing between chapters.

Examples and relevant anecdotes are usually in panels like this, both to allow you to skip them if you wish or find them easily if they might prove useful later.

And points which are particularly salient will be highlighted like this.

The Meikle Matrix is composed of four labelled quadrants. Each represents a different combination of high or low control and high or low responsibility. To save you jumping back to the Meikle Matrix in Chapter One each time, different circumstances will refer instead to each quadrant by their labels listed below and which are explained in the first chapter:

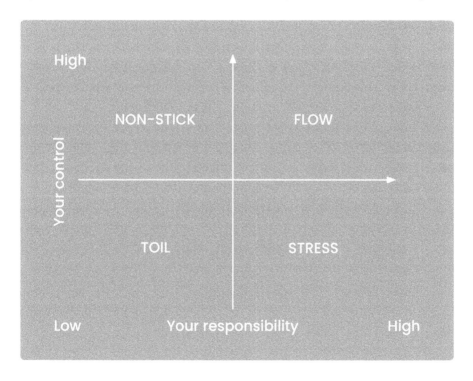

You'll hopefully find a bookmark cheat sheet which you may find useful to keep handy.

Each chapter is summarised at its end so you can either explore whether you want to read it or refresh your memory if you go back to it. However, if you choose to skip chapters, please bear in mind a big part of the effective application of the Meikle Matrix relies on your ability to empathise, so I would encourage you to read those chapters written for the other party involved in any relationship. If you're a marketer, read the agency chapters, and vice versa; if you are being managed, read the chapter for those managing, and vice versa.

By looking at our lives and working relationships through a lens of responsibility and control, we can see things differently almost everywhere. We are able to identify where things need to be *Tuned Up* more quickly and clearly, not least by identifying the causes of our stress, and we see how we are able to improve both transactional relationships and ongoing work and personal relationships by using this model to analyse and manage them.

In *Tuning Up* I have done my best to overcome my default position, which is taking the agency perspective and, more specifically, client service and leadership roles within a creative agency; but, like muscle memory, it can be difficult to adjust. So, for non-agency readers, forgive me if that comes across with any bias; it is not intended.

It is not an overstatement to say that as a direct result of my meeting with the doctor in 2001 my life changed; it certainly did – and for the better. My sincere hope is, through reading this book and sharing this understanding, your experience in work and life will be better, too.

The single most important lesson I can offer, whether you know it or not, is that you are in the driving seat, you are in control. Free will and self-determination are birth rights, and too often we can find ourselves in unreasonable and stressful positions which, had they been offered to us honestly from the outset, we would have refused, but which we easily forget we can *Tune Up*. And if we can't tune them up, we might choose to escape from them entirely.

When responsibility and control are in harmony our jobs feel less like work. We have more energy and we produce better work. But when they're not in harmony, in both work and personal relationships, our mental and physical wellbeing suffers. But they are ultimately our responsibility, and therefore, we should have the control to take care of them – to *Tune Up* and avoid unnecessary stress.

Part One

What's involved in Tuning Up?

Defining the terms of responsibility and control as the two key factors involved in Tuning Up relationships.

Chapter One
The Meikle Matrix

"Unfortunately, no one can be told what the Matrix is. You have to see it for yourself. This is your last chance. After this, there is no turning back."

Morpheus, The Matrix, Lana and Lilly Wachowski.

OK, so Morpheus in The Matrix may be a slight overdramatization, but I would argue once we have looked at our relationships through the Meikle Matrix and the lens of responsibility and control it can be difficult to see them the old way again.

The Meikle Matrix is a simple diagnostic tool to help *Tuning Up*. To *Tune Up* effectively, we must first know if there's a problem and second, what the problem is. There are two key dimensions to the Meikle Matrix, one labelled responsibility and one labelled control. We'll examine their definitions in much more detail in chapters two and three, but, for the time being, imagine each as a line – an abstract continuum. The control line, a vertical axis, represents our level of control. It might be the control over what we do or how we do it, or the control we have over another person, or people, or an entity – like a company or a football team. Or it might be control over us held by another person or other people or an organisation – like our employers, or the police.

The responsibility line is a horizontal axis and is another graduated continuum, measuring our responsibility for, or to, another person, other people, or an entity – or ourselves. That responsibility might be functional, such as to deliver something on time, or moral, such as parenthood, or financial or legal, such as a debt or a duty of care. It might be our accountability for an outcome – a good or bad consequence. It can be an emotional investment, like supporting a sports team, or a responsibility built over time, like loyalty to a life partner or a friend or a company or a boss.

Crucially, how we read both lines is subjective – they are defined based only on how *we feel* about our specific circumstances at a given point in time. They can change as our circumstances change or as we change our circumstances. They are conceptual and they are only to help us – there are no rules for their application, they are deliberately abstract. And the levels of responsibility and control are also judged only by us and based on how *we feel*. Nobody can tell us we're wrong, but we can change how we think about where we are, and our feelings of responsibility and control can change over time, or in the light of new information or circumstances. It's useful to be comfortable with this flexibility; it's normal.

At one extreme of the control continuum we feel we have little or no control at all. Imagine being under the command of the drill instructor in *Full Metal Jacket*. We are told precisely what to do and we have no say in the matter. If we don't like it, the only option we can see is to try to start liking it – or suffer. However, at the other end, we are in complete control over everyone and everything – but only within the relationship to which this line refers when we use it.

Similarly, at one end of the responsibility continuum, we have no responsibility at all. We don't have a care in the world and we are neither responsible for, nor accountable to, anyone or anything – but again, only within the relationship to which we have applied the Matrix. (People invariably have more than one relationship and multiple responsibilities.) We are the children in the unattended sweetshop or the driver of a bumper car at a fairground with no consequences to our actions. At the other end of this line, we could be Atlas with the world on our shoulders. Imagine the responsibility of an open-heart surgeon or Ethan Hunt of *Mission Impossible* grasping his wire cutters, looking at the last few remaining seconds on the nuclear bomb's digital clock and deciding which wire to cut with the future of humanity in the balance.

If we consider any walk of life, any circumstance in which there is a relationship, it's possible to break down that relationship and subjectively assess the level of control and the level of responsibility we or somebody, or a group of people, have.

In combination, responsibility and control therefore create four different circumstances, which can be expressed as a simple matrix:

Figure 1 – The Meikle Matrix framework

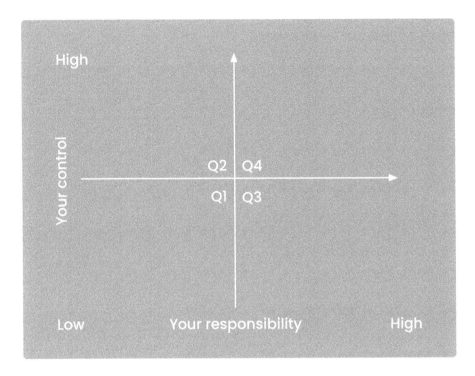

If we think about the different roles and responsibilities we have in life, there are circumstances which fit in every quadrant. To get familiar with this basic model, try to think of where the following roles might fit on the matrix. They don't work in absolutes, so some of these might be in the same quadrant but to greater or lesser degrees on their axes. For the purposes of this exercise, assume all of the following people in these roles are reasonably proficient at what they do. It's not a test, but doing this exercise will get us comfortable with the matrix and make it easier to use and more useful.

Parent of a toddler	Nurse	Rock star
Parent of a teenager	Surgeon	Factory worker
Fighter pilot	Teacher	Airline pilot
Three-year-old	Civil engineer	Police commissioner
Rich socialite	Paparazzo	Rubbish collector

This is an abstract model requiring a number of conventional assumptions, but if our assumptions are similar, your answers might look like this:

Figure 2 – Jobs in the Meikle Matrix

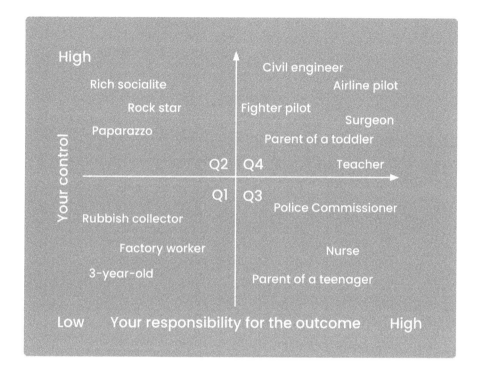

As a guide to these answers, we can look at each quadrant. Labels have been added, which will become clearer later.

Quadrant 1 – Toil
Low Responsibility/Low Control

A three-year-old has few or no responsibilities, at all – if anything, they are just learning about responsibility, and probably reluctantly. They also have little control – they have bedtimes and most have little choice over what they get to eat or how much TV they watch – though obviously this varies depending upon the parenting. They are blissfully unaware of responsibilities and have little idea of the extent of the control continuum, so they may feel and behave like they're in *Non-stick*. **A factory worker** on a production line has a limited function to fulfil – low control – and there are usually other workers or fail-safes in case of human error, so their responsibility is very limited. **A rubbish collector**, likewise, has a specific and limited role – low control. Yes, they have some responsibility, i.e., to take away our rubbish on a specific day, but if they miss our bins one day they usually just get sent back – there's no significant consequence, which is usually a big part of responsibility.

Quadrant 2 – Non-stick
Low Responsibility/High Control

A rich socialite can decide what they might want to do or not: from where in the world they want to live to when they get up in the morning – or not. Most of the responsibilities are at their own discretion. They may choose to start a business or charity, but their wealth allows them to take as little responsibility as they wish – often hiring others to take responsibility on their behalf. Similarly, **rock stars** – although they may have recording contracts exerting some control over them – can behave like divas, safe in the knowledge of their popularity and secure in their wealth. **The paparazzi** will go anywhere, any time, and seemingly do almost anything they like to get their shots. They don't seem to have much responsibility to anybody other than to make a living for themselves – and not to get arrested or assaulted by the people they photograph.

As we cross the vertical line into higher levels of responsibility, we'll see that the nature of the responsibility plays a big part. Responsibility for oneself is very different to the responsibility for others.

Quadrant 3 - Stress
High Responsibility/Low Control

A surgeon might normally be found in Quadrant 4 *Flow*. To see the difference between a surgeon in Q3 *Stress* and Q4 *Flow*, simply imagine it's a military surgeon operating on a battlefield. Surgery is difficult at the best of times, but when we're in a warzone, our normal expectations of control can take a dive. **An NHS** nurse at the best of times is pretty stretched. Prior to the Covid-19 outbreak, there were more than 40,000 nursing vacancies in the UK. This lack of resources increases the number of patients that nurses need to tend each day, reducing their control in terms of their time and resources. Yet they still have the responsibility for their patients' care and are obliged to follow the hospital's protocols and not take short-cuts. More patients make for greater responsibility, and nurses are still accountable to their professional hierarchy and to the patients and their families. **A police commissioner** has a high degree of power (control over their forces). Under ordinary circumstances they are responsible for keeping crime to a minimum. But they don't control the government's social policy, police funding, or the economy – all of which affect crime rates. They are also bound by the rule of law like everybody else, and have no control over the judiciary, which determines what happens to the people they catch in their line of duty. When a teenager develops an appetite for a little adventure or experimentation and self-determination, their parents can likely be found in Q3 *Stress*. **Parents of teenagers** will have feelings of responsibility in the form of their unconditional love for their child, but also a lack of control as the child becomes an adult; then their kids can buy tickets to Glastonbury, travel the world, or go off to university – beyond the controlling reach of their parents.

Quadrant 4 – Flow
High Responsibility/Low Control

While a **surgeon** cannot control what horrors they find inside a patient, they have a team of highly trained people around them hanging on their every word, ready to obey every instruction. The responsibility is, of course, literally life and death. Although a **jet-fighter pilot** would always have high control over their aircraft, their responsibility would be greater when on a mission than it is in exercises. **A civil engineer** is responsible for the safe and sustainable design and construction of a country's infrastructure. The correct calculation of a bridge's weight tolerance is a pretty big responsibility. But they also have high control. Builders and architects must listen to them when they're told to. Finally, a **teacher** is responsible for a class of pupils, but if we imagine a class of ten-year olds, it can be very difficult to control them. Larger classes are more difficult than smaller ones. As students become older and go to university, the nature of the teacher's responsibility and control will change as students becomes more self-reliant for their own learning and the diversity of ability in the student group narrows (the pupils are generally smarter and more motivated because continuing in education is voluntary), making the outcomes of their education less variable.

Moving from quadrant to quadrant

Changing responsibilities and changing controls enable movement from quadrant to quadrant. When trying to get out of *Stress*, there are two directions to travel, clockwise and anti-clockwise. (I haven't yet found an example of the diagonal move from *Stress* to *Non-stick* without passing through *Flow*, even if for only a short time.)

An example of the difference in these directions can be illustrated by the way people play computer games. For example, in a computer game like *Tomb Raider*, the player has to navigate their way through a series of challenges from the simple to the seemingly impossible. Their responsibilities are many: score points, don't die, enjoy the game, win. And their controls, which are at first low for the novice, are learning the game, practicing moves, developing techniques, and increasing the toolbox of their avatar, Lara Croft.

As they practice and learn their control increases and players move from *Stress* to *Flow*. Once they have been in *Flow* for a while and they know that they can win/complete the game, they play for fun. Caring less about the outcomes, a player might move from *Flow* to *Non-stick*.

> Sometimes control can be increased through practice

I, however, take the other direction. I get too stressed and am unable and too impatient to learn the techniques necessary to play well and so I stop caring about the outcome early on. I quickly believe that my efforts are hopeless, so instead of increasing my control I develop learned hopelessness and decrease my responsibility instead. I simply care less about the outcome. When I reluctantly play against my son in a computer game, I usually move quickly from *Stress* to *Toil* while he's moving from *Stress* to *Flow*.

Discretionary responsibility

Once people reach a level of success - call it a critical mass of fame, reputation, or cash - it can be all too easy for them to move into *Non-stick* and
enjoy a life of little responsibility, feeling safe in the knowledge or belief
that nothing can touch them.

From rock stars smashing up hotel rooms, to Oxford's Bullingdon Club
reputedly smashing up restaurants, or TV presenter Jeremey Clarkson
punching his *Top Gear* TV producer and supermodel Naomi Campbell
assaulting airport police and her housekeeper,[1] people in *Non-stick can*
act in a manner entirely confident that there will be no significant consequence to their actions. While it must be comforting not to have a care
in the world, others in such positions of wealth and privilege choose to
increase their responsibility of their own volition.

Microsoft founder Bill Gates didn't have to start a foundation
committed to the eradication of malaria and polio, controlling the spread
of tuberculosis and HIV. Singer songwriter Prince didn't have to secretly
fund solar technology in Oakland, California.[2] John Boyega didn't have
to join Black Lives Matter[3] protests following the death of George Floyd
in police custody in Minneapolis in May 2020. Martin Sheen is reported
to have been arrested more than 60 times for his activism.[4] Sheen and
Boyega both put their causes ahead of their personal interests.

> Discretionary responsibility – it's doing the right thing
> – not because we have to but because we can.

How these conditions make us feel

Having established the different roles and typical circumstances in each
quadrant, we can look at how people must *feel* about these relationships,
how they commonly react to their circumstances:

---

1 The Guardian, 20.6.2008, Naomi Campbell pleads guilty to assaulting airport police
2 Fortune.com, 25.4.2016, Prince Secretly Funded Solar Tech in Oakland
3 The Guardian, 4.6.2020, John Boyega's rousing Black Lives Matter speech wins praise and
   support
4 Thevintagenews.com. 4.4.2019 How Martin Sheen Came to be the Most Arrested Man in
   Hollywood

Figure 3 – Emotional responses to the conditions in The Meikle Matrix

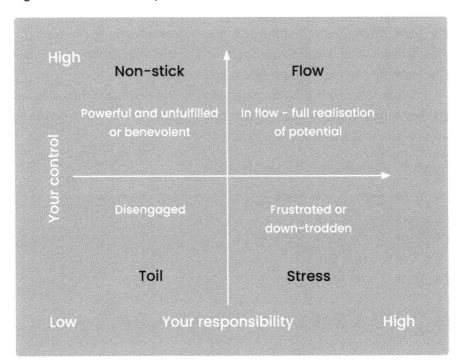

In *Toil*, we couldn't care less. We have no interest in what we're doing or why we're doing it. We are disengaged because the purpose of work is to achieve a basic task, be paid for time and labour, or just to pass the time and little or nothing else.

In *Non-stick* the purpose of our work depends on our discretion. A successful fine artist can choose to paint – or not. If they choose not to paint, they might feel unfulfilled. Wealthy rock stars don't have to write more songs or perform more concerts.

In *Stress*, if we are unhappy with the level of control we have, we are likely frustrated and/or angry, and/or stressed, but feel we are unable to escape due to our responsibilities. Or we may be resigned to staying there and feeling the stresses of that position – conditioned to *Stress* – a life of constant worry.

In *Flow* we can realise our full potential without *Stress*.

Finally, in *Flow*, we are working to the peak of our capabilities. We have significant responsibility and the commensurate control to achieve our goals. Time seems to stand still or go faster, and three hours might pass like one when we are busy "in flow".[5] *Flow* is what some people call "the zone" or software programmers call "wired in".

To conclude, with a little conjecture, we can estimate the value or productivity that these people and their attitudes are likely to produce in each different quadrant (see Figure 4).

Figure 4 – Productivity in the Meikle Matrix

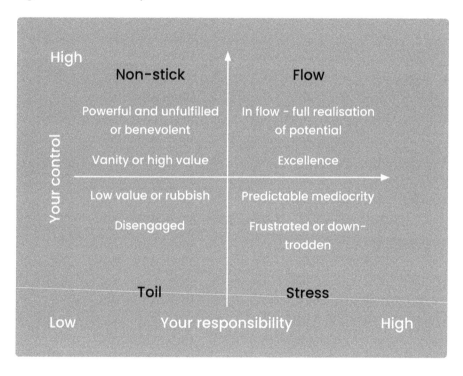

In *Toil*, the value is probably a single simple action in a production line (many students where I grew up in Leicester in the 1980s took summer jobs at Walkers Crisps. One of their more thankless jobs was to stand by a conveyor belt and cut in half potatoes that were too big for the machine – low value.) If somebody works in a fast-food outlet in an

---

5 Flow is a concept developed by Mihaly Csikszentmihalyi (pronounced "CHICK-sent-me-high-ee") and published in 1992

airport putting lettuce in buns for minimum wage, would they care if the lettuce was a little limp and nasty?

In *Non-stick*, people can choose to produce work purely to satisfy themselves, or they can produce work they think or hope will satisfy somebody else; the difference is in their gift because they have limited responsibility. For example, if their work is for themselves, it could be an artist's vanity project – if it's for others it could be Banksy's graffitied artistic comments on society. These are not mutually exclusive.

In *Stress*, the low control means somebody else is determining the 'what' and/or the 'how' of our actions. We are constrained by this and therefore have limited judgement or flexibility. What we can produce is likely more consistent, but therefore and consequently less remarkable.

In *Flow*, we would routinely find the highest value output. People in *Flow* are happy. In *Flow*, people are highly motivated by their responsibility and are in optimal control of what they need to do and how they need to do it. These are the conditions most conducive to value creation because these tasks can be hard to do, but people in *Flow* can do them, and they matter.

It's important to note than it can be easy to think we are in *Flow* when in fact we are in *Stress*. When people see others in *Flow*, they tend to be asked to do more, work longer, take on more responsibility. In this situation, we can be physically in *Stress* but mentally in *Flow* and in danger of burning out.

In my first days of leading Ogilvy Russia, it felt like I was in *Flow*. I had ultimate responsibility and commensurate control, but I was working twelve hours a day – which for me is simply unsustainable. I was actually in *Stress* – even though I was loving it.

> We can think we're in *Flow* but actually be in *Stress* because the pressure is physically and mentally unsustainable.

We are involved in multiple relationships long and short, important and incidental, and each time we can apply the same analysis. Sometimes we are on the receiving end of the responsibility we have and the control we're under – and sometimes, particularly in transactional relationships, as a customer we can determine where the vendor is in the Meikle Matrix by the way we buy from them.

For example, in my twenties, a girlfriend and I had a couple of holidays in the Mediterranean. At lunchtimes we would usually go to a different taverna each day and I would routinely order a Greek salad – because I knew what it was and I liked it. My girlfriend on the other hand always ordered a chef's salad – even when there wasn't one listed on the menu. The first time she did I asked her what it was.

"Oh, it changes from restaurant to restaurant – it's whatever they think makes the best salad."

And every time, without fail, my girlfriend's salad would turn up and it would be magnificent – bigger, more ingredients, better combinations, special dressing, better presented, but rarely much more expensive than my own, if at all. Because my girlfriend didn't mind what was going to be in it, she had given the chef maximum control. The chef's responsibility was for her satisfaction and their own self-esteem, so the chef's salad was always the very best ingredients available assembled the best way they possibly could.

How would you like your steak?

Similarly, in the late, great Anthony Bourdin's book *Kitchen Confidential*, he noted:

"People who order their meat well-done perform a valuable service for those of us in the business who are cost-conscious: they pay for the privilege of eating our garbage. In many kitchens, there's a time-honoured practice called 'save for well-done' (the tray where they keep the ropiest looking steaks)... the philistine who orders his food well-done is not likely to notice the difference between food and flotsam."

If a chef is going to cook the daylights out of a steak, making it juice-less, brittle, and tasteless, why would they use a prime piece of meat? And they cannot overcook "well done", so if it's awful, it's the responsibility of the diner, not the chef – *Toil*.

Since reading *Kitchen Confidential*, whenever I'm asked how I would like my steak, I have a standard response: "*However the chef thinks it best*". As I relinquish total control over how it's cooked, the person to whom I have given control (and who, by the way, should have an immeasurably greater knowledge and vastly broader experience of how best to cook a steak) now has ultimate responsibility for it. Imagine a chef receiving two different steak orders – my order and a "well done". To whom will the chef give the slightly better or bigger cut? In fact, "*However (or whatever) the chef thinks best*" is my standard answer to any question asked of me in a restaurant, ranging from which cheeses to choose from the cheese board to side dishes – *Flow*. (But not the wine; I'm not wealthy enough to cede control of the wine list.)

However, it is crucial to remember here that there must be a shared interest in the outcome. Chefs usually want happy customers for the sake of their own sense of pride and purpose, and hopefully for the restaurant to get repeat business.

If the other person doesn't have a shared interest with us then we've given them control without knowing their sense of responsibility – potentially carte blanche. Although I only have my own experience as evidence, this is why fast food and restaurant service can be so terrible in airports and tourist traps – many of these places don't expect ever to see us again or wouldn't know if they did.[6]

Packing your own parachute

In his entertaining book, Why Did the Policeman Cross the Road? Stevyn Colgan tells a story that appeared in Stars and Stripes magazine explaining perfectly how responsibility can be recalibrated to match peoples' control.

"... In World War II, US paratroopers had a problem with the fact that, allegedly, one in twenty chutes failed in some way. The solution was to require the packers and inspectors to regularly jump out of airplanes using parachutes chosen at random from the store. The quality of the packing then rose to 100% and stayed there."[7]

---

6 Although the birth of Trip Advisor and the like have changed this dynamic a little, I still expect worse service in the walled-garden retail of airports and the like than I do elsewhere

7 Unbound 2016

The final version of the Meikle Matrix below (Figure 6) was actually the first one I drew. It was born when I was developing this line of thinking for my book – *How to Buy a Gorilla* – and I shared a more general observation with two friends who were former colleagues at Ogilvy: Nick Ford and Rory Sutherland. I broadly suggested that advertising agency clients would achieve a diminished return of value from their investment in agencies if they imposed too much control over them. I illustrated it like this:

Figure 5 – The declining return on control

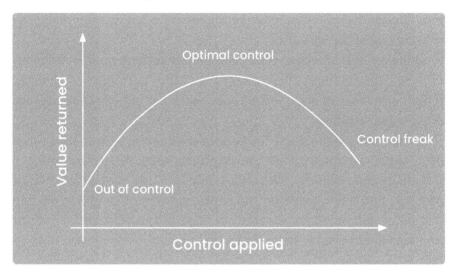

Rory, in particular, was very enthusiastic about this. (As a former MD of a creative agency myself, I can attest that most of us believe we could produce much better and more effective creative work for our clients if only we had the freedom to do it, so as much as I was grateful for his reaction, I was unsurprised by his enthusiasm.) Rory and Nick encouraged me to think about this idea further. So I did: and in the Underground carriage on my way home I drew what Rory later named The Meikle Matrix.

Figure 6 – The Meikle Matrix for client/agency relationships

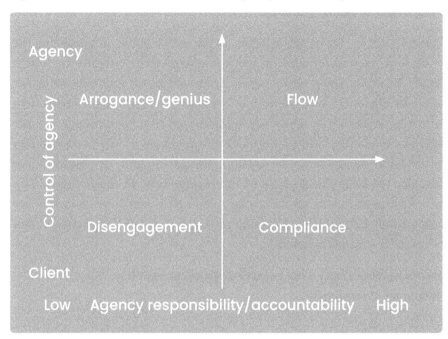

Although it was first created for marketing services agencies, this final version can be applied more broadly.

We can now look specifically at how people *respond* in any given quadrant in an advertising and marketing setting.

Toil – Bottom Left: Low control, low responsibility
Response: Disengagement

In *Toil*, the people have little responsibility for their work and the nature of their work is prescriptive in what they do and how they do it. If their work is sufficiently prescriptive to control the quality of what they do, then their output will be good enough but essentially low value, and predictably so. If there is any variability in the quality or value of the output, there is a higher risk of poor quality/low-value work due the disengagement of the person executing the task. Clients in this sector are largely unimportant to their agencies and therefore allocated the lowest level of agency talent. If the agency were fired by such clients, they would mostly be lost without pain or complaint.

Non-stick Top Left: High control, low responsibility.
Response: Arrogance/Genius

There's a choice for people working in *Non-stick* between producing the work they want to produce or producing work that's best for the task in hand. Of course, these two things are not necessarily mutually exclusive, as we briefly explored earlier. If, for example, we consider a small client who represents a considerable creative opportunity to an agency, the agency could either do work specifically designed to win them industry awards and build agency reputation (arrogance) and/or develop ideas that also will be in the client's best interest (genius). Because there are no serious repercussions for failure, people in *Non-stick* have discretionary responsibility to do the right thing or not, but as I said, the two are not necessarily mutually exclusive.

Stress Bottom Right: Low control, high responsibility.
Response: Compliance

When people are required to maintain high responsibility but have little control, responsibility feels like a burden, an inescapable yoke. Although the reaction is compliance, i.e., an inability to resist control, the outputs can vary between something mediocre and something conservative/predictable in its value. There are some tasks which necessitate high control – for example, imagine the marketing rules set for financial services, pharmaceuticals, and alcohol. Some people can be specialists in this environment, but they will be likely to command a premium salary for it because of the corresponding stress and difficulty. When people are neither compensated for it nor specialists, but find themselves in *Stress* by default, their motivation usually wanes and the calibre of their work – their value – usually diminishes accordingly.

Flow Top Right: High control, high responsibility.
Response: Flow

As responsibility increases in *Flow*, people have a greater sense of purpose, duty, and personal fulfilment. Knowing that we're responsible for something significant and having the control necessary to do our best work is the most motivating state we can find. Client and agency leadership roles will often be here, as long as the stakeholders to whom these managers and leaders report give their people optimal control, such as briefing them for outcomes and allowing them the latitude to do things differently. In *Flow* high responsibility feels more like a duty to be discharged to the best of our abilities rather than a burden.

We'll look at the impact of each of these sets of conditions on the output of agencies in Chapter Six. The responses in Figure 6 were specific to client/agency relationships, so for the rest of the book we'll use one final "master" version of the Meikle Matrix and we'll shorthand the responses by quadrant and name.

Figure 7 – The Meikle Matrix

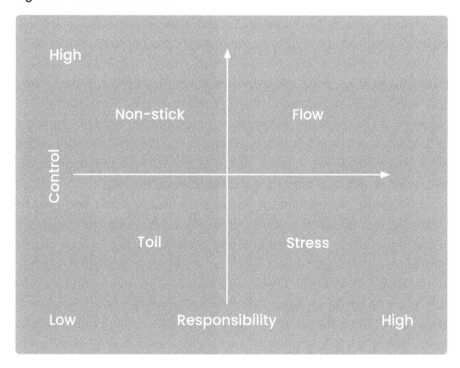

Flow and *Stress* we understand already. *Non-stick* gets its name because, in this quadrant, we can pretty much do what we want and the consequences (responsibility and accountability) somehow just slide off us, and *Toil* is so named because it's just work that must be done and is otherwise not particularly rewarding.

It's also worth taking a moment to differentiate responsibility from pressure. Many people feel the pressure of responsibility – which is just another way of saying that the responsibility they have matters and that it's not necessarily easy to carry because pressure is actually a measure of control; it's about the difficulty of achieving something, not the fact that we might be responsible for it. Two people might have the same financial responsibility, but if one has lots of money and the other has little, then the pressure they are under is different. Lots of money = high control; little money = low control.

> Pressure is different to stress. Stress is a result of pressure.

Pressure relates to responsibility the same way control does, but pressure diminishes our control. Pressure is different to stress. Stress is a result of pressure. Some pressure is constructive or necessary to make things happen. Some people work better under pressure, some worse, and everywhere in between. When people say they work well under pressure, it's because the thing creating pressure (for example, having a limited amount of time) is only one factor of all the controls they might have at their disposal. A good chef might work well under pressure, whereas a novice chef might not be able to stand the heat.

Advertising and marketing represent industries that are used to relatively high pressure as a way of life, as a day-to-day normality. In trying to reconcile responsibility and control I'm not by any means diminishing the need for pressure, nor am I trying to avoid it when it comes along. Frequently, clients and agencies try to respond quickly to pressure to make changes. The Covid-19 pandemic of 2020 is a case in point, whereby the whole marketing and advertising industry came under different kinds of pressure overnight, some to cut their expenditure, some to make new ads appropriate to how society changed overnight. The point I'm making is that under such circumstances we *should* push ourselves, and when we do, we can achieve remarkable outcomes that we might not have thought possible. But, when we are under extraordinarily high pressure, we shouldn't feel as responsible for achieving miraculous outcomes to the degree that it makes us unwell.

Whether in a work setting or not, the impact of the relationship between responsibility and control is consistent. When we have responsibility and control in balanced measure we are largely a lot happier. When the level of both is low, like when we're washing dishes, it's not a huge responsibility and there's not a lot we can do to control it other than to get on with it, but it's not so important, so we just get it done. When we're driving the family along the road and the kids are behaving well and other motorists aren't doing anything stupid, we're in Q4 *Flow* and can contentedly have high control and high responsibility. But any driver will have observed, when other motorists start driving like they're immortal or the kids are screaming, our control diminishes and our stress increases – we're right down in *Stress*. And when we're on our own in the car and the road is empty, some of us, not all, but some, might just enjoy driving a little too fast – *Non-stick*.

Now that we can see the different things that constitute responsibility and the different things that make up control, we can look through this lens to help us see what problems we might have; more importantly, we can see what needs *Tuning Up* to make things better. This is not to say we will always have an answer. There will likely always be bad drivers on the road who force us into *Stress*, and there will always be mundane jobs to do that we don't enjoy in *Toil*. And sometimes we might enjoy the thrill of being out of control in *Stress*, like when we're falling in love – but we'll look at these things and some anomalies in more detail later.

Chapter One Summary

There are varying degrees of responsibility and control in all relationships: at work, at home, at play.

How these variable levels of responsibility and control correspond in these relationships largely determines how we are most likely to react to them and influences the value of relationship's output.

Levels of responsibility and control are subjective to a degree. Their importance is in how they make us feel.

High and low levels of responsibility and control create the Meikle Matrix, which comprises 4 quadrants:

Toil – Low responsibility, Low control: Demotivated low-value chores (anything from completing tax returns to shovelling manure).

Non-stick – Low responsibility, High control: Discretionary effort and responsibility, variable value. Rock star territory.

Stress – High responsibility, Low control: The clinical definition of stress. Too little control prevents us from doing our best work. Danger to our mental health.

Flow – High responsibility, High control: We are at our most motivated and productive, creating the highest possible value from our work.

We can use the Meikle Matrix to better understand and even change our circumstances, but also to create better circumstances for others.

Our position in the Meikle Matrix can change over time as our circumstances change and as our proficiency and experience changes.

If we apply too much control it can diminish the value of the relationship's output.

More often than not, when people are given control commensurate with high responsibility, they will perform at their very best.

Chapter Two
What is control?

"If I was meant to be controlled I would
have come with a remote."

Author unknown.[8]

The Meikle Matrix is the simple combination of two factors: responsibility and control. Both factors are subjective and both factors are relative. They can also be both real or perceived. Equally, we can get it wrong – we might think we have control that we don't. We might think we are more responsible for something than others think we are. Likewise, we might believe somebody else has more or less control or more or less responsibility than they actually do. There is rarely a right and wrong, only what we understand them to be in the moment.

For example, in my son's old primary school, children rarely arrive late, but if they are late, they are not punished. Why not? And why aren't they late all the time? Because the headteacher holds the children's parents responsible for their children being on time. And quite rightly, in my view. The kids are too young to be responsible for getting themselves to school on time – they aren't in control, their parents are, so the parents are held responsible.

> Look for those in control to find those to hold responsible.

Responsibility and control also exist in different levels that have greater or lesser importance, much like Maslow's hierarchy of needs.[9]

---

8   Whoever you are, thank you.
9   Abraham Maslow, A Theory of Human Motivation. Psychological Review 1943.

We can change these levels, as can other parties in our relationships. For example, an individual first may be responsible for their own wellbeing, then, second, that of their family and friends, then, third, responsible to their employer, and finally to their employer's customers. When we fail to negotiate for greater control, on one level we can sometimes switch or escalate to another level in which our control is greater. People will often leave a company for that reason; they escalate their responsibility to themselves over their employer. Interestingly, people can also have very different ideas about which level comes above another.

For example, the interests of our company, our client's company, our company's owners, and indeed our own interests will have different levels of importance to us depending on our situation. Our responsibility for ourselves is probably pretty high, but parents will feel a higher degree of responsibility for their family members than themselves. However, this may but not be the case with their employer. But these levels change over time as our circumstances change. It helps to be comfortable with the changing nature of responsibility.

And levels of control can change over time relative to somebody or something else. We don't work in isolation. We must be comfortable changing the level of control or responsibility we have if we need to, a subject we'll come on to in the last couple of chapters. But a deep understanding of responsibility and control is fundamental to benefit the most from using the Meikle Matrix.

In their 1999 book, *First, Break All the Rules*, Marcus Buckingham and Curt Coffman laid out the findings of their extensive research regarding which qualities make the best managers. They found they could measure the strength of a workplace by asking the following 12 questions:

1. Do I know what is expected of me at work?

2. Do I have the materials and equipment I need to do my work right?

3. At work, do I have the opportunity to do what I do best every day?

4. In the last seven days, have I received recognition or praise for good work?

5. Does my supervisor, or someone at work, seem to care about me as a person?

6. Is there someone at work who encourages my development?

7. At work, do my opinions count?

8. Does the mission/purpose of my company make me feel like my work is important?

9. Are my co-workers committed to doing quality work?

10. Do I have a best friend at work?

11. In the last six months, have I talked with someone about my progress?

12. At work, have I had opportunities to learn and grow?

These 12 questions are in order of their importance. Consider the first two questions, which we could paraphrase:

1. Do I know what I am responsible for doing/delivering at work?

2. Do I have the necessary control to fulfil the requirements of question Number One?

For the purposes of examining client/agency relationships in my first book, *How to Buy a Gorilla*, I broke down the definition of control into two parts: processes and behaviours; the former being *what* we do and the latter being *how* we do it or how we work with others. These in turn could be broken down further into stages of a process and into different types of behaviour.

Process in marketing campaign development could be defined as specific actions: from gathering information and data, writing a strategy, preparing a creative or media idea, executing it and measuring its effectiveness. Whereas behaviour could be defined as how cooperative, inclusive, reasonable, friendly, organised, or chaotic a company or its team is.

For our purposes here, however, i.e., looking at more diverse applications of the Meikle Matrix, controls can be much broader: our obligations, how and when we complete them, our time frame, what we're allowed and not allowed to do – all make up some aspects of the factors of control. It might be the resources we have at our disposal, like a working computer or the condition of the physical resources we have, or the availability of human resources. Our environment is also a key factor of control. I remember arguing with a line manager many years ago that I could be much more productive if I had an office (the agency had decided we should all be open plan), and, when I finally got one, he agreed I was much, much more productive.

Control is also about our level of authority. It can apply to what our company authorises us to do; to buy on its behalf or to say on its behalf. And as we know, knowledge is power, so not knowing what we're doing diminishes our control.

Don't give up your day job ...

Jonathan Newton, a director of long-standing at John Ayling and Associates media agency, bought a small holding in North Wales with his wife. Jonathan commutes to London on a Monday morning and back on a Friday evening, to their Welsh idyll. When they started the small holding, Jonathan went to the livestock market and bought a few chickens. Only they didn't lay eggs – because they were the right species just the wrong gender. Jonathan had excellent experience as a media director; less so as a chicken farmer.

Result: Q3 *Stress* – although it was short-lived. They accepted the cockerels and the huge dose of amusement in exchange for the chickens later.

Control is also procedural. As we'll explore more in the coming chapters, many clients of advertising agencies have their own procedures for the development of ad campaigns; these can be anything from a small booklet to volumes of books. They include things like approvals that are required to develop an idea or the research protocols and action standards that must be met by a new campaign. The agencies of these huge clients usually have to deliver their work while complying to these often very prescriptive controls.

In business and management, people often refer to their roles and responsibilities, but they are often deliberately vague about their controls, i.e., who has ultimate authority. The role is a job description, but rarely in my experience do job descriptions include, for example, what judgements people are expected to make.

It's ironic that an industry that uses so many military terms (target, campaign, contact report) avoids using the clarity of control and responsibility existing in military hierarchy. Particularly in agencies, hierarchy has gone out of management fashion in favour of "flat structures". It's my view that unless the culture of the agency is sufficiently strong (for example, it has values that are universally understood and adhered to) to instil a sense of collective responsibility, flat structures can easily breed confusion, which results in devolved responsibility and blamestorming when things go wrong.

In the marketing environment, the size of the marketing operation will determine to a large degree the level of specialism each marketing role will have. Larger marketing departments will have multiple levels of roles within specialisms, with each position having its own controls and responsibilities. For example, a large organisation might have a head of digital, to whom the head of SEO, PPC, and social and content marketing report, each of those having their own team members, too. By necessity, smaller marketing departments will have broader, more generalist roles. If people move from one organisation to another, from big to small or vice versa, their controls and responsibilities could shift significantly. Larger marketing organisations are generally more capable of providing specific responsibilities and controls in their job descriptions but are also prone to not sticking to them. Ask any agency about their clients' approvals of ad campaigns or general stakeholder management practices and we'll find prevalent inconsistencies between process and practice.

Similarly, large network agencies with the biggest national and international clients, particularly if their clients buy integrated services across multiple communications disciplines, would benefit from clearly defined responsibilities and controls much more than smaller and often independent agencies, which tend to have smaller clients requiring less complex resource structures. However, a powerful culture of collective responsibility and encouragement to take both high responsibility and control can potentially overcome the need for prescriptive definitions of them. Goodstuff, the UK media independent, is an interesting case in point.

Goodstuff, good values

Incorporated in 2004, Goodstuff has grown quickly and steadily to become one of the leading independent media planning and buying agencies in the UK. Its mission is simple and clearly defined:

"To Be the World's Most Inventive Media Agency. Producing ideas that create distinct, famous brands combined with the commercial entrepreneurialism that makes them happen."

But their values are even more striking; the defined behaviours that people must live and breathe. These create a culture which sets them apart from many of their competitors.

1. *Do the Right Thing*
    Always give the best advice for your client's business, ahead of the financial impact on ours.

2. *Keep It Simple*
    Don't come across like a jargon-spouting accountant. What we do is complex; clients are busy and so need clarity of advice.

3. *Move It On*
    Nothing stands still and certainly not around here. Be restless. Be inquisitive. Look for better. How can you top last time?

4. *Give A Shit*
    We must always feel like an ambitious sole trader. Care deeply about what you do. Take pride and go beyond.

5. *Be Inventive*
    Clever solutions aren't found sitting on the shelf. Think around problems and don't take "no" for an answer.

6. *Be Good*
    We are a people business, where other people can help you succeed.
    Be courteous, be decent, and say thanks. Go out of your way to do it.

Now consider these same values through the lens of responsibility and control.

1. *Do the Right Thing* – Delivery of client value is your paramount responsibility, and we're giving you the control to do it.

2. *Keep It Simple* – Don't let anything get in the way of number 1.

3. *Move It On* – Take control to deliver value.

4. *Give A Shit* –Take responsibility for yourself and for Goodstuff.

5. *Be Inventive* – Innovation is found in *Non-stick* and *Flow* – high control. Not taking "no" for an answer is also a high-control behaviour.

6. *Be Good* – The way you do #1 through #5 should be with consideration for others. The key word is "decent" – a shared interest in mutual wellbeing. Collective responsibility.

Goodstuff also tracks clients' satisfaction with its own measures of staff satisfaction working on these accounts – an approach similar to my own. It allows the Goodstuff leadership not only to see what has been good for their clients but also what has been good for their people. While their clients are asked to what degree they would recommend Goodstuff on a score out of ten to a friend or colleague, the staff are also asked to what degree they would recommend a friend or colleague work for that client.

When the results are cross-referenced, they produce four possible outcomes. And like all good directional policy matrices, these different combinations indicate the different actions to take with that client.

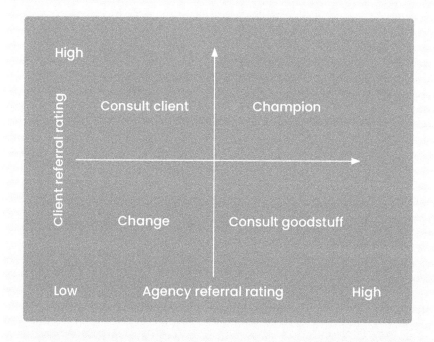

To quote Goodstuff's shortlisted submission to the Campaign Magazine Rapport Report.

Change: Where neither Goodstuff nor client is satisfied.
Action: Crunch talks to make fundamental changes for both.

Consult Client: Where Goodstuffers are satisfied but client is not.
Action: Understand why client is unhappy and address with Goodstuffers.

Champion: Where client and Goodstuff are both highly satisfied.
Action: Avoid complacency by pushing with bigger, braver ideas and thinking.

Consult Goodstuff: Where client is satisfied but Goodstuffers are not.
Action: Understand why Goodstuffers are unhappy and address.

The importance of genuine reciprocity between the business owners and the employees doesn't stop there. Although the business owners of Goodstuff were slightly slower to respond than many other business leaders to the crisis caused by Covid-19, their response when it came was sympathetic, progressive, and valued their employees and their employer brand more than profits. Like most media agencies, Goodstuff saw their billings and revenue fall off a cliff with the announcement of the lockdown in the UK and the subsequent plummet in media value (−60%). Like most agencies, Goodstuff furloughed some staff. Like the more progressive employer brands, some pay cuts were imposed and the greater burden was carried by the higher paid staff. But the business owners, after discussion with the management board, went a significant step further. Having re-forecast their revenues for 2020, the management agreed that staff pay cuts would be repaid before the business would register profit.

Bill Bernbach, known as one of the godfathers of modern advertising and founder of the agency DDB, famously said, 'A principle is not a principle until it costs you money.' Principles are matters of conscience and responsibility, and in the advertising business, it is refreshing to see discretionary responsibility increase to match the owners' control over their business rather than for them to enjoy the more profitable reward of high control.

Does all of this work? Does it make for a better and more successful business? Well, it's difficult to make a direct, causal attribution of how Goodstuff's values contribute to their success. But readers of my first book will be familiar with my use of employer brand strength as a proxy for agency value. The results of a recent survey of employer brand in UK media agencies confirmed Goodstuff as a destination agency for the industry's best talent.

Most interesting in this example is that behaviours like these have made the Goodstuff media agency the success it is today. Goodstuff attracts terrific talent, and with staff turnover 10% below the industry average, Goodstuff tends to retain them. Crucially, of course, all of this makes clients retain them, too; as a result, Goodstuff's revenue has been growing by more than 20% every year.

Control is also hiring and firing. As an employer, we might have control to hire and fire, while also remaining under someone else's control so we can be fired ourselves. In most countries there are some laws, and in most established companies there are some procedures, to which we have to adhere to hire and fire, but it's a level of control of which most employees are conscious from the outset and for many every day thereafter.

For most people in work, it's a big deal to be fired or made redundant. Depending on our age, location, skills, talents, experience, and the job market, we will have a bigger or smaller problem if we lose our job.

Hence, money also provides a useful proxy for control.

"Annual income twenty pounds, annual expenditure nineteen and six, result happiness. Annual income twenty pounds, annual expenditure twenty pounds ought and six, result misery"

David Copperfield – Charles Dickens

Mr Micawber clearly knew the difference between *Flow* and *Stress* in financial terms.

Significant personal wealth – such that we don't have to be as concerned about pounds and pence – provides a high level of control. I observed early in my career that colleagues from wealthier backgrounds, or with their own personal wealth, often – but not always – performed better than those without the same financial security. They performed better because they were fearless, and they were fearless because the company didn't have the ultimate level of control over them it might normally have. People with that kind of security are less afraid of being fired because the prospect of unemployment doesn't carry the same consequences as it does for most other people. Therefore, at times of conflict in the workplace, they can speak as they find, and they can afford to be less agreeable and stand up for their beliefs, not kowtow to hierarchy or be political.

Other people call this kind of personal wealth "fuck you" money, otherwise defined as the amount of money we need to be able to shout "fuck you" to our boss or our client *before* – not after – we slam the phone down on them following an argument.

Power Distance Ratio

It benefits organisations to hire people who will speak truth to power, but they don't have to be independently wealthy. The Power Distance Ratio is an idea developed by Dutch social psychologist Geert Hofstede (1928 - 2020). Power/distance refers to the relationship between those with power and their subordinates, but defined by the subordinates, where power is the degree to which somebody can influence others' ideas or behaviour. Different cultures often have different power/distance ratios. High power/distance cultures are more hierarchical, and subordinates are more deferential to those in power. Malcolm Gladwell cited Korea as a high power/distance culture in his book Outliers[10] as he examined the once poor safety record of Korean Airlines due to the reluctance of co-pilots to question the authority of their pilots by pointing out fast-approaching mountainsides. Other high power/distance ratio cultures include Malaysia, Japan, Russia, and France.

Countries with low power distance ratios include Australia, Iceland, UK, Germany, and New Zealand (super low).

Our level of control is also influenced by our ability. If we take learning to drive as an example, at the beginning of the process our control is pretty low. We progress from an incompetent amateur to a competent learner to a proficient driver to the unconscious competence and even to unconscious proficiency of good and experienced drivers. Our increasing practice affords us greater control. Much of the time, there can be frustration at a lack of responsibility, and those with the power to allocate responsibility are unaware of their employees' proficiencies, which can make the frustration worse. For many years, the advertising business relied on employee self-confidence and "learning on the job" in the absence of any professional qualification.

In contrast to marketing, for a long time, advertising agencies required few if any qualifications. There was no Chartered Institute to recognise anybody's proficiency – and indeed there still isn't. However, one of the most lasting legacies of any president of the Institute of

---

10 Malcolm Gladwell, Little Brown and Company 2008

Practitioners in Advertising (IPA) is that of Stephen Woodford. When Woodford's IPA foundation certificate celebrated its 16th birthday, he reflected on the work that he had begun:

"My inspiration came from my own experience and especially my own incompetence when I started in advertising. Then, in the early '80s, you mainly 'learn by doing', by listening to and copying more experienced colleagues and bosses, hopefully without too much collateral damage along the way. The Foundation Certificate was designed to give new starters a full view across what was an increasingly broad and fragmenting advertising waterfront. So, from very early in their careers, no matter what their discipline or their firm's specialisation, they had a sense of how what they were doing fitted into the overall advertising process. Our objective was to compress what might have taken years of informal absorption from colleagues and experiences into an intensive online learning experience and help people climb the 'advertising proficiency' curve more quickly.

Control can also be a collective concept. It is possible to share control within a team by managed or implicit consent. For example, my wife and I share control over many things; some of them need discussion and revision, some of them are tacit. Business teams work in the same way, sometimes requiring discussion and debate, other times not.

Controls vary depending upon our position, our ability, our capacity, our proficiency, our speed, our resources. It is also important to be mindful of control's mercurial nature when we want to analyse our own situation or help somebody navigate theirs. Although we might have a precise idea of what control feels like to *us* at a given point, when we delegate, it is vital to ensure that there is a *shared* understanding of what control is, as much as it's necessary to have a clear and shared definition of the outcome we want. The same is true when working in a team.

Two common syndromes in marketing and advertising

If control is determined by our ability, it stands to reason that how we perceive our ability can be a form of control. This can go in two directions – neither of which are ideal at their extremes. Either we can have delusions of competence and proficiency or we can be plagued by feelings of inadequacy – the impostor syndrome. The two are not mutually exclusive within any given individual, they're just unlikely to occur at the same time in the same relationship.

> We can simultaneously harbour emotions of insecurity from imposter syndrome and confidence from our delusions of competence – just not around the same issues.

The world of big agency advertising can be a very intimidating one, particularly in account management, if we haven't arrived through the "normal" route of a graduate trainee from Oxbridge or similar top UK university. I remember very clearly sitting in the open plan office of Grey Advertising as that year's head of graduate recruitment walked from pod-to-pod asking each account manager which university they went to and whether they would consider going back there to help with the graduate recruitment drive. It was Oxford here and Exeter or Durham there, until she got to me and asked which was my university.

"*Actually, I didn't go to university.*"

"*Oh my God, I'm sorry!*" was her response, afraid that I was somehow embarrassed by her indiscretion.

Not the best, most inclusive reply she could have made. There's no shortage of chances to feel inadequate or not part of the gang. Early life in ad agencies then made the "who's in and who's out?" social exclusion games of the school yards seem like they had been job training for later life. I hope that these days it's far less the case. Thankfully, I resisted the opportunity to feel like an academic pariah – my sense of control through competence was undiminished by the encounter – though the combination of coming from somewhere north of Watford and without a university degree might have made me look to some like the advertising equivalent of Frank Abagnale.

As Jed Hallam, global head of strategy, Arcadia, Snap, expressed it in a disarming and very moving blog on LinkedIn:

"*So for most of my career to date, I've felt like an imposter. What compounds this is my fear of losing what little sense of belonging and* security I was starting to feel. But being an outsider – or an imposter – just means that you're different from the dominant archetype. For a long time imposter syndrome has been seen as a typically female trait, but I think it's much more intersectional than that. In advertising, if you're not a middle-aged, middle-class, white man with an Oxbridge education, you're going to feel at least a pinch of imposter syndrome."

The crushing lack of confidence that can come from imposter syndrome can make day-to-day work and fear of failure feel easily twice as heavy or twice as difficult. In advertising and marketing, a lack of confidence can be debilitating and the effort required to put on a show of it can be exhausting. This exhaustion is a battle with ourselves for control; control that theoretically we could just, well, *have*. If we're in the same job as somebody from a privileged middle-class background with an Oxbridge education, that's because we're as good as them, you just took a different route to get there. That's a fact for them to adjust to, not a long shadow extending over us against which we must battle for the light of confidence on a daily basis.

> Imposter syndrome can be exhausting – but unless we're materially bad at something it's just a feeling we can learn to manage.

The irony of self-doubt was brilliantly expressed by one of Britain's greatest philosophers:

"One of the painful things about our time is that those who feel certainty are stupid and those with any imagination and understanding are filled with doubt and indecision."

Bertrand Russell (1872 – 1970)

Russell's point was ably demonstrated at the other end of the scale in the Dunning Kruger effect. Named after social psychologists David Dunning and Justin Kruger, their effect results from people's inability to evaluate their own lack of proficiency or even competence. Worse still, the Dunning Kruger effect suggests, as Eaon Pritchard put it in his wonderful book, *Where Did It All Go Wrong?*[11]:

---

11 Art Science Technology, 2017

"If you're incompetent, you can't know you're incompetent because the skills you would need to produce the right answer are exactly the skills you lack in order to know what the right answer is."

Ironically, it has been my experience that people often trust those who are most confident in the advertising and marketing businesses whereas I have much more faith in anybody ready to express their uncertainty. In an industry focused entirely on achieving a higher return on investment in the future, the very fact that the return cannot possibly be certain – *because it's in the future* – makes me question the intelligence of anybody in the business who displays absolute certainty.

To comply or defy? That is the question.

Compliance and defiance form another continuum worth considering, based on the way we respond to control. When I bake a cake, I regularly receive comments of surprise and shock that I could produce something so good (in certain local circles, I have quite the reputation!). This feels almost fraudulent to me because I simply follow the recipe to the letter and – voila! I cede total control to the *Hummingbird Bakery Cookbook*. I execute precisely what their instructions tell me to do with an arguably anal-retentive exactitude and unshakeable, unquestioning compliance; then I sweep up the credit for it from my adoring family, friends, and Facebook followers. My baking is at the total compliance end of the continuum.

At the other end of the scale we might find my son's unwaveringly predictable response to repeated requests to reduce his screen time, switch lights off, practice his trumpet, pick up after himself (ever), and wash his hands before eating – defiance. We should note though that his defiance of screen time is most likely conscious defiance, whereas leaving his stuff lying about is more likely negligence than defiance – a distinction echoed in Hanlon's razor:

"Never attribute to malice that which is adequately explained by stupidity."[12]

Robert J. Hanlon

---

12 Stupidity is probably a bit harsh; I don't believe children have developed sufficient subconscious competence to do many ordinary things automatically; they just don't have the mental bandwidth to process everything they're asked to do. Hence, in every child's household in the land, parents stand by the door shouting, "Shoes … shoes … shoes… " every weekday morning of school term. So, if you're frustrated at not being able to control your kids, it may be helpful to recalibrate your expectations - all I can say is it works for me.

Keep your distance

The most skilled controllers exercise control without us knowing it. They'll likely do it with a clear understanding of the difference between stimulus and response. To illustrate this important difference, anybody who has made the mistake of adorning the rear of their car with a sticker saying "keep your distance" will have noticed, to their likely frustration, how they are nonetheless regularly tailgated – doubtless compounding their perceived need for the sticker. Aggressive drivers noticing these stickers (the stimulus) think to themselves "*Don't tell me how to drive!*" and then go about showing how they feel by driving as close as possible to the offending instructor. In attempting to take control of their personal safety by telling others what to do, "keep your distance" stickers achieve the exact opposite. However, if the same people instead decorated their bumpers with stickers such as, "I brake for no reason whatsoever" or "I'm a terrible/nervous/incompetent driver", they would be far more likely to receive the wide berth they want so much.

In a similar fashion, in April 2020, early in the global lockdown against Covid-19, Gustav Lundblad, the chairman of the environment committee for the council of the university town of Lund in Sweden, needed to deter 30,000 residents from gathering in the park for traditional celebrations to mark Walpurgis Night.[13] Lundblad was concerned his town could become the epicentre for the spread of the coronavirus. The annual festivities are classed as "spontaneous" and therefore they cannot be banned by the local authority, so options for direct control were limited. Instead of appealing to the better nature of the town's residents, Lundblad chose to have a metric tonne of chicken manure spread over the park.

"We get the opportunity to fertilise the lawns, and at the same time it will stink and so it may not be so nice to sit and drink beer in the park."

What do you think they think?

We also tend to control ourselves based on what we think other people think about us. Depending on our disposition, this can be absolutely fine

---

13 Guardian newspapers, 29 April 2020.

or it can make life crushingly difficult as we strive to control ourselves to comply with an _idea_ we have about what somebody else thinks.

This form of control depends equally on our sense of responsibility – put another way – whether we care about what somebody else thinks of us or not. Of course, there are many situations when it is important to consider how other people may feel and thus control our behaviour accordingly. But, and at the same time, we can also selectively choose when not to, and it's vital that we do.

In Sarah Knight's book _The Life-Changing Magic of Not Giving a Fuck_, Knight points out:

"It may take a little getting used to, but you must stop giving a fuck about what other people think."

Crucially, this instruction is followed by a very important caveat:

"I can't over emphasise that when done correctly, not giving a fuck does not mean being an asshole. As long as you contemplate your own reasons for not giving a fuck about something, visualise the effect that your lack of fucks will have on anyone else involved, and mitigate the potential for hurt feelings, you can find a solution – usually through a combination of honesty and politeness – that will stand you in good stead. And minimise the number of anonymous death threats you receive."

If responsibility without control can cause untold stress, we might also find that we make ourselves stressed by imposing self-control based on what other people think. Or, worse still, what we _think_ other people think.

> **We are able make ourselves stressed just by assuming we know what other people think.**

Dealing with difficult people – which is sadly not unfamiliar territory in the fields of advertising and marketing – can also give rise to dangerous forms of control of which many of us may be unaware. Difficult people are often described as such because they're emotionally volatile – one minute they're fine, the world is a happy place and birds are singing, and the next minute it's the apocalypse.

The uncertainty of knowing how somebody we have to live or work with is going to behave can lead to an overwhelming need for, or fear of, control. If we succumb to the fear of difficult people's unpredictability, we can find ourselves second guessing every move we make for fear that we might be about to step on a land mine of their emotional explosion.

Quite sinisterly, I've seen this used by some people as a conscious means of controlling others. I had the misfortune to share my office for a short time with an Account Director colleague, who I will call Wendy – because that was her name – who would flare up at one of her account managers frequently but apparently randomly. After a relatively short time, everyone could see the abject fear in this poor account manager's face (who shall remain nameless) at the prospect of having to deal with Wendy. As much as I am usually reticent to interfere with other people's working relationships without invitation, such was the distress being caused that I could not help myself.

First, I suggested to the account manager that she calmly and politely ask Wendy not to talk to her so angrily and aggressively, that she should do so privately, and that if anything went wrong, I would happily play witness to her need to escalate the issue. Such was Wendy's control that this account manager visibly shook at just the idea of challenging her. After the next flare up, when we were alone in our office, I asked Wendy if it was absolutely necessary for her to be so harsh, angry, and aggressive.

"*It's okay,*" Wendy replied casually.

Wendy seemed to have no issue with me challenging her, which I must say surprised me.

"*This is just my way of breaking them in,*" she continued.

As if her end justified the means.

As much as I did point out that there are ways of establishing how to work with people that did not involve reducing them to tears on an almost daily basis, without the account manager's consent, I couldn't really go much further. But little by little their working relationship improved, though only in the same way the Stockholm Syndrome makes life better for a hostage. But the account manager's value was diminished, because by acceding to Wendy's dictatorial style, her value was entirely limited to whatever Wendy thought or decided. The only ideas or initiatives the account manager would bring would be safely steeped in precedent, a diminished return on control.

Nobody deserves or signs up for that kind of treatment. It's in situations like these that escalating our level of control is so important. Wendy was a bully, and every company must have a zero-tolerance policy for bullies (a subject to which we'll return in Chapter Nine).

Lies, damned lies, and liars

Lying is one of the worst and most insidious forms of control. The complexity of human existence relies on our ability to communicate efficiently with one another based on the reciprocal arrangement that we will tell each other the truth, at least most of the time, and if we don't that it's mostly with good intention. If we spent our lives having to doubt every piece of information that was presented to us without supporting evidence, we would get nowhere.

Liars break this reciprocal agreement. Liars deceitfully take control by providing untruths such that others respond in ways that suit the liars in spite of a reality that otherwise would not. Even those who manipulate others by casually casting doubt or aspersions about someone are guilty of this basic breach of promise. Similarly, people who act in their own interests by knowingly withholding relevant information – something once coined as being *"conservative with the truth"* – are guilty of the same breach. By taking control with their wile, liars leave others out of control, trying to operate effectively under falsehoods and thereby consigned to *Stress*.

Alberto Brandolini's observation, known both as Brandolini's Law and The Bullshit Asymmetry Principle, also observes that even when we know something is a lie:

"The amount of energy needed to refute bullshit is an order of magnitude bigger than to produce it."

Put another way, just to get back to an even keel when a lie has been effectively identified a massive amount of energy is sapped from us to prove it's a lie; energy that we might have otherwise used productively. The liars control our energy but take no responsibility.

> The liars control our energy but take no responsibility.

In our working and personal lives we should make no accommodation for liars. I could hold them in no lower esteem. Once they are identified, they must be called out and revealed to friends and colleagues so that their control is diminished and others cannot be taken in by it.

Gaslighting is arguably the worst form of lying, whereby the liar sows seeds of doubt in the minds of their victims to make them question themselves, their perceptions, their memories, and/or their judgments. Gaslighters' unshakable commitment to their own lies, even when accused and confronted with incontrovertible truths, will guarantee them a special place in hell if there is one.

"Every lie we tell incurs a debt to the truth."

Craig Mazin, Writer, *Chernobyl*, TV miniseries

One comfort is that distortions of the truth and outright lies are usually found out, though too often the damage is already done. Therefore, liars of all kinds are to be avoided at all costs (and must never again be elected to the highest offices of the United States of America, the Russian Federation, the United Kingdom, or any other country for that matter).

Control can take the form or direct authority, skilful influence, or deceitful manipulation. Precedent and tradition are even forms of control by which others must comply because *"that's the way we do things around here"*. Controls can be internal, based on our talents and skills, or our beliefs, our confidence, even our fears and emotionality. And there are external controls manipulating us all the time, too. Some of these we are unable to influence, so instead we must learn not to feel stress when being controlled, but instead recalibrate our responsibility. There's no point screaming in the car when we're stuck in traffic, nor is there anything gained by shouting at the rain. Metaphorically speaking, our only control over such things is to leave time for traffic and to check the weather forecast before arranging our picnic. Sure, we can be cross with ourselves if we don't, but that doesn't achieve much.

Chapter Two Summary

Responsibility and control have different levels to which they can be escalated or de-escalated, working like Maslow's hierarchy of needs. While we may not have control at one level, we might gain control by escalating to the next.

Responsibility and control are also the most fundamental requirements in our working environment: Do we know what is expected of us at work? Do we have the materials and equipment we need to do our work right?

The definitions of control are broad and varied: the stuff we have to do, how we do that stuff, when we do stuff and the time we have to do it, stuff we are allowed to do and the stuff we are not allowed to do to our environment, our authority, our experience, and our proficiency.

How we perceive ourselves and our own proficiency, how we respond to other people's perceptions of us – even how we respond to what we think other people think of us – are factors of control. It's equally possible to overestimate our proficiency as it is to underestimate it.

Control is also hiring and firing, which can be seen from either end of each verb.

Wealth provides a means of control. Those with independent means who are less reliant on their monthly pay cheque have a far greater level of control over themselves and their destiny than those who depend upon it to pay their rent or mortgages.

Individuals' capacity for control at work can depend upon their experience and proficiency. Qualifications are useful markers to indicate levels of competence and hence the control people deserve, whether it is a driving licence or passing the bar exam.

The way people respond to being controlled is on a continuum from defiance at one end to compliance at the other.

Control can also be applied directly or indirectly, consistently or erratically. If we find ourselves stressed by the unpredictable behaviour of others, we need to recognise their behaviour as a means of control and usually either negotiate or escalate our way out of it.

Liars are thieves of control and should be avoided in all walks of life.

Chapter Three
What is responsibility?

"In the long run, we shape our lives, and we shape ourselves. The process never ends until we die. And the choices we make are ultimately our own responsibility."

Eleanor Roosevelt, Diplomat and First Lady of the United States 1884 - 1962

Even more varied in definition than control, 'responsibility' is a spectrum of very different things. On a personal level, responsibility can be an emotional attachment to another person in the form of care or love, or it can be the emotional investment in a sports team's competitive performance. For parents, responsibility is all encompassing, from the well-being and harmony of the family unit to the happiness, nurture, and education of children, to the condition in which we leave the world for them.

We have a responsibility to one another in our friendships, partnerships, and marriages. Partly this responsibility is in our own interest because we should derive pleasure from making another person happy, but our responsibility extends to managing our behaviour, sometimes sacrificing our own interests, such that we please our significant others, or at we least don't upset or hurt them.

At work, the definition of responsibility covers everything from our duty to deliver specific outcomes, to fulfil our obligations and promises, and to satisfy others' interests (such as shareholders). Leaders and managers have a duty of care to people, and workers on the shop floor have an obligation to satisfy clients and customers by providing high quality or good value or by meeting deadlines. Even making sure our *suppliers* are well cared for and treated fairly is a responsibility that ensures they'll do business with us again. These are explicit responsibilities of which we are acutely aware and which we routinely discharge day by day.

Like control, all these definitions of responsibility operate on different levels. It stands to reason that some kinds of responsibility are more important than others and, from time to time, we may have no choice but to fulfil one responsibility at the expense of another. But when we feel the crush of life in *Stress*, we might also decide to escalate our responsibility from the level where we have little control – which is causing us stress – from a responsibility related to our work, say, to a higher responsibility level related to ourselves, where we have control, so we move from *Stress* to *Flow*. These higher and lower levels are something we'll explore further in Chapter Nine.

Implicit responsibility

There are *implicit* responsibilities, too. These more intangible responsibilities are the kinds of qualities that enable us to work more efficiently with others; responsibilities we often take for granted. For example, most of us have a sense of responsibility to be true to our word, to act with integrity and with congruity between what we say and what we do. These responsibilities form the foundation of trust, which not only increases our capacity for responsibility but also allows us to operate more efficiently, not having to second guess whether a colleague will do what they say they will do.

> Recent events have thrown into sharp relief just how much we take these implicit responsibilities for granted. In the middle of the Covid-19 pandemic in the UK, the Mirror and Observer newspapers in a joint investigation revealed that the UK Prime Minister's chief advisor, Dominic Cummings, broke the rules of the pandemic's lockdown of which he had been one of the architects. The ensuing scandal had enough material for a book of its own, but in summary, members of parliament across the political spectrum were incensed by the hypocrisy of Cummings' actions. There was an implicit responsibility to abide by the rules of the lockdown for the public interest. On another level, the lack of integrity shown by Cummings in breaking them, and by the then Prime Minister, Boris Johnson, in defending him, and their subsequent resistance to accountability and absence of apology for the infraction, massively damaged the government's reputation.

Cummings' dereliction of these implicit responsibilities (to act with honour, integrity, accountability, and as an unelected advisor to stay out of the public eye) meant that assumptions about the honour and integrity of other aides, MPs, and civil servants were questioned, too, specifically because there were no direct consequences to Cummings; he took no personal responsibility; *Non-stick.*

Observers have noted that UK politicians' trustworthiness – which we can take as a reliable measure for their personal responsibility – has been waning for many years. Research company IPSOS's Veracity Index of 2019 asked 1020 British adults aged over 15:

"Now I will read you a list of different types of people. For each, would you tell me if you generally trust them to tell the truth or not?"

Nurses, doctors, dentists, and teachers scored highest with 95%, 93%, 90%, and 89%, respectively. Bankers came in at 43%, estate agents at 30%, and 'politicians generally' scraped in at 14%.[14]

The similar change in attitude, which is perhaps due to a lack of tangible consequences, can be seen in the US. Before Jimmy Carter took on the US presidency in 1977, he put his peanut farm into blind trust to avoid even the appearance of a conflict of interest. Yes, A PEANUT FARM. Since assuming presidency in January 2017, Donald Trump abdicated any such responsibility (indeed, his cavalier attitude was a significant part of his appeal), and indeed the US taxpayer has been funding his presidential trips to his own golfing resorts and the restaurant of his Washington hotel is the only place he dines outside the Whitehouse – consequently, it's filled with Washington's political classes hoping to improve their profile; *Non-stick.*

---

14 The only reason why we should be at all grateful for the politicians' score is that it kept advertising executives off the bottom rung with their 17% score, level-pegged with government ministers.

For centuries there has been an implicit understanding that responsibility comes with control, though often control and power are interchangeable terms. Plato's statement nearly 2500 years ago implicitly asserts that anyone with power needs to behave responsibly:

"The measure of a man is what he does with power."

Plato c.425 – 347 BC

Gandhi knew it, too:

"It is wrong and immoral to seek to escape the consequences of one's acts."

Mahatma Gandhi – 1869 – 1948

President Truman had a sign on his desk in the oval office of the Whitehouse, the most powerful position in the country and arguably the world, which simply read:

"The buck stops here." [15]

Even Spider-Man knew that with great power comes great responsibility.

From our early childhood it is drilled into us that we must clean up our own mess. It is implicit that with our control to make a mess comes the commensurate responsibility to clean it up. It teaches us to be in *Flow* when we might otherwise try to be in *Non-stick*. So, when people in power shirk their responsibility – if they slip into *Non-stick* when they ought to be in *Flow* – the sense of betrayal, injustice, and unfairness can be immense, even overwhelming.

Many would consider the behaviour of former prime minister, Boris Johnson, during the Covid-19 lockdowns of 2020, when he broke his own rules on social gatherings, as a perfect example. Johnson's slip from *Flow* to *Non-stick* sparked such a public outcry and such fury that it may have ultimately ended his political career. Well, we can hope it has.

Abuses of power/control are derelictions of the responsibilities that come with it. We all know it. Shakespeare knew it:

———————————

15 Tragically, it appears nobody told the 45th US President.

"O, *it is excellent*
To *have a giant's strength,*
but it is tyrannous
To *use it like a giant.*"

William Shakespeare
Measure for Measure, Act 2, Scene 2.

The important point here is that we shouldn't need to have it spelled out to any of us that we have responsibility, because we understand that it comes automatically with our control, with our power. Whether our control comes from a management position of power or political office or because we've become proficient at a martial art, our implicit responsibility increases as control increases.

Acknowledging our responsibilities when we make a mistake, do something wrong, or neglect our duties is also critically important. When we don't apologise for our infractions, we are failing to recognise our responsibilities and, in so doing, we are making it difficult for others to trust us with that responsibility in future. The most effective way to restore that trust is first to apologise and second to either change our behaviour or ensure that we cannot make the same mistake again; a subject we'll look at again shortly.

We also need to be clear about the locus of responsibility. Although we negotiate responsibility - and who has what share of it - on a routine basis, we're often unclear about what we actually mean. Those responding to a request to undertake a task have grades of responsibility attached from 1) no responsibility to 7) total responsibility:

1. I can't do that

2. I don't think I can do that

3. I'll do my best

4. I think I can do that

5. I can do that

6. I'm sure I can do that

7. Consider it done

1 to 3 imply that the responsibility is still on the person making the request, while 4 to 7 imply that it is on the responder. But responders rarely make the allocation of responsibility explicit, and often these nuanced differences are abused by people trying to devolve responsibility they ought to take. Many people I have dealt with routinely responded to my requests with, 'I'll do my best' or 'I'll see what I can do' to which I routinely reply that I need something more concrete (if it's a habitual rather than a reasonable caveat) to ensure the desired outcome. If there's a risk that we can't do something we're committing to try to do, we ought to be clear about it.

The occasional thrill of *Stress*

Some responsibilities are also present or constructed specifically to be out of our control. A gambler willingly lays their stake (their responsibility) at the hands of a roulette wheel (over which they have no control). The roulette gambler's only control is where they lay their bets and how much they bet and, of course, whether or not to bet at all. Some sporting fans make superstitious attempts to control their team's performance by wearing their lucky underpants or scarves; deep down they know that it doesn't really improve the chances of their team winning (responsibility) in which they're so emotionally invested. Some people derive excitement and entertainment from *Stress*. Some even wilfully reduce their control to derive that stress. As one famous former Formula One Grand Prix winner put it -

"If everything seems under control, you're just not going fast enough."

Mario Andretti

Learning from mistakes

Different responsibilities have different controls commensurate to them. Controls can be before the fact – processes, protocols, or after the fact – sanctions and punishments – the consequences of neglecting our responsibilities. We might assume that external controls before or after the fact (the law, punishment, losing our job) are more effective at ensuring we fulfil our responsibilities than our internal controls (our sense of responsibility, personal integrity, honour). Such is the human condition that a combination of vanity and cognitive dissonance can help us live with ourselves with a dose of post-rationalisation when we've done something wrong. To genuinely and remorsefully accept responsibility for our wrongdoing is far more difficult and far rarer than we might at first like to think.

> To genuinely and remorsefully accept responsibility for our own wrongdoing is far more difficult than the ceremony of saying we're sorry.

Responsibility, rather than control, tends to be more the subject of debate in organisations. Before the fact, we more readily argue and debate over who is ultimately responsible for the outcome than we do about the *way* we do things, i.e., our processes, procedures, and behaviours (control). In my experience, this is much more the case in marketing and advertising than in many other business disciplines where the process has much more attention. After the fact, there are all sorts of claims to responsibility for achievements or, in more toxic working environments, blamestorming exercises when something goes wrong. As the saying goes: success has many fathers, but failure is a bastard.

The tragedy of responsibilities being used as a buck to pass, rather than recognising that it might stop with us, is the degree to which it stifles organisations' ability to learn and grow through mistakes and failure. Companies in which employees understand that their employers will have their backs if the employee fails are far more likely to succeed than organisations in which an employee's failure would lose them their job. That's not carte blanche for irresponsibility – employees would also understand that it's their responsibility to succeed, and they would try hard to do it; but it's a lot easier to take on more responsibility when we know our mortgage payments don't necessarily depend on our success in fulfilling it.

This is not to say that responsibility can be taken more lightly because failure is safe, but that in the event of failure our responsibility should switch from the achievement missed to learning from it instead. As my brother, Andrew, says to his software development team in Lancaster University:

"I don't mind if we make mistakes, let's just make sure they're new and interesting."

Consider, too, the impact of the way we expend our energy at work. In working environments where blame is apportioned and consequences are routinely felt, too much time is spent on defensive/protective behaviour and aggressive behaviour (what we might call arse-covering and arguing) compared to creative/constructive behaviour (cooperating doing stuff, making stuff, making things happen). Imagine how much more productive companies could be if defensive, protective, and aggressive behaviours were sacrificed in favour of creative/constructive behaviour because there's clarity over responsibility and control.

Before the fact, most debates over responsibility are conducted by people wanting more of it. When we have these debates and when we achieve the additional responsibility, it's because we believe we will also be given the commensurate control. Though frequently we don't, likely because it is easier to argue over responsibility for outcomes than the detail of more tangible things, like steps in a procedure or equipment requirements to achieve those outcomes. Briefing for outcomes is far more motivating than control-freakish micro-management or negotiating processes and equipment. But in the creative industries, avoiding the commensurate-controls conversation can be a cop-out by leadership who is afraid of conflict or putting noses out of joint if one person were to be given more control than another over how an outcome is achieved.

Leadership in advertising agencies can dodge the responsibility of avoiding conflict by transferring the responsibility (and the conflict) to more junior people. For example, I have both experienced and witnessed situations where junior account executives are allocated to two different bosses. When the inevitable diary clash occurs between the bosses over the junior's time, the junior is told to resolve it. They might try to negotiate with each boss how they best spend their time to determine which to prioritise, but it can quickly turn into a battle of egos between their two bosses, both unwilling to let go but not taking responsibility for the situation by talking to one another. In such a situation the two leaders are acting with control but not responsibility – *Non-stick* – by delegating to the unfortunate junior and thereby putting them in *Stress* because their diary won't let them be in two places at once.

Success vs the avoidance of failure

The kind of responsibility being negotiated could be either an achievement to be fulfilled or, equally, a question of where the buck will stop. These two are also not mutually exclusive. In the health crisis of the Covid-19 pandemic, doctors, nurses, carers, and bus and train drivers were massively stressed because they had a huge responsibility for the performance of their ordinary duties. However, they also had low control because many didn't have the staff resources, testing facilities, personal protective equipment (PPE), or hospital equipment, like ventilators, they needed.

These key worker roles had further responsibility heaped upon them by labelling them as heroes – a word that suggested personal risk and sacrifice. All credit and unending thanks must go to all key workers for having done what they did, but they didn't sign up for having their lives put at risk by governmental negligence or incompetence. With so much at stake – with lives literally on the line – rather than saying, "I *can't do my job without the correct PPE*" and leaving patients unattended, key workers continued to do their jobs, putting themselves at risk instead of insisting to the health secretary and the prime minister that it's their responsibility to provide proper PPE first. And no small number of them paid the ultimate price.

To fully understand the key to managing a balance of responsibility and control relies on our own awareness of both, the nature or form they might take, and the influence we may or may not have over them. By thinking about these things and addressing them in advance, we can either manage expectations, in ways such as avoiding guarantees or promises, or we can set our own conditions, the necessary "if, then" statements for us to take responsibility being given to us but commensurate with control.

The RACI Model

The RACI management model is an interesting business tool to review in the context of responsibility and control given that the R stands for responsibility. For those unfamiliar with the model, RACI stands for Responsible, Accountable, Consulted, Informed, and is used to identify the variable roles of different stakeholders in complex business processes. I routinely use the RACI model when running agency pitches so that my clients can see the different requirements I will have of them and their people and also what they can expect of me. The differing nature of these four roles will benefit from further explanation before we can examine them in the context of the Meikle Matrix:

Responsible (R)
Those who do the work on the task. One or more people.

Accountable (A)
The one ultimately answerable for the correct and thorough completion of the task. One person only.

Consulted (C)
Those whose opinions are sought (typically subject matter experts) and with whom there is two-way communication. They have the power of veto over R.

Informed (I)
Those who are kept up to date on progress.

What is particularly interesting about the RACI model is that its effectiveness is entirely reliant on a shared vision or objective, to ensure everybody is pulling in the same direction. When this shared endeavour is clear, then the different roles could be applied to the Meikle Matrix as follows – with everybody with an active role performing their best in *Flow*:

Figure 8 – RACI in the Meikle Matrix

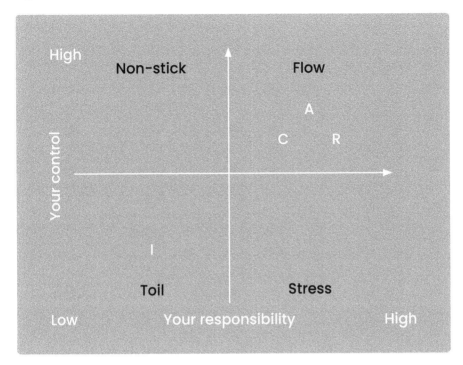

However, if the people being consulted, C, are not on board with the overall objective or the means by which it will be achieved, then the roles in the Meikle Matrix begin to look like that in Figure 9, because as soon as C doesn't share the objective or the means by which to achieve it, they could veto and go straight into *Non-stick*, and in so doing they force R in to *Stress*.

Ultimately, A might have the authority to override a veto and support R but the stress and the conflict has already happened because interests weren't aligned in the first place.

Figure 9 – Dysfunctional RACI in the Meikle Matrix

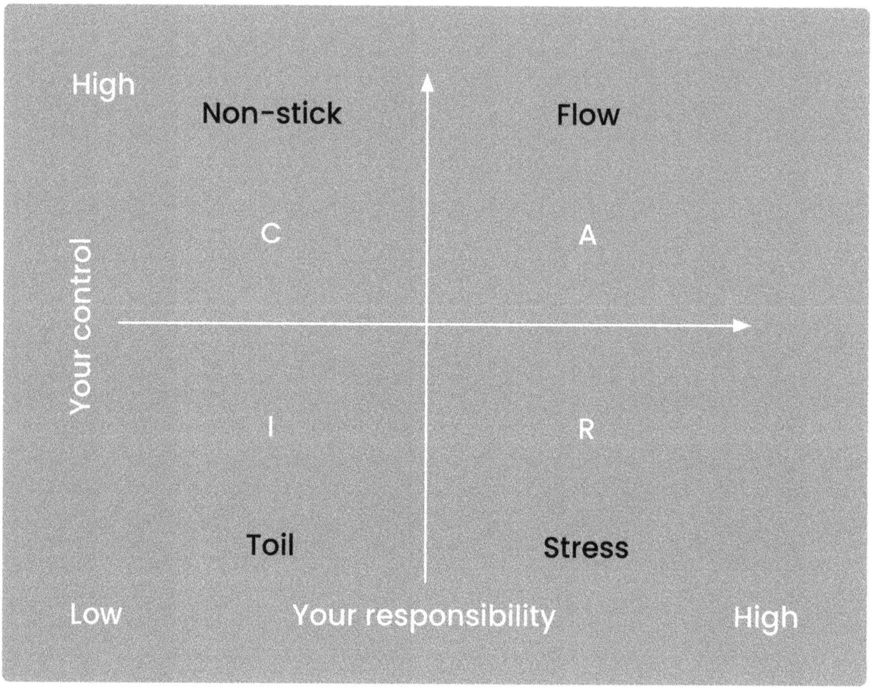

Building consensus

My friend and former client, Paul Harvey, was the marketing director for Abellio, one of the train services franchise owners in the UK. Paul's previous role was global marketing director for Merlin Entertainments – this was one of the key reasons he was the preferred candidate for Abellio. Merlin Entertainments is a global company running theme parks, resorts. and attractions across a number of brands, including Madame Tussauds, Sea Life, and LEGOLAND, from Denmark, to Japan, to California. Each attraction had its own profit and loss account, each had its own sales target, and sales were their primary key performance measure. In short, each attraction had their own responsibilities. One of Paul's primary tasks was to develop ads for LEGOLAND that could be deployed internationally. Using the principles of a RACI model, Paul's role was R, the marketing directors of each local LEGOLAND were C, and Paul's boss, Hans Aksel, the group managing director, was A.

The skilful approach devised by Paul and Hans for this new global role enabled all these roles to reside in *Flow*, despite the individual responsibilities of each marketing director.

1. Hans made it clear that Paul reported to and was accountable to him.

2. Hans informed all local CEOs of the LEGOLAND operations that Paul had his full confidence and that Paul spoke with Hans' authority.

3. Paul shared his objectives and his approach with each LEGOLAND marketing director so they could all see that his and their objectives were aligned.

4. Influence, openness, and shared objectives were enough, but Paul also had a Sheriff's badge if it was necessary.

I love the idea of the Sherriff's badge. Importantly, it's worn under the coat; it's not a constant display of authority. It's revealed only when required and as a last resort when reasoned debate and dialogue have failed. It's a safety net for people who would otherwise be in the stressful position of relying only on their influence without authority. In Paul's position, the Sherriff's badge was largely unnecessary, because he had the skill and experience to form and manage consensus and is extremely good at evaluating, developing, and deploying creative work. Had the Sherriff's badge been needed, it would have essentially made Paul A and R in the RACI model with C reporting to him. That, in turn, could have felt stressful for the country-level marketing directors, who could have felt they were therefore in *Stress*.

On top of having the Sherriff's badge, in his new global role, Paul also provided the markets with a degree of protection – what was coined the "shit-storm umbrella" – another new term I shall be borrowing. So, support for Paul from the marketing directors was reciprocated by him, because in the event of something going badly wrong, Paul would act as the umbrella and take the initial faecal downpour, protecting the markets.

The ads Paul produced for LEGOLAND with his agency BMB represented a radical departure from where they had been. Blonde-haired and blue-eyed Danes had to be replaced with a more international-looking cast. The theme park advertising maxim "show me the metal" (meaning ads are all about the rides, so show the rides as much as possible) was abandoned.

Aimee Luther was the managing director of BMB at the time:

"Developing creative ideas for multiple countries to use is often the stuff of nightmares for agencies. Initial ideas are sliced and diced and compromised beyond recognition as agencies try to satisfy multiple stakeholders in multiple countries with different points of view all at the same time. Creativity's death by compromise. But working with Paul was a delight for BMB by comparison. We could focus on developing brilliant ideas for LEGOLAND, and we knew that all the tricky stakeholder stuff was being managed by Paul."

Paul and Hans had *Tuned Up*.

Strategy without consensus

In a series of gut-wrenching scenes from the superb 2011 movie *Moneyball*, we witness what happens when people are aligned on their responsibility but unaligned on strategy. Brad Pitt plays the Oakland Athletics baseball team's general manager, Billy Beane.

Based on a true story, Beane needs to replace a bunch of players who have been poached by bigger teams with deeper pockets. However, Beane's budget seems far too limited to replace the same level of talent – *Stress*. Beane meets Peter Brand, an economics graduate from Yale who uses an objective empirical analysis of players to identify a team they can afford that can get them to the pro season.[16] However, some of the players they buy in are intended to be deployed in positions other than the ones for which they are known.

The late, great Philip Seymour Hoffman plays Art Howe, the Athletics' coach. It's Howe's job to decide which player to field and who to bench and, crucially, which positions they play. As much as Howe has an equal desire for his team to win, he doesn't believe in Beane and Brand's strategy and so plays the right players in the wrong positions. Of course, Howe wants Oakland Athletics to win, but he also is trying to satisfy his higher-level responsibility for his own reputation by not appearing

---

16 I know this makes it seem like I understand baseball, but I don't. All I know is that making it to the pro season was important – a big responsibility.

mad and putting players in different positions to their usual ones. As the battle for control between Beane and Howe continues and games are consecutively lost, their opposite positions on strategy make them both play a lose-lose game. Howe continues to put players in the wrong positions (but that look right to the outside world) and Beane ends up trading these players away, diminishing Howe's stock until has he has no choice but to bend to Beane's will.

Although I usually fail miserably to get excited about sports, helped by the dramatization of a movie format, the tension between responsibility and control had me on the edge of my sofa.

When we encounter incompetence

From time to time, we might also come across people who don't fully understand either the extent of their responsibilities or their inability to fulfil them. These happy souls blithely go about their daily business, unaware of how much of their success may have had little to do with them or their ability … until a serious problem arises.

One of the more challenging tasks I had while running Ogilvy Moscow in the early 2000s was to move offices. When I took over the business, we were only 65 people, but we had grown rapidly to significantly over 100 and were running out of space in which to cram extra desks. The ownership transition of the agency was still ongoing, so I needed to manage the interests of both WPP, who were buying the agency, and Leonid who owned it, against our practical needs and finances. To comply with WPP standards, we engaged their preferred global commercial estate agent. I provided a thorough brief to the agent, approved by all stakeholders, and we agreed a six-figure dollar fee according to their contract with WPP. Unfamiliar with managing commercial leases, in our first meeting I used the principles of the Meikle Matrix to explain my position to our agent in words something like this:

"I really have no idea what I'm doing, but here we are and I'm the one doing it, so I'm going to be relying on you 100% to get me through this. I will need to be led by you on matters of what we do, when we do it, and how we do it. Assume I know nothing and understand less."

To anybody acting as a consultant, this should be music to their ears. It was also an opportunity at the outset of the process for them to reject either the task or these conditions. Basically, I was saying that I wanted them to have an optimal level of control and the greatest responsibility – *Flow*. The agent had to get the agency I was managing from where it was then to where it needed to be, and I would do everything in my power to cooperate with them fully. However, I had been working on the assumption that the recommendation to use this nominated estate agent came with an assurance of their competence and that they would naturally accept the responsibility I gave them. It transpired that this was not the case.

Having looked at a number of absolutely awful buildings (too far out of town, too small, too crushingly depressing, too near to a former nuclear testing site …) the agent had found a building under renovation in a different part of town to our existing office – but I use the word "renovation" very loosely. As I recall, it was late autumn when I first visited the site of an enormous red brick building that looked as if it had been bombed during a distant war. However, the size and flexibility of the space was good, the location was OK, and the price was very competitive in an inflationary market.

What followed was unnervingly few indications of much activity or progress on the building site, but I was assured by the agent that Russian builders are capable of incredible feats, and they were entirely confident that it would be habitable by the end of March when our current contract expired. (This might sound crazy, but I had both experienced and read of the Russian people being better motivated to achieve tasks that are either impossible or require other-worldly effort than they are to do the most basic task in a reasonable amount of time. As Alain De Botton observed, "*Work begins when the fear of doing nothing at all finally trumps the terror of doing it badly.*"[17])

Having agreed all of this with my stakeholders, we paid the property developer a deposit for the new office space, but, somewhat cynical of their guarantees, I reiterated my total reliance on the agent to get this right and that the agent was not only responsible for managing this

---

17 A principle that I find applies particularly well to DIY tasks.

process but would be accountable for its success, too. Without hesitation, the agent confidently agreed.

Every month or six weeks thereafter, a representative from the estate agent and I would go and visit the site of the new office to see the work in progress. It was the beginning of December when I said to the agent that I had seen too little evidence of progress and was highly sceptical that the project would be finished on time. Once again, I got the same feedback: that I would be amazed by what Russian workers can do under pressure, that I should not worry. When I asked specifically, I was reassured that I should give notice on our current office lease. And, once again, I checked with my stakeholders who gave me their consent to proceed, too, on the basis that our agent had said it would be OK.

Over the next two site visits I saw a little improvement, but my concern and my cynicism increased greatly. On the second of these visits, I was shown the specific office space we would occupy and how it had been wired and decorated in readiness for our move, although it looked as though it had been protected by some kind of force field when the bombing of the rest of the building had taken place, such was the contrast between our space and the rest of the site.

I pointed out that the rest of the building was in a state of dangerous disrepair, that access to our office space was both difficult and dangerous, and that working on a building site is not exactly conducive to producing the best strategic and creative ideas if we were to be surrounded by drilling and banging for months to come thereafter. I gave the matter a little more thought and called the estate agent. I instructed them to remind the property developer of their contractual obligations and to triple check that the offices would be ready for our occupation at the end of March. A couple of hours later they came back to me.

"I'm sorry to say it looks like you were right," they said. "Although they are confident that your office space will be ready to be occupied, the rest of the building will still need a few months to be finished. And another thing, your offices won't be registered for a while."

Holding my temper as best as I could, because although I had thought this situation might arise, I nonetheless found it difficult to believe the degree of incompetence I was having to deal with from both the agent and the developer, I calmly asked what *"won't be registered"* meant.

"It means it won't officially exist for the purposes of public records and mail delivery and what not."

"What not". I may have used some more industrial language at this point in an uncharacteristic lapse of professionalism, but it felt entirely warranted. I now had to assume both responsibility and control of the situation in the belief that if a child could have made a better job of this than my well-paid estate agent, then I could, too. Reluctantly, I moved to *Stress*.

"We are Ogilvy & Mather," I replied. *"We are part of WPP, which is why I used your company in the first place, to what is now my profound regret. I have an obligation to make this company Sarbanes Oxley compliant, which I doubt very much I will be able to do if our address is an office that doesn't officially exist, to which post therefore cannot be sent and I would find rather tricky to insure. That is before I deal with issues of health and safety and my duty of care for my people, clients, suppliers, and anyone else who might be unfortunate enough to have to visit our offices."*

Putting my mind to the resolution of my limited time before notice on our existing offices ran out, I considered what I had learnt in my first few months in Russia – that there are only three conditions of business-to-business relationships: one is no relationship at all; two is wilful and happy cooperation with a shared interest; but if there is a conflict of interest it moves to the three – all-out conflict. We were in condition three, where the only option is to take control.

"Here's what's going to happen," I said. *"Your company is going to reimburse Ogilvy every cent of the fee we have paid you without complaint and immediately. You will confirm this by the end of the day or I will be bringing the matter up with WPP. Next, you will provide the details of the property developer I will have to sue for breach of contract. Then we're done."*[18]

---

18 The agent's surprising response was: "Yes, of course we will. But you know the same thing happened to us? We were all set to move into our new offices and our new landlord didn't get them ready on time!" The cobbler's defence – that his own children were shoeless – was not well received.

As comedian Ricky Gervais noted:

"Remember, when you are dead, you do not know you are dead. It is only painful for others. The same applies when you are stupid."

I had to apply the all-out aggression approach to the property developer, too, from whom I needed to recover a six-figure deposit, so I briefed our agency's solicitor to sue them. What I particularly enjoyed was the contrast between the utterly ill-deserved confidence of my assigned estate agent (*"Dunning, Kruger, come in please, you're needed"*) and the response that I got from our solicitor. The firm, Firestone Duncan, had a reputation as a bit of a rottweiler. The firm's partner, Jamison Firestone, responded to my request to sue the developer for our deposit, demonstrating his own proficient grasp of responsibility and control. Jamison agreed with my aggressive strategy, saying that any openness to a negotiation would only serve to make me look weak. To my unending regret, I didn't keep a copy of the letter from Jamison, but the last lines read something like this:

"It is essential that you understand the owner of the property development company is not only a business oligarch, but he is also a member of Russian parliament. Although you are, of course, well within your rights to demand the return of your full deposit for their breach of contract, if this matter was to go to court, I must advise that you might not be able to rely on the impartiality of the judges."

(I'm happy to say that my strategy did pay off and all fees and deposits were returned.)

Dealing with incompetence isn't easy. We must weigh up risks and outcomes and decide whether to step in and take responsibility and control for ourselves or increase responsibility such that the other party might be forced to improve/increase their control. But the application of the Meikle Matrix in these circumstances can help identify the options available to us and the best option for a given situation.

The need for empathy

The manifestations of responsibility and control are endless. They are subjective, many layered, and can be different for two parties in the same relationship. For example, the responsibility of a criminal to themselves to escape capture is usually far more important than that of their pursuer to catch them – hence in the film *Butch Cassidy and the Sundance Kid* the anti-heroes jumped into a river from a height they thought would probably kill them, but their trackers understandably didn't.

Hence, to use the lens of responsibility and control, we must be able to calibrate it according to both how we see the relationship, but also to how the other party might see it. We must not assume they're responding to either responsibility, control, or both in the same way as us, but consider that they may be on a different level to us, or even considering responsibility and control in an entirely different way to us.

We can better manage our responses to the variable levels of responsibility and control if we can empathise, accurately deduce, or just ask the other party how they see their situation. We must be practiced and skilled at knowing positions in the Meikle Matrix both for ourselves and for others. We may have to ask careful, sensitive questions to truly understand our own situations and theirs. When we do, and we can see our own circumstances and theirs with more clarity, then we can consider how to effect change or at least we can understand what our options might be to achieve resolution.

When high responsibility and high control come together in *Flow*

When our whole work life is in *Flow*, I'm yet to find a better feeling. My first days in Russia serve as an ideal example, notwithstanding my comments earlier about the sustainability of 12-hour days.

During the summer of 2003, I was working as a Board Account Director at Ogilvy & Mather in Canary Wharf, London. The phone on my desk rang, and I found myself speaking to Leonid Shutov. He introduced himself to me as the owner of Propaganda Ogilvy, our Russian office, which was an affiliate to the Ogilvy network, and was about to enter a process of acquisition by WPP to become Ogilvy proper. After a meeting in London, I was invited to Moscow to see the office, meet the MD, and consider a role as Client Services Director. Although I decided it wasn't for me, and gratefully I declined, the phone again rang in October that year. It was Leonid again. This time, he said something like:

"I know the role we talked about in the summer wasn't right for you, but how would you feel about the MD job?"

We met in London soon after. We spoke fairly loosely about the role, what I would have to do, what kind of control I would have in the organisation, and we struck a deal. I was only 34 years old, and I had never been a head of department, let alone senior management, but if he believed I could do it, why should I doubt his judgement? My only personal responsibility was a mortgage on my London flat, so by late November I was on my way.

On Sunday November 23rd, I was a new resident of the Moscow Mezhdunarodnaya Hotel, a bizarre hotel that I was assured was conveniently located for the Propaganda Ogilvy Offices, on the banks of the Moskva River in the west side of the city. The following day would be my first day of work in my new role, and Leonid had popped into my hotel to welcome me and have a chat the evening before.

Leonid was a true entrepreneur with interests in a number of businesses, but he had been hands-on in the agency for a few months prior to my arrival. He briefed me fairly lightly about the clients and the agency people, readying me for the next morning. During the course of our conversation, I thought it would be a good idea to re-establish my responsibilities and the degree of control I should assume the following day. So, to introduce the topic, I said:

"I assume that over the next few months we'll figure out what involvement you want to continue to have in the decisions I have to take day-to-day."

"No," he said and continued something like this: *"They're all yours, starting tomorrow. You know the growth objectives we have, and I want you to be motivated to achieve them, but other than that, it's over to you. I'll be around if you have questions or need help, but don't assume you have to check anything with me if you think it's the right thing to do."*

My objective was clear – grow the top line revenue of the business by 30% year-on-year. In my first year, I hired and installed a management team, recruited people, and invested in equipment. Although I reduced the percentage of profitability (though it was still one of the most profitable offices in Europe), I doubled the revenue in year one; by year four, it was up more than 500%. All I all, my life was mostly in *Flow*. For times when I found myself in *Stress*, I had Leonid's unwavering support.

Knowing when to quit and when to commit

We also need to put some of our responsibilities into perspective. If we take all of our responsibilities with equal dedication, we are likely to explode or dissolve into a nervous breakdown.

The kind of perspective we need was perfectly illustrated in the children's book *The Boy, The Mole, The Fox and The Horse*, by Charlie Mackesy:

"Do you have a favourite saying?" asked the boy.
"Yes," said the Mole.
"What is it?"
"If at first you don't succeed, have some cake."
"I see, does it work?"
"Every time."

(Except if making a cake is the endeavour in which we may not have succeeded, as my son Daniel keenly observed.)

How to get a man on the moon

In his eulogy for John F Kennedy in 1964, Ralph Webster Yarborough, an American congressman, provided a superb illustration for how to impel ourselves to achieve difficult objectives when referring to JFK's commitment to put a man on the moon:

"Frank O'Connor, The Irish writer, tells in one of his books how, as a boy, he and his friends would make their way across the countryside and when they came to an orchard wall that seemed too high and too doubtful to try and too difficult to permit their voyage to continue, they took off their hats and tossed them over the wall – and then they had no choice but to follow them. This nation has tossed its cap over the wall of space, and we have no choice but to follow it.

When considering our responsibilities or those we expect of others, it's vital to consider what really matters and what doesn't. If everything is important, then nothing is important: we cannot prioritise anything and we'll exhaust ourselves equally over the trivial and the vital, taking us to the furthest reaches of *Stress*.

At the same time, we can also create additional responsibility to control ourselves and prevent ourselves from giving up or giving in.

When I set out writing *How to Buy a Gorilla*, I was conscious of the failure rate of writers and how easy it would be to give up, even long after I started (not least because I had given up once before). Admittedly, although my task was slightly less ambitious than landing on the moon (but at times it felt comparable), I needed a way of throwing my own cap over the wall. So, I told as many people as I could that I was doing it, people whose opinions and respect mattered to me, my family included. Consequently, I would regularly be asked how it was going, whether I had found a publisher, what the book would be called. I had massively increased my responsibility to them in the form of their interest in what I was doing. And it worked so well I did the same with this one.

Filmaker, Alice Wu, found a different way to motivate herself.

"Prone to procrastination, she went to extreme measures. 'I wrote a check for a thousand dollars to the NRA and gave it to one of my best friends,' she reveals. 'I gave myself five weeks and said if I don't have a first draft, you are sending that check in.'"[19]

Responsibility motivates

Crucially, we must recognise that for most people responsibility itself is highly motivating because it is the route to more control.

Control in all its forms, but in particular autonomy, self-determination, and decision making, are powerful motivators. As Edward L. Deci put it in *Why We Do What We Do*[20]:

---

19 www.variety.com
20 G. P. Putnam's Sons, New York, 1995.

"To be autonomous means to act in accord with oneself – it means feeling free and volitional in one's actions. When autonomous, people are fully willing to do what they are doing, and they embrace the activity with a sense of interest and commitment. Their actions emanate from their true sense of self, so they are being authentic."

From our earliest years, we are taught that the more responsible we prove ourselves to be, the more our autonomy will increase. The same is true in most lines of work with supervision decreasing over time as we fulfil our responsibilities with increasing regularity and competence.

Responsibility is therefore a route to control, and control is motivational. Dan Pink takes this connection further by suggesting three foundations for motivation. From Pink's 2000 TED talk:

"Autonomy: the urge to direct our own lives.
Mastery: the desire to get better and better at something that matters.
Purpose: the yearn to do what we do in the service of something larger than ourselves."

Purpose is not dissimilar to the apex of Maslow's hierarchy of needs: self-actualization. So, in fulfilling our hierarchy of responsibilities, we move toward self-actualization. This is the nature of aspiration and ambition.

With self-actualization as our goal, the route to it increases our responsibility, which requires us to increase our autonomy and therefore control.

> To increase our responsibility is our purpose.

Chapter Three Summary

Like control, responsibility has a variety of meanings and multiple levels; it can be both implicit or explicit, specific and deliverable, or day-to-day.

Implicit responsibilities include honesty, integrity, congruity between word and deed, default pro-sociality in our behaviour – and it increases as our control increases.

Explicit responsibilities are delivering against commitments, promises, contracts, expectations, and honouring a duty of care for people in our charge.

We must be clear about the language of responsibility and beware of the overuse of phrases that typically try to evade responsibility, such as "I'll see what I can do".

Responsibility has a thrilling and playful side, too. (Gambling is the relinquishing of control over our responsibility to our stake.)

When we sometimes fail to meet our responsibilities, we must ensure that we learn from them and move on, not dwell on unintended failure.

RACI models are a useful tool to manage responsibilities in complex projects with multiple stakeholders, but care must be taken in their application; there must be a clear and shared objective – a RACI will not resolve hidden conflicts effectively.

When we delegate responsibility, we do not absolve ourselves of it, because the delegation was within our control. The buck should always stop at the top.

The most effective relationships are built with empathy of other parties' responsibilities – and these responsibilities may not be immediately apparent.

Knowing when to quit and knowing when to overcommit are skills worth learning.

Responsibility is highly motivating, not least because for many it is the route to control, which means the freedom of self-determination and self-actualization – which is our purpose.

Part Two

Tuning Up marketing and advertising

Examining more specifically how responsibility and control manifest and relate to one another in marketing and advertising, and how we can Tune Up relationships using the Meikle Matrix.

Chapter Four
The Meikle Matrix
for marketers

"Don't blame the marketing department. The buck stops with the chief executive."

John D. Rockefeller– 1839 – 1937

Marketing is a form of corporate gambling – in the same way any other business investment is a gamble. As Peter Drucker pointed out, "*All profit is derived from risk.*" Depending on the marketer's stakes and the outcome, gambling is either exciting or stressful. There's a point at which we've put our chips on the roulette table and the Monte Carlo croupier calls, "*Les jeux sont faits*" – after which all we can do is wait for the result. In the same way, there's a point when a marketing campaign goes live, at which the marketer says "go", and then all they can do is wait to see if they won or lost market share.

In both cases the money is on the table.
In both cases there's no going back after a certain point.
In both cases they're hoping for more back than they put down.

Crucially, the point when the ball is released onto the roulette wheel, the point when the marketing campaign is green-lit and activated, is the point at which control is relinquished but responsibility remains high; *Stress*. If the marketer is confident in their campaign and they've had control commensurate with the responsibility to produce it, this stress will feel more like excitement. If they haven't had that control, *Stress* will feel, well, stressful.

The key difference is that gambling for entertainment is just that – it's for fun. Unless we have a gambling problem, then we're prepared to lose (and usually able to lose) our stake without any consequence other than disappointment. But, for the marketer, a failed campaign can be a career-limiting moment – as can a successful blockbuster campaign be a career-defining moment.

There are two blindingly obvious features of gambling, which nonetheless evade too many conversations about advertising and marketing and would be to everybody's benefit if we were to address them regularly.

The first is that marketers are commonly asked by the CEO or the company board to "guarantee" the results of their marketing investments, or at least to give reasonable personal assurance that the investments will generate a positive return in an attempt to make marketers responsible for the future. In turn, marketers will often seek reassurance from their colleagues, advisors, and agencies that the campaign they are developing/running will work and will provide that return. Then agencies often fall into the trap of reassuring their clients that their strategies and ideas will "definitely" work (agency taking responsibility for the future).[21]

Essentially, this is a game of responsibility hot potato, where responsibility is passed on to those at the end of the supply chain – because they have no choice but to speak with confidence or risk not running the campaign - or having a reason to exist. The reason that a guarantee is both unrealistic and unreasonable is that *the results will be in the future*. If the Covid-19 events of 2020 and 2021 have taught us anything, it should be that the future is unknowable. But throughout my advertising career I have seen agencies aggrandise themselves for their genius when a campaign proves effective and find every reason under the sun other than their advertising's effectiveness if a campaign disappoints or fails. (That said, as Bernbach pointed out as eloquently as always – a good ad campaign will make a bad product fail faster – so failures in sales are not necessarily always the responsibility of the advertising.)

> The future is unknowable – so we can't take full responsibility for it not turning out as we want despite high levels of control.

---

21 Making very fertile ground for Mr Dunning and Mr Kruger. See: Two common syndromes in marketing and advertising, chapter two.

The second point follows from the first: insofar as the future is unknowable, it is therefore *beyond the marketer's control*. During the "normal" course of events (and I use the word "normal" more carefully since the Covid-19 pandemic), nobody in the marketing community can be in complete control of their brand and its performance. Marketers can attempt to control how their brand is represented, in which channels it is exposed, and to what degree of reach and frequency or to what audience they run their campaigns, but they can't control individuals' responses. British Airways couldn't control Margaret Thatcher snubbing their new tail designs in 1997, resulting in their expensive abandonment. Nike couldn't control people burning their trainers in 2018 following Nike's support for Colin Kaepernick's peaceful take-a-knee protest against racist police brutality (although, unlike BA, Nike didn't back down[22]), and most people in advertising and marketing and the remaining wearers of Nike would consider the latter a desirable response. Public interference with, adaptation, mockery, and even aggressive rejection of brands is a new normal in an age of social media, taking a lot of control over brands from marketers.

Just as YouTube became popular, videos emerged of people creating everything from explosions to carefully timed and choreographed displays of fountains by adding mentos to Diet Coke. By all accounts I have heard, Mentos didn't have a problem with this, but Diet Coke sought to control who could do what with their product and had to go through a painful and fast learning curve that they have little control over the public domain.

In the light of the unpredictability of what's going to happen, it's understandable that marketers want to do whatever is feasible to mitigate the risk of campaign failure and to improve the chances of campaign success prior to that point of no return. Any such measures would help move marketers from a default position of *Stress* closer to *Flow*.

---

22 A Nike ad supporting Colin Kaepernick's protest against racial injustice met with some backlash from white Nike customers whose response was to burn their trainers and post the videos online. Nike's reply was to run another ad titled "How to burn our products safely", taking responsibility for their stance and control of the narrative.

Some of the variables influencing campaign effectiveness are often interdependent (e.g., the message and the medium) or multiple other marketing investments have a dependency on one variable. For example:

- The effectiveness of a creative idea will impact on the effectiveness of every channel in which it is deployed.

- A delayed creative idea delays a campaign start date, impacting the time value of money on the marketer's return on investment.

- A miscalculated target audience can have the right ad addressing the wrong people.

Other variables include the weather, the economy, a competitor's launch of a superior product, a competitor vastly outspending a marketer's brilliant campaign with a mediocre one (or just being second to market with a new product), or an unexpected PR disaster. Just ask the sponsorship managers at Nike and Trek about Lance Armstrong to understand about a marketer's lack of control. Marketing is stressful.

With so many things out of a marketers control, it's hardly a surprise that marketers will want to control the things they can.

Marketing investments work like any other. There are two ways to increase its return.

1. If a marketer wants to minimise risk to achieve a more predictable outcome, they must either increase their investment and use safer odds or invest in finding ways to better predict the outcome (which is also increasing investment, just indirectly in the likes of advertising creative research, econometrics modelling, etc.). More control has a cost.

2. If they want a higher return from a lower investment, they must increase their risk. Less control.

It is impossible to increase return without doing either of these. However, if marketers think they can, then they have just moved their risk and they haven't identified where or how they have done it, or they've increased their investment and haven't identified where or how they've done it.

It might help to consider risk as a proxy for control (or rather a lack thereof) and responsibility as a proxy for return on investment.

Right ad, just the wrong audience

Nearly 20 years ago, I worked with GlaxoSmithKline (GSK) on their Oxy brand – an acne treatment for teenagers. The brand had passed its heyday of brand leadership, but still advertised on TV with ads intended to appeal to teenage users. When I took on the brand I went back to basics: sales data and distribution, targeting, etc. But something didn't add up, so I politely challenged the marketing team.

"Your target audience is male and female teens, right? But you're buying daytime TV spots." I asked.

"Yes, it's cheap airtime and there's evidence it's working", they replied, confidently.

"But your distribution is exclusively supermarkets. Do you believe teenagers are shopping specifically for your product in supermarkets?"

"Yes. They must be."

The marketing team believed they knew and were in control of who they were targeting and who therefore was buying their product.

I asked them to check. We duly discovered, as I had suspected, that the TV campaigns were being seen by parents who were then buying the product for their spotty kids with the weekly shop in supermarkets. Teenagers don't shop alone in Sainsbury's, and wild horses would have to drag most of them there to accompany a parent for the weekly shop.

The interesting learning here is when identifying an advertising target, there is often an important difference between who chooses, who uses, who buys, and who benefits. For example, if we consider the responsibility and control of the different family members when buying a car, these differences are critically important.

Crucially, what the GSK marketing team did right was to accept that they didn't have the control they thought they did over how people responded to their advertising so they changed course to a media selection targeting teenagers – the users and beneficiaries of the brand.

Figure 10 – Investment and return in the Meikle Matrix

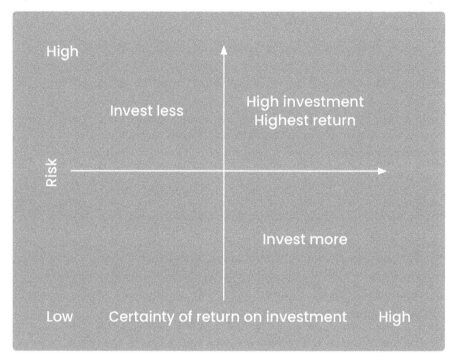

These two ways to increase return are pivotal to the marketer's responsibility because huge amounts of time and energy are spent trying to mitigate risks and achieve certainty of returns on investment. Every pound and minute spent mitigating risk is either increasing a marketer's investment (albeit indirectly) or reducing their return – because a) it takes longer to get to market or b) the riskier, more distinctive qualities of the idea have to be knocked off or toned down to make a campaign more like something seen before – and therefore more predictable. Marketers mitigate risk in the belief they are increasing control and thereby moving from *Stress* to *Flow*, but they are also investing more and could therefore be moving from *Flow* to *Stress* in *Figure* 10.

Whichever way we look at marketing through the lens of responsibility, it is a series of gambles – like spins of the roulette wheel. The variables of risk are whether the marketer takes the low-odds gambles on red and black or if they're a high-risk double zero kind of player. When marketers are good at their job, they can win; if they're not so good at it, they will watch their gambling chips diminish on each spin and their market share shrink.

Essentially, marketers' responsibility for their brands' performance is unpredictable and cannot be neatly managed by more robust processes or tougher research action standards. A huge amount of marketers' success or failure comes down to their judgement. Sometimes even conservative campaigns won't work or don't work to the degree that might have been hoped. That doesn't necessarily mean that a marketer's poor judgement was to blame, it may be that on that spin of the roulette wheel the ball landed on red and not black and they lost their stake due to one or several of the gazillion other variables – or just bad luck.

Compounding the challenges of life for marketers in *Stress* is the personal responsibility marketers have – failure could put their livelihoods on the line. So, it's little wonder so many marketers play safe and enjoy lower, more reliable returns. But I wonder whether we'd find that marketers with a lower burden of responsibility for outcomes, with a lower fear of failure, could deliver higher returns than those with higher burdens of responsibility because they weren't so reluctant to take greater risks.

While there's much marketers cannot control, Chief Marketing Officers (CMOs), in particular, usually have a reasonable degree of control over their resources – the people in their departments and their outside agencies. Indeed, most of the marketer's job is the intelligent and strategic application of different controls over their resources to achieve the ends for which they are responsible. While a CMO may have the control to hire or fire people or agencies, they must also rely on them: on their proficiency, their effort, their integrity, and their motivation. What is more, they will have to relinquish some control and rely on their own teams and agencies to cooperate with one another to fulfil the marketer's objectives.

Marketers as orchestral conductors

Like conductors of orchestras, marketers coordinate, balance, and harmonise each of their different external resources, as well as their own resources, to perform an effective tune. Marketers cannot play all the instruments themselves, so their direct control is more limited, but their responsibility for the tune remains high. Within their orchestra of external resources, some sections are reliant on others. For example, if the conclusions of marketing's market researchers are wrong or inaccurate then the value of the agencies acting on those conclusions can be anything between compromised to totally useless to actually damaging. But the opposite is equally true.

However, it's only on concert night when it has all to come together, that our marketer will know if they got it right. Because we mustn't forget, our marketer is competing with other marketers, who are all putting on their own concerts for their own brands with their own musicians (who might be significantly better or worse than their own). All these other marketers are managing all these variables and investments in their own efforts, too, to gain higher returns - but specifically at our marketer's expense.

> We can't always predict or know what competitive brands might be planning – and most likely at our expense.

Figure 11 – The CMO's orchestra of resources

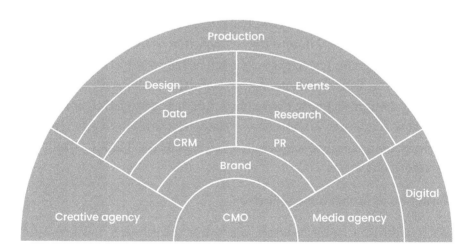

While it seems that our marketer is therefore moving further into the bottom right-hand corner of the Meikle Matrix *Stress*, there's more …

Our marketers have stakeholders, too (see Figure 12 below), who will often impose their own points of view about how marketing bets should be placed and how much they should gamble, while often continuing to hold the marketer responsible for the outcome. Cuts can be imposed on marketing expenditure or on the marketing department headcount by their finance department; procurement might find "savings" that then vanish from our marketer's total budgets; demands can be made on marketing from sales departments or even from manufacture, all of which can act as controls over marketing.

Figure 12 – Marketing stakeholders.

Within this turmoil of controls, marketers must forge, broker, negotiate, persuade, and execute marketing strategies to achieve their business objectives.

Through the lens of responsibility and control, how can marketers survive such chaos? Not only that, but orchestrate their resources within the chaos to deliver what they need to perform in tempo and in tune?

On the face of it, from the marketer's perspective, the situation can appear to have little in their favour. As we go through Figure 13 below, we can see that marketing's stakeholders can have high control over marketing but still hold them responsible for marketing performance – putting a) stakeholders in *Non-stick* from marketing's perspective and b) putting marketing in *Stress*.

The marketer's agencies are doing the work of campaign development and thus are controlling what they do in that respect. Although the agencies are likely incentivised by their results, they are not as dependent upon the return on investment as marketing. Once again, marketing is in *Stress* because c) they feel their agencies are in control without proper responsibility. Without understanding the perspective of the other parties, marketing can feel like they're the only ones in Stress and everyone else has it easy.

Figure 13 – Marketing, their stakeholders and agencies, part 1

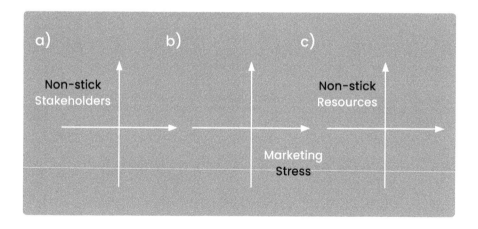

But looking at the same situation again from the perspective of each party, and with the right balance of responsibility and control, it can appear to be quite different.

The stakeholders' day-to-day control over marketing ought to be relatively low; but the stakeholders shouldn't be involved in marketing day-to-day – their control is in the selection of the CMO – *Flow*. They have other fish to fry – see Chapter Eleven. After that, they should be leaving them to it. These stakeholders do have high responsibility for marketing returns, but in the same way they do over all major business operations. It's just that some need to be dissuaded from bikeshedding (see panel below). When they practice properly, stakeholders and marketers can both be in *Flow*.

> Bikeshedding is a term derived from C. Northcote Parkinson's law of triviality.[23]
>
> Parkinson observed a committee which had been convened to approve plans for a nuclear power plant. Committee members avoided spending much time discussing the more important, difficult, and complicated issues relating to the power plant and spent more time discussing the materials they should use for the employees' bike shed.
>
> Parkinson's Law of Triviality states: The time spent on any item of the agenda will be in inverse proportion to the sum of money involved.

Marketers' controls over their agencies are many, including: the selection of agencies, how they work with them, how much to pay them, how well they brief them and incentivise them, and so on. They also have total responsibility for the agency's work because of all of those controls. Again, high control and high responsibility put marketers in *Flow*.

From the agency's perspective, if they're being told what to do by the marketer, then the agency cannot also be so responsible for it. In this case, the agency's responsibility is to satisfy their client by accepting their control and thereby not upsetting them and retaining the client's business. However, the agency should also defer *responsibility* for their work to the client who instructed them, putting the agency in *Toil*, however most agencies *retain* responsibility despite not having control and are therefore in *Stress* with such clients.

---

23 Parkinson's Law, Publisher John Murray 1958

Satisfy my responsibilities and you can have control.

When a client of mine once requested further changes to a script, which was probably about idea number 12, draft 20, I said something like this – which I'll now paraphrase and condense for the sake of expediency:

"OK, if you insist, but you have to recognise that this isn't our ad anymore. You've changed it so much, it's now your ad. So, if you'll agree to give us a B rating for our agency performance bonus on this ad regardless of what it achieves, then we can do whatever you like."

My agency couldn't be responsible for the performance of an ad that bore no resemblance to the one we recommended, but I was still responsible for the revenue from the performance bonus.

But aside from the prospect of losing a client, in most circumstances, when agencies are given the responsibility to achieve specific campaign objectives, the agency will work much harder to achieve them if they are also given more control over how to do so. It's no different to managing employees for outcomes, it's just a group of people instead of one person who works directly for us. So again, this high control and high responsibility puts agencies in *Flow*.

Figure 14 – Marketing, their stakeholders and agencies, part II

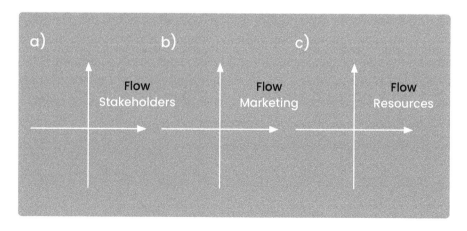

a) Stakeholders are in *Flow* because they choose the CMO and agree what they need to achieve.

a) Marketing is in *Flow* because the marketers know what they have to do, they know how to do it, and they have the resources to do it.

a) Their resources should be in *Flow*, too, because they've been selected for their ability to fulfil their role and usually specialise in it.

Lead agencies and free-for-all briefs

It's not quite that straight forward, however, when dealing with multiple agencies which have a cross-over of capabilities. Throughout my career I've witnessed a growing trend away from the idea of a 'lead agency' and toward some sort of pseudo-democratic free-for-all briefing of all agencies in all disciplines. In the latter scenario, one communication's brief is issued and all the agencies can independently pitch their ideas to the client about how to address it. There are some circumstances, although rare, where I could appreciate the need for this approach. For example, if a rapid response was required to an unexpected event in the market or a business crisis meant the overall marketing investment was being radically reduced so that the conventional allocation of budget across channels had to be revised. But as a day-to-day practice, the free-for-all is an example of how *not* to allocate responsibility and control.

If the 'winning' idea determines which agency leads the others for a campaign and it is won by an agency that does not normally lead, then the agency that would normally be responsible for the development of such ideas is moved from *Flow* to *Stress* in an instant. This applies to the campaign in hand but also for future campaigns where the other agencies get a free shot at increasing their scope of work (and thereby revenue and reputation) in a we've-nothing-to-lose-but-some-time-and-effort beauty parade of ideas.

Figure 15 – Competing roster agencies in the Meikle Matrix

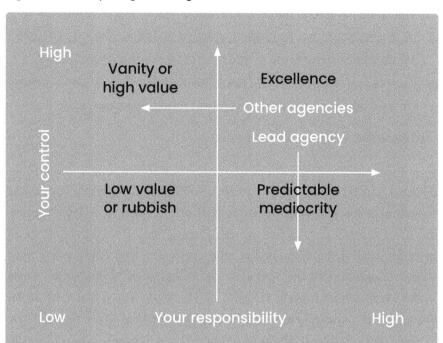

The greater danger here is that lead agencies, for fear of losing the lead to their competitors, are much more likely to give clients what they think the clients want rather than what they might need. They'll be more reluctant to speak their truth to the client's power because they've been put in *Stress* where the output is Predictable mediocrity. More often than not, the lead agency is the creative advertising agency, so if the very thing they do, their raison d'etre to be engaged with the client, is up for grabs, they'll be more likely to elevate their responsibility to protecting their revenue rather than doing what they think is right.

Agencies both perform better and cooperate better when they have clear responsibilities and control with the client and each other. That is not to say that they should have master-servant relationships between each other, but rather the principles of their cooperation should be clear, and in the event of an impasse or disagreement, there should be a route to resolve it, either by a carrying vote being given to the agency most responsible for the outcome (essentially a sheriff's badge) or the marketer having to make a choice.

As part of relinquishing control to agencies, marketers should also consider the agencies' talent resource as a form of control that I encourage clients to use lightly, if at all. For example, if a client tells its agency how much team resource they need, i.e., what kind of people in what kind of roles with what kind of experience, then there are a number of obvious problems:

1. How does the client know?

2. Why is the client managing the agency's resources?

3. If something goes wrong – who's responsible/accountable?

Instead, I advocate saying, *"This is the budget, these are the tasks that need to be completed, please can you match talent to task to deliver what I need?"* By all means, listen to the agency's feedback. By all means, have an ongoing dialogue about it, not least because the scope of work may change. But marketers need to be careful not to fall into the trap of diminishing their agencies' responsibility because they have increased their control over their agencies' resource.

An increasingly common occurrence is heavy-handed negotiations being made over agency fees and thereby agency resources. Such heavy handedness is usually driven by procurement and can even involve the use of threats to go to an alternate agency over agency fee disputes. Such practices almost always result in the client buying less value for less money from the agency. The client decreases the agency's control while maintaining their responsibility and suffering the compromised output of *Stress*. The most dangerous thing about having an agency in *Stress* is that their natural centre of gravity from that situation is *Toil* – which is the lowest possible agency value. To *Tune Up* an agency, moving them from *Stress* to *Flow*, takes a plan and takes effort.

Marketers' organisations are different, but it's still not uncommon to hear of their procurement departments taking the reins in a pitch when the subject of money arises. Whether by forensic examination of agencies' overheads and resource plans or encouraging competing agencies to cut their own throats with the use of reverse auctions, these are forms of control that ought to bring responsibility with them. However, it's very rare for the same procurement departments who exercise such high levels of control in these circumstances to have any direct responsibility for the marketing performance their actions are affecting (*see panel titled Unaligned Interests in Chapter Eight*).

People in marketing procurement have a responsibility to procure agency services for marketing that represent the best available value, but they almost universally have another level of responsibility – to themselves.

Those in marketing procurement are often incentivised to make savings with personal bonuses for targets reached. Consequently, they may negotiate harder to reduce the investment in agencies with little responsibility to marketing but more to themselves. Ironically, given another role of procurement is to mitigate risk; such action increases the risk of agencies allocating less expensive, less experienced, and less talented people to these accounts. Thus increasing the risk of failure to achieve the best possible return. Put simply: procurement can often meet its objective by buying cheaper, less effective advertising.

In this situation, the distribution of responsibility and control sees marketers and agencies move from *Flow* to *Stress* and marketing procurement, enjoying their "savings" bonuses in *Non-stick*.

Figure 16 – Procurement incentives in the Meikle Matrix

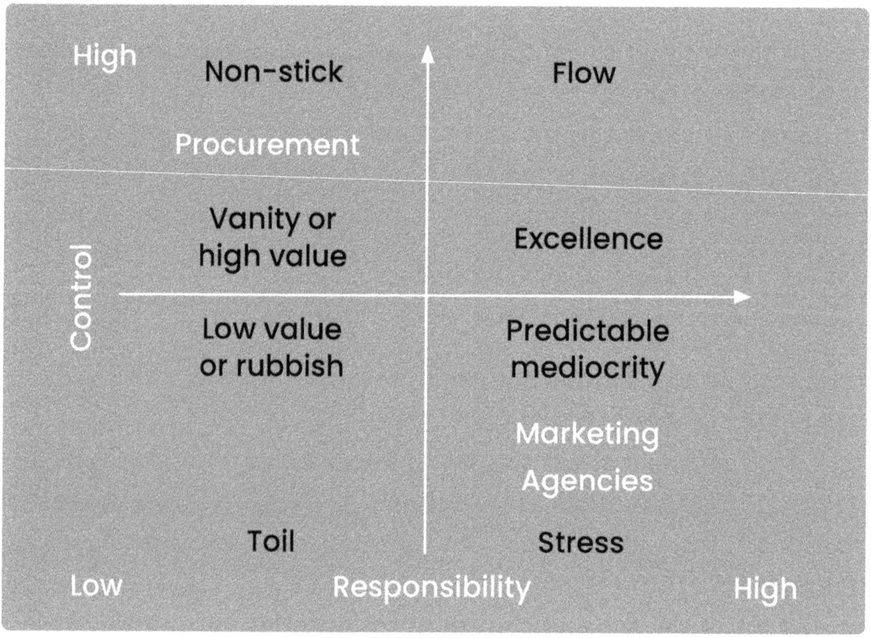

> The ultimate control a marketer has over their agency is the choice of agency.

In the light of marketers' needs to confidently delegate to agencies for outcomes, agencies might better understand why so often their positions are reassessed by incoming marketing directors and CMOs. That's not to say it's necessarily a reasonable thing to do, but it is understandable, because the ultimate control a marketer has over their agency's performance is the choice of agency.

Time is a factor of control

"I love deadlines. I love the whooshing noise they make as they go by."

Douglas Adams, The Salmon of Doubt

Time pressure is a staple condition of advertising and marketing, and it is a phenomenal source of external control, as well as control that can be imposed on one party by another. Time pressure acts on us often without our knowing how it's affecting our ability to think, judge, or make decisions. Time's relentless march in one direction makes it a constant of control like no other, so the only way to rebalance its power is to get ahead of it. I've encountered lots of people who say they respond well to time pressure. The truth is more likely that they make decisions more quickly under time pressure, largely because they have no choice.

Carsten de Dreu, Dutch Professor of Social and Organizational Psychology at Leiden University and Professor of Behavioural Economics at the University of Amsterdam, has demonstrated that time pressure closes people's minds; it does not open them to possibility. Instead of being able to accommodate others' points of view, time pressure actually does the opposite, reducing integrative thinking and making it more difficult to take other people's interests into account objectively or effectively. It's the catalyst to achieve the zero-sum game, arguably the worst outcome of any negotiation.[24]

---

24 Bar the minus two-sum game, which is favoured only by a few sociopaths.

> Time pressure closes minds; it reduces integrative
> thinking is the catalyst to the zero-sum game.

To pee or not to pee

While participating in European negotiations in Brussels In 2011,
the Guardian newspaper reported of the UK's then prime minister,
David Cameron, that he had used his tried and tested "full-bladder
technique". Cameron claimed by intentionally making himself
need to pee, he achieved the greatest focus and clarity of thought
during the lengthy negotiation sessions and formal dinner.[25]

While Cameron might believe that creating his own time pressure
provides him with focus and clarity, those who have studied the
effect of time pressure disagree.

In client/agency relationships, which have been established to solve complex strategic and creative problems through cooperation and collaboration, time pressure is therefore one of the worst possible conditions for success, yet it is one which is so often taken as a given – as a constant condition of the industry.

One of the simplest ways marketers can improve their performance and that of their agencies is better forward planning. The best clients I've worked for provided detailed scopes of work for the year ahead, far in advance of the year to which it applied, and even prioritised the year's projects from the most important to the least. The result wasn't just better work, but when the agency knows the brief ought to be coming, they can ask for it. And as an agency they would be far more accountable to these clients for delivering good work on time than to those working for clients who left the briefing a little too late.

---

25 Leo Hickman, The Guardian Online December 12, 2011

Knowing when not to use control

It's critically important to exert control as a marketer to focus on what matters rather than what might otherwise be a more ceremonial reflex of control. An example here:

A case study in the wise use of power

In the summer of 2018, The HTBAG Co[26] was approached by Greater Anglia (GA), a UK train franchise owned by Abellio, to run a review for their creative advertising account. GA's network was at the start of an unprecedented £1.4 billion investment to replace every single train in East Anglia and upgrade a number of stations over the coming years. Marketing's role was to follow suit and transform the network's advertising, both to hail the arrival of the new trains when they came and to fill the extra seats they would be providing.

We agreed a process to identify the right size and profile of ad agency and proceeded to execute it.

I call the second round of the HTBAG Co's selection process an Acid Test. As the name suggests, it's a form of chemistry session only tougher, designed to test the mettle of five agencies through case studies and rigorous, two-way, question-and-answer sessions. My client, David Metherell, GA's Head of Commercial Development, and I had seen one or two of our shortlist of five and were grabbing some lunch at a pub, 100 yards down the road from our next meeting with the agency Atomic.

David and I were revisiting the reasons we'd shortlisted them when my phone rang. Jon Goulding, Atomic's CEO, wanted to know if they were in the right place for the meeting – i.e., where the conference room was at GA's station in Chelmsford. The problem was the Acid Test was planned to be held in Atomic's office in Farringdon, 200 yards from David and me and more than thirty miles away from Jon and his team.

Just imagine the silence that hung there on the other end of the phone when I explained where we were. Such a major logistical cock-up doesn't usually make the best impression when an agency is trying to get selected for a pitch shortlist.

---

26 AKA The How to Buy a Gorilla Company, or rather, me.

As Jon's heart audibly sank, I asked him to hold the line, muted my phone and turned to David and explained what had happened.

"As I see it, we have three options," I said.

"Option one, we drop Atomic from the process. Option two: we can reschedule. Option three: Jon reckons they can be back in 40 minutes maximum, so we can have a cheeky pint of Guinness here while they head back from Chelmsford faster than Roadrunner. On the face of it, Option one is justifiable but it could be a mistake. We know why we wanted to see them; I doubt very much this is normal for them, and I can pretty much guarantee it will never happen again if you end up choosing them. Furthermore, if we give them a pass on this, they will move heaven and earth for you now and likely forever; plus, we will have unlimited piss-taking rights from here to eternity."

David would probably admit being a man of few words. He simply paused, smiled, and said,

"You'd better get the beers in then."

And I went to the bar.

Contrary to the Atomic team's expectations a couple of hours earlier, the meeting went very well, and Atomic went through to the final three.

On the day of the pitch, Atomic was the last agency to present their ideas. The GA pitch team included David, Ela Hawran-Beaumont, GA's Senior Marketing Manager, Martin Moran their Commercial Director, and me.

The first two agencies' presentations were both excellent, but the first one in particular was outstanding. The creative idea was spot on the brief and the whole team was visibly excited by the agency, their team, their approach, and their idea. They knocked it out of the park. But, last to present, Atomic also knocked it out the park – just that bit further.

The idea Atomic developed personified the GA brand as an animated hare made of a mesh of triangles that changed shape and size as it moved and in GA's red and grey colourways; what is termed "low poly" in computer graphics. Simply, the hare represented speed, agility, technology, modernity and reflected it all through a beloved feature of wildlife from this rural region. All of which would have been lost, indeed would never have been seen, had David Metherell's decision gone another way.

David said,

"It perhaps would have been a natural instinct to drop Atomic from the competition. But although the mistake was embarrassing for them, it didn't really matter that much. People make mistakes, but not every mistake needs a consequence. When we arrived at the meeting you could see they were gutted about what had happened. It wouldn't have served us well to throw them out of a process when we didn't yet know what they could do. As it happened, Atomic were fantastic and our whole organisation immediately got behind their idea. Their GA hare is now even on the trains. We would have missed out on all that if we'd been picky over a little mix up."

As is so often the case when we haven't walked a mile in somebody else's shoes, agencies often fail to realise the stress that marketers can feel. Depending on their organisations, marketers can be in *Stress* or *Flow* and often move between the two, but it's very rare for them to have low levels of responsibility.

Things go wrong when neither the client nor the agency recognise where the other is in the Meikle Matrix. It's one of the many reasons why leadership qualities of empathy, maturity, and emotional intelligence are so important. Likewise, it would be helpful for their mutual understanding and productivity for them to have more open conversations about where they are with other relationships, such as the marketer's relationship with the board or the agency's relationship with third-party production resources or another agency. With some time and dialogue, there's little reason why most of these relationships can't be in *Flow* for both parties. In the next chapter we'll look at *Tuning Up* these relationships if they're not in *Flow* and how sometimes we must deal with *Stress* and just learn to manage it better.

Chapter Four Summary

Marketing is a form of business gambling: placing stakes in the hope that they will transform into greater fortunes. The process of this transformation can never be entirely controlled and the future can never be 100% reliably predicted.

Marketers are managing a million moving parts on a day-to-day basis of internal stakeholders and pressures, external resources and demands, all of which need to be managed and coordinated like a conductor manages an orchestra.

Micro-management is not only counterproductive to the value marketers want their agencies to create, but it is also impractical from the sheer volume of instructions that would need to be given. Therefore, the interests (the responsibilities) of marketers and agencies need to be aligned and guided to *Flow*. Marketers and their agencies need to *Tune Up*.

The responsibility a marketer takes for a return on marketing investment must be risk savvy. Low investments seeking high yields will need to be riskier than high investments requiring lower yields.

It is essential for marketing and marketing procurement to have the shared objectives, responsibilities, strategies to achieve them, and incentives to do so. This is *Tuning Up* between departments.

Agency rosters need clearly defined roles and responsibilities and must agree in principle the way in which they'll work and collaborate with their client's other resources.

Time pressure is one of the worst and most commons forms of control over marketing activity and is not conducive to better judgment and decision-making. It limits our ability to see things from other's perspectives and to accommodate each other's interests.

With so much control in their hands, marketers must use it judiciously, according to what really matters and the value they want to create, not according to convention or expectation. Sometimes the opposite of the expected delivers a better outcome.

Chapter Five
Tuning Up for marketers

"The best way to predict your future is to create it."

Peter Drucker, Management Consultant 1909 – 2005

Before we get into moving within the Meikle Matrix – *Tuning Up* – it's worth remembering that what we are addressing here doesn't include marketing strategies or advertising ideas; we're focusing exclusively on the *environment* within which they are created. We're doing so in the belief that by *Tuning Up*, moving within the Meikle Matrix to *Flow*, we are likely to manage ourselves and our own performance better, and those of our teams and resources - and consequently it will indirectly benefit strategies and ideas.

It is also critical that we recognise how often set processes and procedures inform our marketing strategy rather than the other way around. Our processes (controls) have largely been developed to maximise efficiency and minimise risk, but, as we shall explore, if our strategy requires more risk, our processes may not be fit for purpose.

Everything starts with control. If a marketer doesn't have enough control, then they're straight into *Stress*. It's as simple as that, because it's pretty likely they'll have been given more than enough responsibility.

Most senior marketers I have known throughout my career report that they mostly feel they're in *Stress*. The challenge with marketing is that many of the influences affecting marketing performance are impossible to control – but most marketers nonetheless feel responsible for their influence. Even if they don't, marketers are often held responsible for them anyway, like unsuccessful lawnmower sales during a rainy spring. So, the first step for a marketer is to know the difference.

125

Step 1 – Challenge the system for more control

The fact that marketers cannot be responsible for the weather, or increased competitor spend, or a new competitor entering their market, doesn't mean they're not going to be held responsible for marketing performance, despite any intervention by such variables. Unexpected recessions, global pandemics, and other acts of God provide the only performance downturns for which marketers are not (usually) held responsible. Such black-swan events are out of everybody's control, and in their wake there's nothing any of us can do other than our best under very challenging circumstances.

> Black-swan events are out of everybody's control, in these circumstances there's nothing we can do other than our best.

However, weather, competitive activity and the like are factors marketers ought to be able to anticipate or for which they could have and should have prepared. If marketers are operating in a new and fast-growing market, they should anticipate new brands entering it, even if they don't know of any. Playing war games can establish basic scenario plans for competitive activity, so when such deleterious events happen the prepared marketers can assume more control and move quickly. Sometimes, it's possible to determine how some competitors will act in the future based on their actions in the past; for example, some brands will continue to spend during a financial downturn when the relative cost of media is low; others will not. And agencies should be helping their clients with these analyses.

But, in the face of a new competitor or a new product, a marketer must be able to adapt plans, change processes, make judgement calls between good, quick, and cheap when briefing their agencies,[27] in order to create the most effective response. These choices, judgements, and priorities are marketers' controls.

---

27 When briefing agencies on strategic and/or creative problems, the rule is you can choose any two from good, quick, and cheap.

Likewise, in the absence of an unforeseen intervention of a competitor or other extraneous variable, things change, go wrong, or just don't turn out as anticipated *anyway*. Nothing is entirely reliable. As we saw in the last chapter, marketing operations consist of innumerable moving parts, reliant on different people and different companies, and they're all changing all the time. The skill of the marketer is to be aware of them, to control these moving parts skilfully, and to do so whilst remaining conscious of time and money *and* remaining focused such that they are all aligned to achieve specific objectives. Under these circumstances, marketers' ability to navigate the inevitable mess can be significantly hampered by unnecessary or inappropriate procedures, protocols, or meddling stakeholders. Even the most gifted and experienced marketers can find themselves in *Stress*, with the result being potentially compromised performance.

The answer can be to recognise and challenge the standard ways of doing things – the structures, processes, and conventions, by presenting a business case for how it hampers (or might hamper) marketing performance. Arguing the principle and changing the procedures *in advance* is far better than fighting battles for control as they arise. When we only do the latter, the system snaps back afterwards to make us unprepared in the same way the next time.

Tuning up for new tech in travel

By way of an example unrelated to marketing but illustrative of both the problem and the solution, a friend of mine since school, Harvey Tate, now works in International Airlines Group (IAG) in their digital business transformation team, aptly named Hangar 51. These guys are not responsible for the technology that might be going into the smoother and more efficient running of Heathrow Terminal 5 next week or next month; they're responsible for transformational change – the stuff most of us haven't heard of or even thought of – ideas and technology that are being developed now that might be implemented in the years to come. But the long lead time between ideation and implementation belies the sensitivity and speed of timings required when they go to market today to find the technological capabilities they may need in the long-term.

Like any business, IAG wants to see a return on their investments through Hangar 51. Projects must therefore be industry-changing – much more akin to research and development than change management. However, the innovative and sometimes embryonic nature of these initiatives makes it very difficult to develop a conventional business case for them where timelines are usually shorter, specific, and predictable.

As with any business of scale, cost control is an essential part of good governance, so initially, in the normal run of events, the Hangar 51 team would have developed a business case with 1-, 2-, and 5-year key performance indicators. They would then present this business case to the management board for budgetary approval. Then, once approved, they would have to develop a specific business case for a specific supplier to use some of the budget. For example, if they were investigating the feasibility of automated luggage carts, they would need external resources for the tech and internal resources in the form of project managers to run the project. Such requests would then require all sorts of local procedures and authorisations before they could even engage with the supplier they found. By the time they had jumped through all the administrative and procedural hoops, the new, small company they wanted to engage may have found another source of business and taken the development of their tech in a totally different direction, sending Harvey and his team back to the drawing board – responsibility without control – *Stress*.

The solution was to design a fast-track approval process for a ring-fenced pot of investment capital and to write a digital framework agreement with procurement. Initiatives could then get underway before it was too late. The process was much more suited to Hangar 51's need for short-term trials rather than long-term implementation. Instead of waiting for cycles of meetings to come around, one-pager propositions could be emailed to key stakeholders and authorised weeks and months faster than the previous procedure would have taken. The Hangar 51 team moved from *Stress* to *Flow*.

Many more ambitious marketers feel hamstrung on a day-to-day basis by their own companies' protocols and approvals. (This is also a near constant source of frustration for agencies, but they seldom seem to empathise that their clients are in similar positions.) If marketers are to increase their levels of control, then some of the things they believe are inflexible aspects of their company's processes might need to be challenged. Marketers need to be more prepared to challenge the apparent rigidity of existing processes to see whether a more suitable process for their needs is viable. *Tuning Up* is a means of creating a case for them to do that.

The first task is to determine what's fixed and what's a variable.

Step 2 – Define the objective as specifically as possible

Problems generally occur between parties when they have conflicting interests, divergent interests, or have no shared interest at all. In establishing a healthy and productive relationship, it's essential to understand what the other party or parties want from it. When people have a shared interest, they understand that their disputes or arguments are for the same purpose. A shared endeavour creates trust and a willingness to cede control from one to another on the understanding that in so doing we will still, ultimately, achieve what we want (this is a subject we'll explore further at the end of Chapter Ten).

> A shared interest engenders trust and a willingness to cede control to our collaborators.

The next stage is to define this objective as clearly as possible. In Chapter Seven we'll look at how clients and agencies are often divided by a common language, but that can happen just as easily within organisations as it can with business-to-business relationships. We spend too little time defining our terms only to discover our definitions can be worlds apart when it's most critical that they're identical. In advertising and marketing, we readily use words like "breakthrough", "creative", and "cutting-edge" when describing creative work, but we rarely sit down and agree what they actually mean. To one person these words might mean one thing (again, we'll see this in Chapter Seven), but when we're dealing with internal stakeholders, it might mean another. I would always encourage the exploration of both the definitions of such terms and their implications.

Even words like objective and strategy can easily become conflated or confused. In one relationship, the strategy to achieve a goal can define the objective of another relationship, so it's equally important to be clear about which is which and with whom and exactly what they are.

For example, the shared objective with the board might be to increase sales by 10% in the next 18 months. The strategy to achieve that could be to both increase and more effectively deploy investment in advertising media and to develop significantly more effective advertising creative work. The internal *objective* (between the marketer and the CEO) has created a *strategy* that in turn defines the shared *objective* of the client and their media agency and the client and their creative agency. Subordinate strategies are then required and must be agreed between the marketer and each agency. Such improved clarity increases marketers' and their agencies' control alike, and not least through marketers' better stakeholder management.

The implications that need to be discussed and agreed with the board are the broader dynamics implicated in the achievement of the objective. There are usually multiple ways to achieve a goal, but some will be acceptable and others less so. For example, if we take the 10% sales growth example, examine a one litre carton of a branded juice in the supermarket chiller – it might surprise some that one leading brand is not in fact one litre but 850ml. That will have reduced a significant part of the brand's cost of goods. It may also increase all the 850ml SKU's rate of sale (customers run out more quickly and so buy more frequently), not necessarily by the same amount, but by some. On the other hand, it may have also reduced the loyal customer base if some people feel they've been deceived and are cross about it (150ml less is one fewer of our five a day) – so the implication to be discussed is the relative risk to the potential return of this strategy.

It may be that fiddling with the product and cost of goods is not an option. A toothpaste manufacturer might increase the calibre of the toothpaste nozzle by 10% to achieve the same increase in sales because people judge the amount of toothpaste they squeeze by length. But again, it presents a risk if it's discovered. There are also implications for the tube's manufacture and stock management; would it work in the travel - size tube or look weird?

Another route might be to expand distribution into another sales channel or distribution area or to invest much more in the advertising's creative work or more in media or in new media channels. All of these could achieve or contribute to the same objective of a 10% increase in sales, but all have their own implications, some of which might be more palatable than others to the brand's board. Marketers must know which of these levers are at their disposal, as well as having a shared endeavour with whomever they need to cooperate.

The point here is that if we want the future to be different to the past then we have to do something differently, *and inherent in that is risk*. If we have an agreed objective with our stakeholders but they don't recognise that risk is a necessary part of achieving it, then we can find ourselves in *Stress* right off the bat. This recognition and agreement with stakeholders is also essential if we're dealing with, or dependent on, other departments or other markets, as in the LEGOLAND example in Chapter Three.

But not everybody will get the Sherriff's badge we saw in the LEGOLAND example. As an alternative, in Adam Morgan's book *The Pirate Inside*,[28] he advocates having a sponsor – somebody very high up in the organisation who has authority and is ready to intervene on the marketer's behalf if they encounter a blocker. Morgan calls them smokejumpers:

Fire fighting in dense woodland is a difficult task once the blaze has caught. Smokejumpers are people who fly low over forests in North America and, once they see a plume of smoke rising from out of the trees that indicates the beginning of a more dangerous blaze (if left unmanaged), parachute in on their own and cut a fire break around it to limit its poten-tial effect. That is, they proactively look to stop it before it causes a bigger problem – while it is still warning smoke, rather than an actual fire.

If a marketer is charged with achieving a new sales objective that is inconsistent with natural organic growth, they *must* do something

---

28 Wiley 2004.

differently. If the board with which the marketer agrees this objective can't give them the authority (control) to do things differently, they could provide a smokejumper instead who can be called upon should the need arise. While it's not a Sherriff's Badge, a smokejumper is an advocate who can break down, or find ways around, barriers as they arise from their position of authority. The job of the marketing leader is to spot the smoke before it becomes a raging fire.

Once marketers have a shared objective, they must agree *how* they're going to achieve it …

Step 3 – Define and agree the strategy to achieve that objective

It is equally important for a marketer to agree *how* they're going to achieve something as it is to agree *what* it is they want to achieve.

The Brad Pitt movie *Moneyball* I referred to in Chapter Three, in the section *Strategy without consensus*, indicates how damaging it can be to have a difference of opinion about how to do something, and the same is true of advertising strategy.

In the early 2000s, I was working with a large multinational client launching a new hay fever treatment. Their business already had a market leading tablet for hay fever, plus they had a twice-a-day hay fever spray under a different brand, but they now had regulatory approval to launch their once-a-day hay fever spray that was previously only available on prescription – under yet another brand name.

It took very little time at all for me and my team to find ourselves in *Stress*. The agency's role was to develop a creative strategy and idea that would meet the client's approval and subsequently their specific action standards for pre-test research. So far so good; none of this is particularly unusual. However, Marketing 101 states:

1. Marketers must identify an audience with a desire or need that their product fulfils …

2. … to whom they can present a proposition for their product in a persuasive way …

3. … such that prospects will try, and then hopefully adopt, their brand.

Within the population segment of hay fever sufferers there are three groups: those who do not treat their symptoms at all, those who treat their symptoms with tablets (the majority), and those who treat with sprays (a smaller group because many people find snorting liquids unpleasant). But sprays are a more effective treatment because they prevent the allergic reaction from happening at all, whereas tablets treat the symptoms after the allergic reaction. Our question to the client was, "What's our source of business? Which of these groups are we meant to persuade to do what?" Their reply was ...

"We don't want to target tablet users because we'll cannibalise our tablet business. We don't want to target existing spray users, because we have most of them, too, on our twice-a-day spray. We want to target non-users to use our new spray."

Now it is the case, and it stands to reason, that sprays are both the least popular and the most effective because they are less pleasant to use than tablets. Therefore, those who use sprays are those worst affected by their allergy – i.e., their hay fever is so bad they are willing to endure the discomfort of sniffing a liquid up their nose to avoid it. And we knew all this from the client's own research. So, the client wanted to target the group who didn't even find it necessary to treat themselves with a tablet (mild sufferers) with the most unpleasant yet effective spray available. The strategy made no sense.

We asked the client what the proposition was they wanted to use to attract this market segment given these conditions.

"The most effective once-a-day spray treatment for hay fever."

Our heads really started to hurt now. How could this proposition avoid automatically appealing to their existing twice-a-day spray users? What would we do, start the ad by saying, "*If you already buy a twice-a-day spray – stop watching now*"? Surely a proposition to target tablet users with a more effective treatment than their tablet and one that's half as unpleasant to use (one spray per day vs two) would be better? It would achieve growth at the expense of all tablets, although some would be from their own brand.

> No amount of control will compensate for a flawed strategy.

The debate raged as time ticked away. The season-sensitive launch was approaching, so the client insisted on using creative work as a means of overcoming a strategic impasse. I escalated the problem internally, twice, and repeatedly engaged the client in the debate. My senior management capitulated to the client's control, twice, and the process continued, with my team having continued responsibility for the outcome without control.

The consequence of *Stress* is either to feel the stress or to stop caring. Nobody wanted to work on the project, especially in the creative department where the brief bounced around from one reluctant team to another week by week, dodged only by those who would have left if they'd been asked to do it. My team and I were all fed up, demotivated, and lost all respect for our client's and our own management's failure to deal with the real issue. Nonetheless, we tried proposition workshops, research groups, and a creative hothouse in an exotic location with the most senior client close at hand to judge ideas. Our team must have presented at least 30 different concepts. Finally, the client put another of their roster agencies on the brief, which I warned my agency's leadership was going to happen – the brand was pitched, and we lost.

Normally, if somebody loses a piece of business it's a body blow to the team and the agency. This felt more like emancipation. We did our best in the pitch and we all worked hard, but the outcome was inevitable. There was no point in caring about the loss because the situation had become futile. We had reached a point of learned hopelessness, the inevitable outcome of spending too long in *Stress*.

> The inevitable outcome of too long spent under stress is learned hopelessness – essentially we quit and leave or we quit and stay.

The work the client bought from the other agency was pretty much the same as an idea we had developed months before; one we had researched and knew wouldn't work. But for the client it was somehow progress. After the predictably poor product launch, within a couple of years the product had to be launched again – this time under the same brand as the client's marketing-leading tablet, a suggestion we had made in the original briefing around three years earlier.

There are no two ways about it: capitulation as a strategy to avoid conflict does not work if the problem remains unsolved. Had we dealt with the real problem at the outset, the client would have saved themselves from a failed launch; they would have also saved huge agency fees and the time value of money returned on their investment from a more successful, earlier launch.

An unofficial post-mortem later revealed that the UK Marketing Director lost his job and the international client was moved to another category. The problem had been that neither had stood up to their boss and pointed out the flawed strategy. Instead, they fluffed the strategy in the hope that creativity might solve it, somehow – as if by magic. That's one of the problems with advertising and marketing: if we'd been in construction and disagreed about whether we were building a house out of timber or brick, we wouldn't have been able to say, "Well, let's just start building and it'll sort itself out when we decorate it."

Step 4 – Make sure all interests are aligned

We've already recognised that we can escalate our responsibilities and our controls if necessary, but it is equally vital to appreciate that others can do the same. It may not be enough to collectively declare that we have a shared interest; some may also have a conflicting interest on a higher or different level.

Racing to the bottom

As an example, I once advised a client's procurement department that their planned use of a reverse auction[29] was a very bad idea; they were running a media pitch for their marketing team. I was consulting for the client at the time on other aspects of their marketing operations, so I made my thoughts heard in marketing, too. Sadly, the most I achieved was procurement reassuring marketing they would be running the tender for the best value proposal, not necessarily the lowest price, i.e., that their auction was not the single determining factor. However, like most procurement departments, they had a higher-level responsibility in the form of savings targets to reach.

---

29 For the uninitiated, a reverse auction is one where agencies have to bid lower and lower rates against each other either to win an account or to count towards their score in winning it. It's an exercise in seeing how deeply a business will cut its own throat to win.

I knew the leader of one of the larger competing media agencies and asked her what she thought of the auction afterwards. She told me it was extraordinary to witness how two companies continued bidding after her agency had pulled out because it obviously wouldn't be possible to service the business properly at that level. And indeed it wasn't. The new agency relationship was an unmitigated disaster. The account was woefully under-resourced, and the media agency performed abysmally. As they say, you get what you pay for. The slow process of building the account team up to competence, which required an increase in fees, became marketing's responsibility, not procurement's. Procurement's savings targets were not adjusted retrospectively either. A damaging and unworkable "saving" paid out for them. Procurement successfully bought less for less, despite a shared objective to buy for value. Procurement was in *Non-stick,* leaving both the agency and the client in *Stress.*

Step 5 – Ensure you have an honest environment

"Deferred to, agreed with, acquiesced in. Who can flourish on such a daily diet of compliance? "

The Madness of King George
Alan Bennett, 1994

If we successfully *Tune Up*, or indeed if we already have the control commensurate with our responsibility, it's essential that we check our environment for undue deference. One of a successful marketers' greatest strengths is their judgement, but if their teams are deferential, they may only be given what their teams believe to be what marketing leadership want to hear or see.

This is the source of one of agencies' biggest frustrations – they see their strategies and ideas altered and second-guessed *before* they are presented for approval.

Not music to my ears

In the early noughties I had a client for whom we made a 60 second commercial for a budget investment of c. £1m. The client presented the ad to his boss, who said he "wasn't sure about the music". The problem was that the ad had been shot and edited specifically to work with the music track, such was the nature of the idea. The music had been presented and agreed with my senior client at the pre-production meeting, for the same reason. Nonetheless, this senior client had our agency frantically spend an additional £50,000 commissioning new music tracks to be composed and recorded, searching for other existing music that would fit the rhythm of the edit, all with only a week before the air date. When the client's boss saw the alternatives they said, *"None of these are as good as the original, but it wasn't that big a deal."* And we proceeded as if the last week and £50k down the toilet had never happened. Everybody perceived his boss's response as unshakeable determination to impose his will—it wasn't. A simple question like, *"How unsure are you of it? The ad was shot and edited to the music track."* posed earlier might have avoided lost time and money. Instead, control was ceded because of a perception of senior client authority, not because of his will.

When Ogilvy Russia had to launch the American Express card, I attended a meeting to discuss the launch campaign idea and end line with the owner of the bank who had the contract to distribute the card. The owner of the bank (one guy!) was surrounded by five or six very senior advisors and his American Express marketing director. Everybody was happy with the advertising ideas, but the bank owner favoured an end line that we felt significantly diminished the power of the idea. When I spoke up to politely challenge him the room went silent. I swear the temperature dropped a few degrees. This client was used to complete, unquestioning compliance. We ran his choice of end line, and a double meaning – which made the idea much more engaging – was lost.

In contrast, in a more inclusive and cooperative banking environment, when Pete Markey was the CMO of TSB in the UK, he had three direct reports and a department of c. 50 across locations in London and Bristol.

"There's no point hiring smart people if they don't get to be smart. My team has greatest value to me when they tell me exactly what they think – especially when they disagree with me. It's not my job to have all the solutions or know precisely how to achieve any given objective all on my own. My job is to manage my team's performance and use my judgement to get the best out of them. For that to work they have to feel totally unafraid of voicing potentially conflicting views."

Pete Markey, CMO, TSB.

The ultimate endline

Almost as an antidote to my experience on American Express, above, I was fortunate enough to hear a story from Robin Wight when he received his fellowship award from the marketing society. As I recall the tale, Robin's European BMW client had been told the brand had a new line which had been developed in the US, "The ultimate driving machine", which he decided he didn't like, so he briefed Robin's agency, WCRS, to develop an alternative line. They worked on the brief for weeks until Robin finally told his client that they hadn't been able to produce anything better. Apparently, Robin's client bellowed, "What the hell do I pay you for then?" to which Robin replied, "My judgement."

Trying to do the right thing, make the right decisions and judgements, is everybody's responsibility at work. To fulfil that responsibility, we may have to ask questions of those with power and authority to direct us, but that doesn't mean we shouldn't ask. Not everybody has a Pete Markey who actively encourages different points of view and ideas – but equally it's important that we don't assume we haven't. We have a duty to ask.

Step 6 – Consider what's needed for success

Sometimes the stress and chaos of life in *Stress* makes it a challenge just to know where to start when we want to affect meaningful change. So, when we can't see the wood for the trees, start with the end in mind and work backwards from there.

Dependency modelling

A dependency model is a technique for doing just that. It works backwards from an overarching objective right through to an action list.

David Abrahams, author of *Brand Risk*,[30] has refined this approach to suit problem-solving by marketers. It was inspired by a methodology originally used by engineers for the preventive analysis of complex system failure, such as jet engine shutdown in flight. The adapted technique takes challenging marketing issues or opportunities and breaks them down into intelligible, manageable pieces.

In the first place, David Abrahams advocates flipping from a narrow focus on risk to a broader perspective on success. Instead of using dependency modelling only to determine what could go wrong, we start with a definition of success and work backwards to determine what therefore needs to be achieved – and progressively how it needs to be achieved. The logical flow of necessary conditions cascades into a rich and informative family tree of dependencies. At the very end of each branch and twig, we then have a list of the concrete actions we must take to achieve success.

For instance, our dependency model could be based on the familiar assessments of Product, Place, Price, and Promotion. Each of these will have its own hierarchy of dependencies. A viable product depends on its reliability or its efficacy or its appeal. Effective promotion may depend upon advertising, media planning and buying, and/or PR, and/or point-of sale, and/or e-commerce. Each of these elements will in turn have other factors upon which it relies – such as appropriate resources and strategies. A dependency model allows us to map not only a single sequence of elements, but also to consider alternatives to any single component in the event of its failure or inadequacy. Where appropriate, we can go beyond simple expressions of adequacy, adding and consolidating relevant metrics.

By way of a simple domestic illustration, if we wanted to bake a great cake, success would have three primary components: the right ingredients, the right equipment, the right method. So now we can check what we have and look at options.

_____

30 Gower, 2008

Figure 17 – David Abraham's dependency model

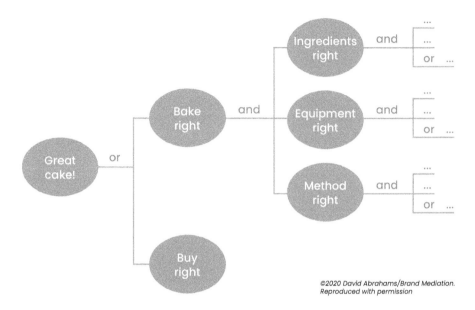

©2020 David Abrahams/Brand Mediation.
Reproduced with permission

Populating and elaborating our dependencies helps by mapping our dependent relationships with the more intangible factors affecting success, too. First, we draw the Meikle Matrix on a sheet of paper for each of our relationships. It is important that each relationship has its own Matrix. For each one, we state the shared objective. (If there isn't a shared objective, then we need one – see Step 2 above). For each one we also state the shared strategy to achieve the objective (If there isn't one, see Step 3 above – we need one). We track where we think we are and where we think they are in the Matrix. Importantly, thinking of the other party's stakeholders, we ask ourselves where they think they are in those relationships. Often, being in *Stress* cascades through organisations (see Figure 25, Chapter Eleven).

Once we have identified where we feel we are on the Matrix, we can capture every reason why we are there and determine which of them we can change or influence. Then we fit the desired Matrix outcome(s) into our dependency model. Once every dependency line is complete, the end points form a list of things to do. As they get done, we can check our confidence in their integrity against how much they are needed to contribute to overall success.

Determine if the change we want is possible

Two of the most useful questions we can always ask are:

"What are the circumstances I need to create in order to achieve my objective?" and

"What are the circumstances I need to create for you *in order to get the control I need?"*

These phrases are useful because they force us and others to confess whether change is possible and put the onus where it's due to identify what's necessary to make change happen. They each ask for one or several "if you, then I" responses – which are at least tangible. For example, "IF *you let me hire two more digital project managers,* THEN I *will meet your earlier deadline."* It makes us (or them) recognise the specific controls necessary to achieve our objectives.

Sense checking all the variables in our dependency models for feasibility is another way to achieve this. Also worth remembering, particularly if we're given a new and demanding challenge:

"These are the circumstances I need you to create for me to achieve your objective."

Sometimes, we will hit a dead end, whereby we can't be certain of the dependencies or conditions we need, in which case we've been able to identify the risk of failure instead. All of which can be very useful if we have conversations or negotiations over increasing our control commensurate with our responsibility.

Other times we may find that the change we want to make isn't available to us. It might be because of the people or the processes or the company's culture. If we find ourselves in *Stress* in these circumstances we should escalate. We must take responsibility for our own wellbeing and take the controls necessary to ensure it.

Chapter Five Summary

For marketers to move within the Meikle Matrix, it usually implies a need for greater control because responsibility comes with the territory and rarely is it less than the control available.

It's important to be clear about variables affecting marketing performance that are within the marketer's direct control, indirect control, influence, or are simply uncontrollable risks.

Interventions and discussions to increase control are better had before the control is needed than during a project – it is easier to argue in principle.

Everything stems from marketing objectives which must be defined as clearly as possible. If marketers don't have all the authority they feel they need to fulfil the objectives, they could seek a senior sponsor – a smokejumper.

Define and agree the strategy by which the assembled team (and external resources) will achieve the objective.

Ensure individuals' interests are aligned; personal agendas must not be pulling in a different direction to group objectives.

We must build safe environments in which our teams can speak freely and candidly. One of our controls is the most complete information – whether it's good or bad news or ideas and strategies different to our own. One of the most valuable qualities of a marketer is their judgement.

A dependency model can help us identify areas of risk and reduced control before embarking on a project.

Marketers can't do everything. Instead, they should consider what circumstances need to be created for success such that they can confidently relinquish controls to their team and their agencies.

Chapter Six
Agencies in the Meikle Matrix

"Most agencies run scared, most of the time ...
Frightened people are powerless to produce
good advertising."

David Ogilvy, Founder of Ogilvy & Mather 1911 – 1999

On the whole, marketing services agencies are *Stress* businesses – they generally have Low Control and High Responsibility. Agencies are usually dependent on only a small number of their clients to spend enough money to keep the agency's doors open. Of a portfolio of twenty clients, we could expect a small handful to represent the difference between the agency's success or failure.

Matters are made worse in an economic downturn when agencies are typically first to financially suffer and last to recover. A key difference between agencies and their clients is that most clients have thousands or millions more consumers than agencies have clients. If a client loses a consumer, it's not usually a body blow to their bottom line; sometimes the drop in revenue is little more than a rounding error in accounting terms. Economic downturns affect clients, of course, but the degree varies depending upon the category, and the consequences are more variable. Distress purchase categories like fuel are affected less, categories depending upon disposable income can be more vulnerable, but few are as inflexible as agencies.

In an agency, the loss of any sizeable client can have much further-reaching implications. On a scale of bad to worse, failing agencies might have to consider redundancies, mergers, being acquired, closing offices, or going out of business altogether.

Agencies' direct control over their businesses may be high, but it is forever hamstrung on a greater scale of control in the form of revenue because it relies entirely on clients – over which agencies only have influence as best.

Agencies' one-to-one influence on their clients determines how efficient the agency can be. Difficult clients or untrusting ones put weightier (and often impossible) demands on agencies, including burdens of proof for agency recommendations, or they require multiple options for campaign strategies and ideas, which are highly inefficient. More efficient work is usually much more profitable for the agency. Likewise, better work is usually more profitable for the agency in the long run; if a client buys high calibre work it improves their agency's reputation and their ability to win more business and grow. Agencies and their greater or lesser control effects their employer brand status – which influences the calibre of talent that the agency can recruit and how well it can retain it. The agency's size and standing influence its buying power over suppliers from media owners to production companies. But agencies cannot compel their clients to behave efficiently, or to spend more; likewise, they cannot compel their people to stay or for prospective hires to join them.

The most successful agencies balance their influence and their responsibilities (to clients, staff, suppliers, and to the balance sheet) and are in *Flow*. When agencies or the people within them feel like they are losing their influence in any of these areas, they move directly to *Stress*. But the route back from *Stress* to *Flow* is extremely difficult. Agencies who have thrived in *Flow* have also quickly slid into *Stress* the moment they withdrew even part of the effort required to fight the gravitational pull of high client control.

Few, if any, agencies are in *Non-stick*. Those that come closest are mostly category specialists or boutiques, but their businesses are rarely scalable. Agencies in *Toil* are more likely not to be agencies at all but high-street design and print shops with a one-to-many client profile rather than the one-to-few of established ad agencies.

The gravitational pull to *Stress* is the combination of a number of trends and dynamics in client/agency relationships. It's worth looking at them in more detail to fully understand the force against which agencies must fight to get to, or stay in, *Flow*.

Strategic partners

Many clients may think my assessment unfair because they believe their agencies are their "strategic partners". "Strategic partner" is a label that clients often give to their creative and media agencies. Countless times I have asked clients and agencies alike what "strategic partner" means. Responses vary, and the definitions are largely quite different between marketers, marketing procurement, and agencies. Marketers generally agree that strategic partners are important, and, if pressed, they add notions of shared risk and payment incentives by results. Marketing procurement usually use the label for suppliers with whom they spend a lot of money but will also reference shared risk and incentives.

Agency leaders, to whom I have also asked this question, also answered similarly to marketers, largely because the whole notion of strategic partners was initiated by clients, albeit by my judgement either naively, disingenuously, or with the knowledge that it is little more than an empty, vague promise.

Clients pay agencies. Unless they form some kind of joint venture, whereby they both invest, risk, and profit or lose from their marketing campaigns' effectiveness, then the term "partner" is misplaced. Unless the success of the agency is a strategic objective for their client.

As the buyers in the transactional relationship, clients have control. Therefore, they must take discretionary responsibility to match that control in the management of their strategic suppliers for the agencies to thrive. That's what makes them *strategic* partners instead of business partners. Clients benefit from their agencies' success indirectly: the more successful the agency, the better the people, and the better the people the better the work, and the better the work the better the return on marketing investment.

What clients frequently forget is that agencies' number one responsibility is to create value for their clients, so further words of encouragement or vacuous and empty talk of partnership are not necessarily helping to create the right dynamic as much as they might like to think. Paying agencies properly, talking up their successes, crediting their contributions, referring other clients to them, referring talent to them, consolidating and growing accounts with them are acts of strategic partnership and help keep agencies in *Flow* – which is where their clients should want them to be.

Is the agency market oversupplied?

An oversupplied market is one within which those competing have reduced control over pricing. But there is a world of difference between a market being competitive and being oversupplied. The agency market is certainly competitive – which can be a source of stress in itself, not least if the competition is better than our own agency. "Oversupplied" suggests that there is a burden of riches for clients when it comes to choosing an agency – and that would mean agencies are all much of a muchness.

> Agencies' oversupply is a myth initiated by procurement and – ironically – perpetuated by agencies.

Oversupply in the agency market is a myth – one that ironically is perpetuated by agencies in defence of their often-poor growth, but started by clients' procurement departments as a means of leveraging price negotiations. There are many advertising agencies of all shapes and sizes, with creative, media, CRM, PR, interactive specialisms, and integrated agencies in any combination, but to suggest that the market is over supplied is to argue that any one client's need can be equally and well fulfilled by an unnecessarily large number of agencies with that specialism. However, by the time a client has found the agencies ...

a.   ... with the right disciplines

b.   ... who haven't got other clients in the same category

c.   ... who aren't too big or too small

d.   ... who have been around long enough to be stable and reliable

e.   ... who show they can solve similar problems and have done so

f.   ... with terrific people – who they ...

g.   ... are ready to assign to the client's account

h.   ... who the client likes and wants to work with

... the oversupplied market looks pretty limited. It feels paradoxical that at the same time as clients use pitches to identify the different qualities they need from agencies, they also say the market is oversupplied to their need. Agencies are either different or they're not.

But the perception of oversupply is the reality for agencies, and the gravitational pull to a compliant and therefore stressful relationship with their clients in *Stress* is perpetuated by marketing procurement retelling this myth to the agency community. The perception is reinforced by some of the heavier handed marketers saying to their agencies, "*If you won't do what we want there are plenty of others who will*" when they meet significant resistance. Thankfully, such clients are few, but they still exist, and I've known a few.

Client/staff turnover

A business that relies on influence relies on relationships, but these aren't built overnight. Longstanding relationships are difficult to build when senior marketers move from company to company as often as they do. It is still the commonly held belief that the average tenure for marketing leaders is 18 months. Whatever the figure, high turnover means marketing relationships with agencies often must be built from scratch, not to mention relationships with the rest of the marketing team if they, too, have a high turnover. In turn, new marketing leadership often prompts agency pitches, and the whole relationship thing starts again.

The pressures of this situation also include, of course, the dynamics of a marketer's position in the Meikle Matrix, as outlined in previous chapters, and their desire for control. Collectively, these create the gravitational pull to *Stress*, to which agencies feel they are constantly subjected.

Returning to agencies' responsibilities, they are myriad and diverse:

1. Satisfy and retain their clients

2. Produce reputation-building ideas and strategies

3. Produce campaigns that deliver returns on their clients' investments

4. Attract and retain its talent

5. Be sustainably profitable

6. Maintain a competitive, differentiated reputation

7. Win new clients and grow and/or acquire and/or diversify

It is important to recognise that these responsibilities are felt beyond the management team. However, not all agency departments have the same responsibilities.

The agency management team and the client service department (account management) will have a high sense of responsibility from 1 to 7, though mysteriously in many agencies account management is still not responsible for the profitability of their accounts. Strategy and planning will mostly feel responsible for 3 but also for 1 and 2. Creative departments usually only feel any responsibility for 2 and 6, but most roles in the agency are driven by a desire to make brilliant ads and win pitches. That said, when creative teams develop a really good idea it is often taken from them by other agency departments and clients – *Stress*. And all creatives have are their ideas, so although their responsibilities are fewer, they are greater.

When we consider that account management feels it carries responsibilities of 1–7 in the above list and that it relies almost solely on influence for control rather than authority, we'd be forgiven for thinking the role of account management was designed to be the most stressful.

Who are we?

The David Ogilvy quote at the beginning of this chapter is no understatement. My friend and former colleague Ed Commander (undoubtedly, one of the best names in advertising) once told me of a terrible client meeting that he and two creative directors had in New York in the late 90s. Ed and I had worked together in London, but he had gone to New York a couple of years previously to work on a notoriously difficult account in a notoriously difficult product category. The client's global marketing director had a reputation to make Genghis Khan look like Mother Theresa, and in Ed's meeting he lived up to it, mercilessly ripping into the agency's work, aggressively questioning their worth and ability.

Deflated, despondent, and depressed, Ed and his two colleagues went to the bar in Chin Chin, once a restaurant in Midtown Manhattan, to drink and lick their wounds in silence. After a while, Ed turned to his creative colleagues and asked with an air of desperation but genuine curiosity:

"Who are we? What have we become? What kind of people are we that we can be spoken to like that?"

More prolonged silence was finally broken by one of Ed's colleagues, who said in a soft, resigned tone,

"Ed, we're just a bunch of frightened people helping thieves sell crap to morons."

Ed and his colleagues were off the charts in *Stress*.

Would we think it fair to say that any client of any advertising agency would not really want the people working on their account to feel like that about them or their business? People must know that happier people, those who don't dread having a meeting with their client, those who feel – dare I say? – empowered, will work harder and produce better work. Many clients understand this, but unfortunately, it has also been my experience that this logic doesn't make a sufficiently compelling argument for some clients to change their behaviour.

In addition, multiple priority conflicts can arise between an agency's responsibilities, making the management of them that much more difficult. For example, the process of developing brilliant creative ideas, persuading the client to buy them, and producing these ideas is not always comfortable and easy and therefore not conducive to client satisfaction. As we explored in Chapter Four, many clients are under enormous stress themselves, and ground-breaking work, even though it might be good for the client's business and the agency's reputation, isn't always easy for clients to buy. New ideas represent risk – good for the agency, scary for the client. Therefore, it is easy to be stuck between the agency's creative agenda and the client's wish for either more assurance or less risky work. Agencies can then fall into an irreconcilable argument between:

"We can't make any ads for clients we haven't got"

from account management trying to reduce their responsibility for selling more innovative creative ideas and

"We're not going to get any new clients if all we do is this boring crap."

or words to that effect from the frustrated creative teams and creative directors who know that the agency is only as good as its latest campaign – as a prospect for better talent and better clients alike.

Furthermore, the responsibility to retain the agency's best talent does not necessarily mean agency leadership can deploy their best talent on whatever accounts they like. The best people usually have a choice of which accounts they work on, so there can be a conflict between client satisfaction and talent retention. It's easy to imagine that an account director might want the best creative team to work on their account, giving them some control to match the responsibility of their client's satisfaction, only to find that the best creative team don't really want to.

The agency's business profile makes a big difference to its responsibility and control. Big networks that are publicly traded have far higher levels of control over their local branches in each country while also having a responsibility to their shareholders. If individual offices are performing financially, they would largely be left alone. I was once told at Grey Advertising in the late nineties that its global CEO, Ed Meyer, had said,

"You can turn the office into a brothel for all I care, as long as you hit the numbers."[31]

In the case of independents, they have much greater freedom – much higher control – to do what they want and as they see fit, as we saw in the case of Goodstuff in Chapter Two.

Account management, however, has the largest number of internal stakeholders to satisfy because of their varied responsibilities. They are accountable to client service leadership, MDs, and CEOs because they're responsible for client satisfaction (both in terms of service and the agency's work). Account management is accountable to agency finance departments for their accounts' profitability (or at least they should be). They're accountable, too, to planning/strategy for getting the information and data they need to develop strategies and for keeping the client on board with the agency's recommendations. They're often responsible

---

31 Although I cannot speak to the veracity of this statement, we could be forgiven for believing it is based solely on the choices of office décor at the time.

for presenting and selling the agency's creative work to its clients, so they're accountable to the creative director and creative teams, though sometimes account management has little control or even influence on the ideas themselves. They're responsible for protecting ideas from interference. And because they are the negotiators of time and money with the client, account management is also accountable to production and project management.

Figure 18 – Account management's stakeholders

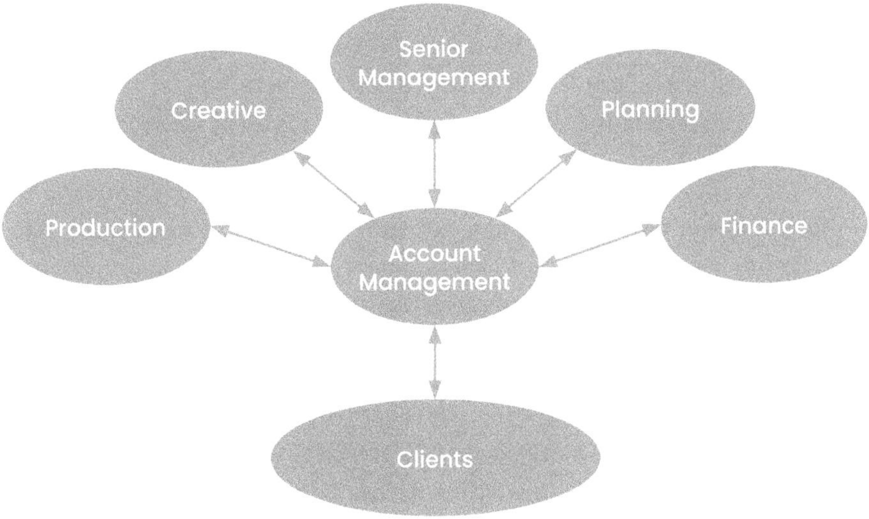

When everything is going well and, like the good marketer, an account manager is conducting an orchestra of resources all playing in harmony and at tempo, it's a wonderful job. But as we saw in the introduction with my near heart attack response to being deep into *Stress*, life in account management can be unbearable, too. Although there is a higher level of awareness and support for mental health now than there was twenty years ago, still, diagnosis and treatment of poor mental health is mostly left to the individual to instigate for their own well-being.

The second part to the LA story I began in the introduction serves as an example of the benefit of getting help (in my case resulting in the epiphany about responsibility and control) but also illustrates how account management's position in the Meikle Matrix is often indicative of the entire client account's position for the rest of the agency.

After the stresses of our LA shoot and after my realisation about the crucial relationship between responsibility and control, I received a call from Jack, Ogilvy's global head of BP retail in Chicago. Jack told me that we now needed to produce a new campaign for BP fuels to run in the UK and ten other markets across Europe, but that the creative work would be developed in Chicago and New York, not London where I was based. Now that I understood about responsibility and control, my composed response surprised even me. Calmly and with genuine sincerity, I replied,

"That's fine, Jack, if that's what you want to do. But if I don't have a developmental role [if I don't have any control], *you really don't need me on the BP Retail account, so I'll go and ask for something else to work on. I can't be responsible for BP's European Retail business if my office isn't doing the work."*

Jack told me not to overreact, not to take it so personally, and that, *"It's not like that."* But when I asked, again completely dispassionately, what it was like then, it seemed I was beginning to make some progress. I told Jack,

"This office produces work that runs across Europe for Ford, American Express, IBM, Dove, and many more. It's precisely what we're set up to do. We're familiar with the Ogilvy offices across Europe, the cultural and the language differences, but if you guys want to take on all that responsibility, that's fine – I'll just work on something else – no hard feelings."

When I had made it clear that with the control of making the work would come the responsibility for it, too, for countries from Belgium to Greece, Jack stopped to think and went back to the client, Dave.

Instead of taking the brief in the US, Dave and Jack decided first to hold a kick-off conference in Paris with the two of them, me, and the other BP and agency representatives from all the countries involved in the launch. Not long after everybody returned home, I got another call from Jack.

"Fantastic news!" he said. *"The conference was terrific, and we want you to lead the creative out of London, but Dave also wants every market involved to input into the process. They'll all take the brief, they'll all submit*

work to you, and your guys can work on it too of course, and then we'll select the best route and develop it."

By now I was getting quite good at remaining detached and clear about responsibility and control.

"No, Jack, I can't do that. Sorry. If you want me to be responsible for the campaign, that's fine, but then l must determine the resource I need, and it'll be out of London. On the other hand, if you would prefer to go straight to the other countries and have them submit scripts to you, that's fine, too – as I said, I'll find something else to do. But I cannot be responsible for meeting the launch date if I must coordinate probably between thirty and forty scripts which must be translated, back-translated, shortlisted, researched, and approved."

While it would have been typical to swallow Jack's first instruction and accept responsibility without control, *Stress*, persistent reasoned argument prevailed. Most interesting is that Jack had had no intention of pushing me into *Stress*, he simply wanted creative development to be more closely under his control. Similarly, once he and Dave were comfortable that the work would not be done in the US, they had intended to help by suggesting all countries contribute to the process. It was only through the lens of responsibility and control that I could see why that would cause me problems rather than help me so I could effectively argue against it. And it was only through the same lens that I could explain it and *Tune Up* the relationship.

It is crucial to recognise that the relationship between responsibility and control and the need for one to be commensurate with the other is mostly inarguable. Although we'll look at how to manage it more for ourselves or as managers or leaders in Part Three, my experience has clearly shown that – if presented fairly and dispassionately – levels of control and/or responsibility can be more easily negotiated than we might first think.

> Levels of control and responsibility can often be more easily negotiated than we might first think.

Buying creativity for others

In addition to the stresses caused by the responsibilities above, another big area of stress for agencies is in the production of expensive creative work. After an advertising idea has been presented, scripts and storyboards agreed upon, they are often researched and amended (rinse and repeat until finished). Then it needs to be developed from an agreed idea on a storyboard to a finished film for TV or an ad for a magazine or website.

The number of variables to be nailed down are innumerable, as are the variabilities of the variables. To have an idea of how difficult it is to buy something on somebody else's behalf, we can consider what it would be like to have a house built for our partner. Even after the plans are agreed, how much reassurance of the specifications would we want before we begin to build? Imagine then, while the house is under construction, our partner changes their mind, adds new details, and even new specifications. Our control is decreasing but not our responsibility. Then imagine, instead of one partner, we have several, and they're not in agreement about the changes in specifications we're being given, indeed some are at odds with them. Then consider that we fulfil our responsibility to build the house within the given time and budget.

If clients don't want the houses their agencies build for them to either be an eye-sore or a health and safety risk, they need to apportion commensurate responsibility and control to the agency to do it. Production processes and pre-production meetings exist specifically to do this, but often interference still follows.

Agency models and the Meikle Matrix

Different agency models in creative and media agencies can impact how and who might find themselves in *Flow* or *Stress*.

Agencies that have client contracts for global businesses and brands can differ significantly to agencies that operate nationally. When a client aligns their global brand exclusively to one agency network, it's on the assumption that all agencies in all markets will satisfy a threshold of competence. If a marketer in a particular country finds themself saddled with an agency that they feel doesn't meet that threshold, then the client is immediately in *Stress*, being responsible for an agency's effectiveness but unable to control the selection of agency. Similarly, a country's agency leader matched to a bad client will find themselves with little choice but to continue servicing that client despite the negative impact it might have on the agency – *Stress*.

With media agencies there is an additional consideration in relation to how media is traded and bought, which can also influence their position in the matrix. Although negotiating competitive media rates with media owners is an entry level requirement for all media agencies, some do volume deals based on the forecast of all their clients' spends (let's call them Volume dealers) and some negotiate on a client-by-client basis (let's call them Client-by-client agencies). These models exist in network and independent agencies alike and can even exist at the same time within an agency across different clients. The volume deals can only be done by agencies with the critical mass to ensure that their volume thresholds will be met. The volume deals will be designed to accommodate some flexibility in clients' plans or even the loss of a client or two. When Volume dealers' forecasts are accurate and targets well calibrated, media planners can operate in *Flow*, recommending what they think is best for their client. However, poorly estimated forecasts can find the agency planners needing to compromise and favour some media choices over others so they can hit volume targets – *Stress*.

Ever-rising stars

In 2005 three friends and colleagues, Jenny Biggam, Mark Jarvis and Colin Mills were working together at one of the larger and more successful networked media agencies in London. The three shared a growing frustration derived from the responsibility of growing and developing the business but without the control to reinvest in its people and talent. Instead, they saw its profits consumed by their parent company to support its other offices in the same network.

So, Jenny, Mark and Colin started a new agency, the7stars, with their own set of principles and values. And with the benefit of hindsight, it's clear that well-aligned responsibility and control were at the heart of their success.

The7stars' growth has been consistent and aggressive. Gross billings, i.e., the amount of their clients' budgets spent with media owners has grown by an average of nearly £30m a year for the last 15 years, hindered only temporarily by the Covid- 19 pandemic.

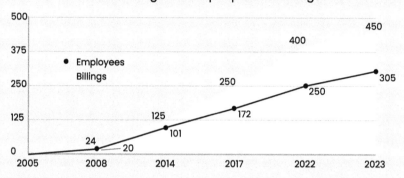

the7stars' growth of people and billings

It's not easy to achieve scale in the media agency market per se, let alone at this kind of speed, especially without mergers or acquisitions. The key to the company's growth has been the combination of the7stars values and their people. But their numbers only tell part of the story. Walking into the7stars' reception you can immediately see a wall of awards for effectiveness, creativity, agency of the year, and of course best places to work. And who doesn't want to work in an award-winning environment? Their mission statement sums up their attraction to talent and clients alike: "Inspire the exceptional, defeat the bad and the boring".

As an example of how the7stars' management of responsibility and control enables their growth, many organisations suffer from the bottleneck of hierarchy. There are only so many hours in the day in which the leadership can make the decisions that direct and unleash the efforts of others to achieve growth. But when people are empowered from the minute they join an organisation, which – and at the same time – is not hindered by either centralised decision-making or a layer of middle management, the result is that people can be left alone to do what they do best. Jenny said:

"All we needed was to create the conditions for optimal performance and then put great talent in it. That's all most organisations need to do, but too few hire well enough or have faith enough in their people to achieve their potential."

Although she is the last of the original founders of the business, Jenny Biggam doesn't like to refer to herself as the CEO.

"When people need to give me a title I'll reluctantly agree to using 'founder'. We don't use titles much here, mostly just to describe specialisms or indicate areas of responsibilities like "Head of biddable media", but not so much for hierarchical purposes with the usual proliferation of executives, managers, supervisors and directors all over the place. Complex ladders of management don't fit with our culture, it's not about achieving status at the7stars, it's about delivering value for clients and developing your career."

There is a quote from Henry Ford that they use a lot at the7stars:

"It is not the employer who pays the wages. Employers only handle the money. It is the customer who pays the wages."

Which plays directly to the7stars first value – "Clients come first".

By putting the creation of client value at the forefront of everything they do, the7stars has immediately created a common purpose, the foundation of building an environment of trust.

Their second value speaks volumes about the faith the7stars has in its employees. "People above process." Hence the7stars has abandoned many of the things that organisations of comparable scale rely on to control their people. Time sheets, holiday forms, job titles and other management tools and conventions have been replaced with a culture of trust, intelligent risk-taking, teamwork and devolved responsibility and control. It explains why since 2013, when the7stars first had enough employees to enter The Sunday Times' Best Companies to Work For competition, they have featured every year and have regularly received numerous other titles with similar recognition.

It is the industry convention for media agencies to demonstrate their success based on their gross billings because it indicates an agency's buying power when negotiating with media owners on their clients' behalf. However, this is another area where the7stars have been market disruptors. As conventional agencies evolve and grow they tend to prioritise their larger clients over their smaller ones – which stands to reason because they're worth more. But one of the fundamental values of the7stars' is to treat large and small clients just the same. And with their people empowered to walk that talk, the result has been an astonishing rate of client retention – large and small.

When the7stars' clients are asked if they would recommend the agency to a colleague or business acquaintance they score an average of 8.9 out of 10. That's an average across all clients, billing from as little as £50,000 a year to £100m and representing nearly 100 different brands.

Whereas most agencies are to some degree or another filling a leaky bucket, the7stars doesn't leak that much at all, they just need an ever-bigger bucket.

When I'm looking for a new agency for one of my clients, one way I usually segment an agency market is by assessing how important the new client's billings would be to the agency. Would it be big enough to engender sufficient priority within the agency's portfolio of clients? Or would it be too big, such that the agency might be too deferential to them? The7stars model throws a spanner into my use of the Goldilocks zone, because their clients' satisfaction shows little if any difference across their entire portfolio.

The7stars combines the effective distribution of responsibility and control with a relatively flat structure and trust as a default relationship with all their people. It's a powerful combination; and an example of the virtuous circle I introduced in *How to Buy a Gorilla:*

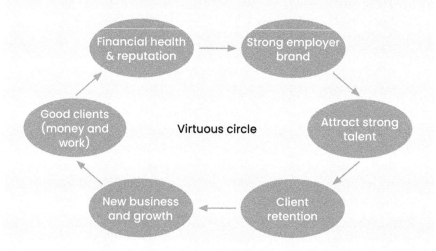

And it all began when three colleagues started *Tuning Up*. They increased their personal control over their working lives and decided on a new vision, a new culture, and a new way of working that would be their ambition – their responsibility – to realise.

It began when as they sat in a pub one lunchtime in 2005 where they agreed to take control, they agreed to share responsibility and they agreed on a name for their business.

The pub's name was The Seven Stars.

When all things are equal, media planners in client-by-client agencies that don't do volume deals will also find themselves in *Flow* – able to recommend what they think is best because they negotiate case-by-case with the media owners. But when it comes to competing with Volume dealers, Client-by-client agencies are more reliant on the media owners delivering the discounted value, resulting in their own kind of *Stress*, than the Volume dealers, who can sometimes distribute discounted value unevenly across all their clients to be more competitive.

While some clients favour the transparency of the Client-by-client model, others prefer the often-greater buying power of the Volume dealers.

In these last three chapters I have aimed to illustrate how marketers and agency folk alike can have a propensity to sit firmly in *Stress*. It is only by *Tuning Up* – firmly establishing a shared interest, clearly defined terms and ambitions, and clearly acknowledging the distribution of responsibility and control – that both groups can be elevated into *Flow* for better work, better results, and greater satisfaction all round.

Chapter Six Summary

Marketing services business are inherently more stressful than many due to their dependence upon a relatively small number of clients to spend with them consistently; in recessions they are usually the first to suffer and the last to recover, indicative of this dependency. Agencies cannot control their clients; they can only attempt to influence them.

Agencies often believe they have less control over pricing because the market for agencies is oversupplied. For the market to be over supplied any one client could be equally satisfied by any of an unnecessarily large number of agencies. This false perception and often poor differentiation among agencies perpetuate many agencies' positions in *Stress*.

Agencies have myriad responsibilities, and they are felt way beyond the management team, but not all departments have the same responsibilities, account management probably carrying the most after agency leadership.

Frightened, unconfident agencies are less able to produce their best work for their clients. So, agencies must be skilful persuaders to achieve and remain in *Flow*. Agencies are often torn between the fear of losing a client and pushing for the best thing for them.

The calm and reasoned assertion of a need for control commensurate with responsibility is hard for anybody to refute. At worst, responsibility can be recalibrated to match a limited amount of control.

Creative agencies buying creative production services for clients must carefully manage their control of the process given the almost infinite variability of outcome for the likes of film production, photography, and original art.

Media agency models need to have their responsibilities scrutinised to avoid conflicts of interest between buying obligations that some may make to media owners and the best interests of their clients.

Chapter Seven
Tuning Up
for agencies

"Millions of years of evolution have wired a network of biological certainties into the human organism. There is the need to eat. There is the need to sleep. And then, right before the need to procreate, is the client need to change every ad his agency shows him. This need is spinal. Nothing you can say, no facts you lay down, no prayers you send up, will stop a client from diddling with your concept. It's something you need to accept as reality as early in your career as you can."

Luke Sullivan. Hey Whipple, Squeeze This![32]

The first useful thing anybody from an agency can do is read Chapters Four and Five of this book to start from their client's point of view. Not just to understand it but to try to empathise with it, to imagine how it feels. In my experience, agencies are often blinkered by the control they perceive from their clients and often ignorant of the pressures their clients may be under themselves. Agency folk must fully understand the responsibilities and controls of their client before they can productively engage with them.

Furthermore, agencies must do more than just understand and empathise with the pressures the client is under, but a recurrent complaint from clients is agencies not understanding their business.

Taking the initiative

When my friend Paul Burns was an account director at Saatchi & Saatchi, he was once assigned to work on a building society account. It was a prestigious piece of business, making ads with high production values, so Paul wanted to make a good impression when he took on the account. Gathering people from the other Saatchi & Saatchi agencies in media and direct marketing, Paul convinced them that they should initiate and develop a campaign idea to take to the client together.

32 Wiley, 2015

The client had a mortgage product linked to earning Airmiles, and their TV campaign at the time leant itself to a travel theme. The media agency was excited by the idea and looked at how they could target their market through travel pages; the direct marketing guys had creative ideas using postcards instead of envelopes, and Paul's immediate team pulled together edits of the existing TV ads to complete this fully integrated campaign about earning air miles with your mortgage.

They arranged a meeting and presented the integrated campaign all together as one team but, as the presentation went on, Paul could sense there was something wrong. At the end of the presentation he recalled,

'The client said something like, "Thanks for the presentation and all the hard work –" "Phew!" we thought, then they added, "– but don't ever come to my office again until you have a proper grasp of my business and our products." We were all dumbstruck – mortified. It transpired that this product was an albatross around the client's neck. It wasn't selling because the interest rate had to be higher than their other products to pay for the airmiles and nobody in their right mind would choose that, so the client had been taking a regular kicking from the board for even launching the product in the first place. No amount of advertising was going to save it. I felt massively ashamed. But I spent the next six weeks getting all over and under their business so there wasn't a thing I didn't know or understand about it.'

In the end we knew the client's business so well that his trust for us and our judgement was enormous. We attained the holy grail of status that every agency searches for – the trusted advisor.

Agencies wishing to improve their relationships with clients are usually trying to increase their control – most frequently attempting to move from *Stress* to *Flow*. Unless handled carefully, conflict is likely to arise because clients generally don't want to decrease their control over agencies.

From my time in agencies, I've witnessed many clients alter their agency relationship so they have more control over their agency teams.

Without exception, this has resulted in unhappier, less motivated, and less productive teams and less effective work by any objective measure. And if agencies resist such change and fight to maintain their control, it's not unusual for clients to escalate their own control and pitch their business. (Ironically, unless the pitch is very well run, some clients will only find out if they are in a preferable situation with their new agency after the change has been made.) So, agencies need to find ways of increasing their control to get themselves in *Flow* without destabilising the relationship such that they risk losing the client's business.

> The challenge for agencies is to increase their control without destabilising and risking the client relationship.

Creative agencies and clients often have real problems working together, which arise from the very reason the agency was chosen in the first place – their creativity. Creative objectives easily end up ill-defined and misunderstood – *Stress* for both parties. Much like the joke about the British and Americans being divided by a common language, so, too, are creative agencies and their clients, and often.

It is rare to see a brief from a client that doesn't ask for "break-through" work. It's a word that has agencies excited to do something new and innovative. But for many clients it has simply meant that the advertising needs to be noticed, not necessarily that being noticed needs to be achieved in a ground-breaking and innovative way, which is gener-ally the agencies' understanding of the term "breakthrough".

Some agency teams and creative directors will make great efforts to better define the kind of advertising their clients want. They'll review multiple reels and examples of outstanding, award-winning work with their clients, but even when they reach a shared definition, a different problem arises. Seldom has the brilliant work they have reviewed been analysed in terms of how they were developed and produced. And often these ads are appreciated for the core idea but not the things that are absent and that make that idea more powerful – like unnecessary voice-overs, sciency-bit demonstration sequences, or any number of other advertising conventions. The levels of responsibility and control in client relationships that produce the best and most innovative creative work are very rarely the same as those that produce the more mundane, run-of-the-mill creative ideas that dominate our airtime, screen time, and poster sites.

Also, creative agencies often believe that almost all briefs must represent a creative opportunity to produce outstanding work. Even for very prescriptive briefs that may have been given to junior creative teams, while not presenting opportunities for industry awards, they will still be used by that team to demonstrate to their creative director what they can do. It sometimes won't matter to the creative team developing the ads whether the work they write is on strategy or not, saleable to the client or not, will be a nightmare for account management, or not. All that counts to them is that the creative director recognises their talent. If they can write brilliant ads that are on brief then all the better, but their responsibility to themselves and their relationship to their boss often trumps the responsibility the rest of the team has to getting the right work out. The truth is: not every brief demands or even wants outstanding creative work.

It's not just garbage in garbage out

"Garbage in garbage out" was coined in the IT industry, meaning if the data we put into a computer is flawed then what comes out will be flawed. Advertising agencies are very much the same as computers in that respect. Poor briefs beget poor strategies, which beget poor ideas; likewise, poor processes and behaviours beget demotivated teams, reduced effort, and so on. (We saw this in the value outputs of the Meikle Matrix in Figure 4 in Chapter One.) However, sometimes a value lower than the agency's full potential is *preferable* to the client – it's entirely possible for advertising to be too effective.

For example, if one brand is cannibalising another brand owned by the same company, it makes sense to increase the control over the agency to mitigate the effectiveness of the campaign and prevent the losses of the second brand – essentially stopping the agency from robbing Peter to pay Paul with the client's brand sales.

An ad that's just too good

Nick Schon spent a significant part of his career as an art director for Saatchi & Saatchi. Among other things, Nick worked on a famous anti-dandruff shampoo. One of the ads he and his creative partner developed proved extraordinarily successful compared to the others they had written. Nick was told that the first monthly sales report had shown the brand sales going through the roof. Nick and his partner were delighted of course; there is an immense amount of satisfaction derived from witnessing such effectiveness.

Then, shortly afterwards, he was told that the ad had been pulled off air by the client and that it would never run again. Understandably exasperated, Nick asked why on earth they would do such a thing. What could they possible want? Whereupon the account director explained that their ad was so effective it had started diminishing sales of the client's other, non-dandruff related hair products. Nick's ad was literally too good.

Certain categories, like financial services, pharmaceuticals, and alcohol, have higher levels of control in the form of advertising regulation. So, while the garbage-in garbage-out maxim is true when all things are equal, things aren't always equal. Agencies are often quick to judge a client frustratedly as one who doesn't buy their outstanding creative work or breakthrough strategies without fully understanding their client's broader business context.

Planning our journey from *Stress* to *Flow*

The reason I draw attention to this example is that when an agency's potential feels stifled, it might not be by accident. It might be that the client's bigger business problem hasn't been fully understood. So, when agencies find themselves feeling like they're in *Stress* they must ask themselves a few questions:

1. **Why am I here? Is it me or the nature of the account and the brand?**

I have often found that agencies haven't fully understood their client's business or their business problem. In addition to the example above, there are advertisers in distress purchase categories (that is, products that people need to buy, such as car fuel or pharmaceuticals) in which sales are largely driven by unavoidable demand, and advertising's role is far less than it is in discretionary purchase categories such as consumer-packaged goods (CPG) brands or holidays. Also, some companies are risk-averse and happier with the certainty of lower, regular, steady returns on their investments than the implicit risk from more creative campaigns.

2. Am I missing any context or information?

Always remember, we don't know what we don't know. Are there personal responsibilities or perceived responsibilities that are making our client use a high level of control? Is there a global context we need to understand? (For some multinationals, different countries receive different levels of investment and brand freedom.) These are just two examples; it is of course impossible to know everything, but always useful to dig.

3. Is high control a regulatory requirement?

As much as it would be marvellous to run funny ads about how alcohol brands make us more attractive, it's against the law. Such constraints are usually conspicuous, though. Other companies impose higher standards upon themselves or have reasons for restrictions that we may not have considered. I remember being asked in 2001 the rhetorical question by a senior BP executive, "What should Sir John Brown (then CEO of BP) say to Tony Blair (then the Prime Minister) when he asks why we're advertising alcoholic drinks in our petrol stations?" We won't be able to anticipate every restriction, but if the higher controls are unavoidable and procedural, it may be that our route to *Flow* is to recalibrate our responsibility in line with the control available to us.

4. Are the processes themselves determining control?

The purpose of creative processes is to impose control, limit chaos, and create efficiency in an otherwise inefficient situation. The whole notion of control is limiting, and the whole notion of creativity is inventing something new beyond limits, so of course processes are not conducive to creativity in the broadest sense. But larger advertisers often have volumes of step-by-step "best practice" guides for how to produce superb advertising. These include timing plans, briefing templates, stakeholder approvals, and budget ratios for investment in creative development, production, and media. They have been developed with all good intention to guard against marketing failures, but routinely they fail to recognise that originality cannot be derived by formula. (In my first book, *How to Buy a Gorilla*, I discuss how procedures must change to suit business problems.)

> Larger advertisers' detailed "best practice" guides fail to recognise that originality cannot be derived from formula.

When the development of a large proportion of ads mostly follows the same processes (often laid down by their clients) and ideas have to achieve the same research action standards and include the same components (like product demonstration sequences), they can all start to look the same. It doesn't matter what kind of meat we put in the sausage machine: the result is always going to be a sausage.

Following years of conventional advertising style and content, I can publish here the advertising sausage template. It looks like this:

Figure 19 – The advertising sausage template

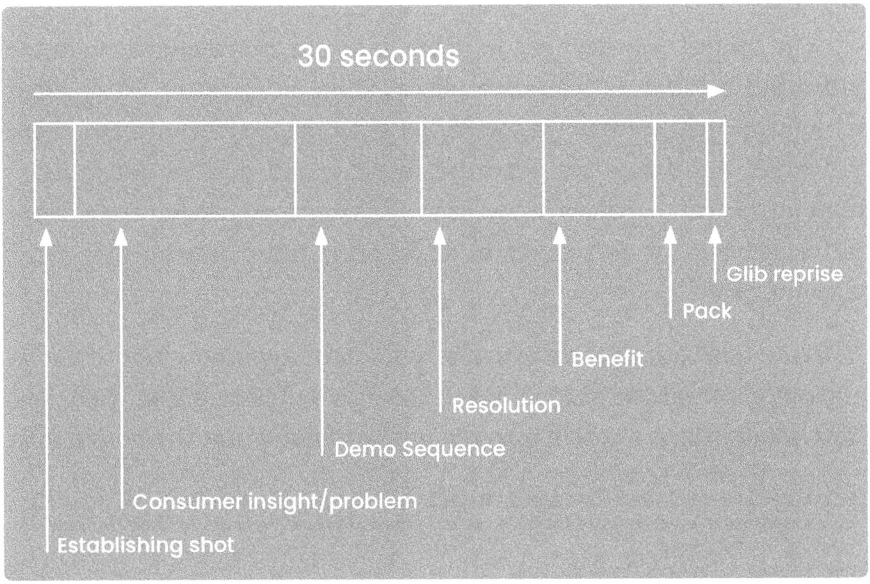

After drawing this template I challenged myself to find a formulaic match. It took me about 90 seconds. This commercial for Nurofen was the first one I found. www.tuningup.co.uk/videos.

But if the performance of such formulaic ads is this poor, this predictable, why and how do ads like this get made?[33]

Again, it's partly the result of controls in the process. When I was making ads, ideas that conformed to my sausage template would have probably hit the necessary key performance indicators to pass in the most popular quantitative testing systems. It's heavily branded (and from the point of highest drama, of course), it has a demonstration sequence to explain the product's mode of action, and it has a nice long pack shot. Many quantitative research methodologies have become echo chambers for this kind of advertising. As such, if an agency's proposed ad needs to pass these tests, the agency will propose the kind of creative work that it knows will pass. Indeed, many creative departments have identified the creative teams most adept at writing ads that will pass these tests. And so the circle of mediocre advertising life continues ... and if we always do what we've always done, then we'll always get what we always got – more sausages.

As Blair Enns notes in his excellent book of 2010 – *The Win Without Pitching Manifesto*[34]:

"The control that we need in order to do our best work includes the imperative to bring our own methodology to the engagement. Throughout the buying cycle we are constantly gauging whether or not the client recognises and values our expertise to the extent that he is willing to grant us this control. Does he see us as the experts who merit the reins of the engagement, or does he see us as the order taker supplier that needs to be directed?"

There are notable advertisers who have ignored their creative research findings and instead taken the risk and played their hunches. The Cadbury Gorilla, which inspired my first book's title, died more than

---

33 One answer is that brand sales research has shown that on average, brands can expect a 0.5% increase in market share for a 10% excess share of voice. The brands could be simply buying market share.
34 Rockbench Publishing, Nashville, 2010

one death in research, and in its first test the death was quite brutal. Nonetheless, with bloody-minded determination and a lot of arguments, the ad got made, and after more arguments it finally got on air. Then it sold a lot of chocolate and made advertising history. There were multiple reasons why this happened:

1. The agency and the client were aligned on the role of the advertising.

2. The client, Phil Rumbol, fought for control over the creative work from his stakeholders.

3. Rumbol was ready to take responsibility for its results.

When we look at the most celebrated, most popular, and most effective advertising ideas, they tend not to comply with the controls of conventions or formulae. As Bill Bernbach, founder of DDB and one of the godfathers of modern advertising, said decades ago:

> *"Rules are what the artist breaks; the memorable never emerged from a formula."*
>
> Bill Bernbach 1911–1982
> Founder, Doyle Dane Bernbach

However, if agencies want to make such original work then it takes more than a convincing presentation and some slick salesmanship. There needs to be a civil discussion between client and agency about campaign objectives and who has responsibility and who has control over what – *before* the work is done.

In recent years it has become trendier for creative agencies to be "collaborative" in their approach to developing creative ideas for their clients. But I would seek to make a clear distinction between keeping clients close to the work – which I favour – and collaboration or co-creation, which I would not. As David Ogilvy put it to his clients – *"why have a dog and bark yourself?"*

Ideas that seek to persuade must be single-minded and convincing. Pushing, pulling, stretching, and bending ideas to accommodate multiple people's perspectives – all of whose minds' eyes could have strikingly different end results – creates compromise after compromise. Put another way, collective yet devolved responsibility comes from collective and devolved control – so once again we're back to the sausage machine.

5. Is client behaviour driving high control?

As much as it may not feel like it for agency folk in *Stress*, their clients are human, too, and prone to behave the way humans do. They are susceptible to feelings and influences that may adversely affect their behaviour. This is one of the reasons why developing close relationships with clients can be beneficial, because it instils trust and confidence, and agencies are more likely to understand what's driving their client's behaviour. On a more conspicuous level, think back to the influences and pressures from the previous two chapters and probe not only where problems might lie for the client but what can be done to help solve them.

Similarly, throughout my advertising career, I have found that many clients in multiple business categories (and using multiple advertising research companies) have held as gospel some maxims about creativity. These maxims became rules, which are frequently repeated to agencies in efforts to course-correct and improve their creative work. Because the rules have become accepted wisdom, it means breaking them makes advertising even more distinctive. Rejecting accepted wisdom is one of the things that makes advertising notable. But it doesn't make bad advertising.

> Rejecting accepted wisdom is one of the things that makes advertising notable.

Here are only a few of these rules:

1. Don't make the consumer look like an idiot
2. Always use a voiceover with a visual to deliver the selling message
3. Introduce the brand in the ad's story at the point of highest drama
4. Demonstration sequences provide necessary reasons to believe in products' effectiveness
5. Ads should have a call to action

On the surface of it, they seem perfectly logical and the reasons to adopt them seem reasonable and legitimate. But it doesn't take long to find the brilliant work that would never have been made if these had rules been applied. For example:

a. Don't make the consumer look like an idiot
    Hamlet photobooth

b. Always use a voiceover to deliver the selling message, as well as a visual.
    Cadbury's gorilla

c. Introduce the brand in the ad at the point of highest drama
    Sony Bravia – 250,000 rubber balls in San Francisco

d. Demonstration sequences provide necessary reasons to believe
    Tide – it's a Tide ad

e. Ads must have a call to action
    Nike – Nothing beats a Londoner

    Links to ads can be found at www.tuningup.co.uk/videos

The problem is that for advertising to be effective it must engage – it must stand out. And therefore, if advertising submits to the control of such ideas of best practice, it cannot be as distinctive as advertising that does not comply with them. And when we examine some of the most effective, engaging advertising, we find that usually they have not been bound to the rules as to what makes for "the best" advertising.

A client's pursuit of the certainty of return on investment is under-standable, but – when the creative product is a key determinant of that return, and the creative idea doesn't yet exist because the agency hasn't written it yet – it's understandable that clients want to exert control to mitigate against poor creative work. But unless agencies know their craft well enough and are ready to respond with evidence about why these rules of thumb don't serve their clients well, then such conventional wisdom will prevail, despite it largely defeating the purpose of the creative process.

6. Have our own company's behaviours and processes forced us into Stress?

It's worth us remembering Marcus Buckingham's list of 12 conditions (see Chapter Two). Without meeting most of those conditions, we're unlikely to have the headspace to effect meaningful change. We should ask: Have I got too much on? Have I got enough support from above and below? As much as we can step back to look at whether our client's processes are conducive to producing the best work for them, the same can be asked of our own processes.

For example, as an account director I was often told the creative team would come back to me with ideas once they'd been approved by the creative director. Often, the creative director would then approve something that didn't match the strategy but that I would be under increased pressure to "sell" to the client by virtue of the creative director's approval. So, I had to develop relationships with creative teams so that I could see ideas before they were shown to the creative director. This way, the creative team, the planner, and I could agree on, and have more control over, which ideas went forward to the client.

If we need to change an internal process for the client's benefit (and thereby ours, too), it's important to get the support we need from our management. After all, that's what they're there for.

My first TV commercial

In the mid-nineties I made my first TV commercial. I was an account manager in Grey Advertising for Ribena. Creative development had been tortuous, but we finally produced a decent, animated ad for No-Added-Sugar Ribena. However, between the creative treatment being approved by the client and the broadcaster (what was then the BACC, now Clearcast) and the production, the TV producer recorded the voiceover from the unapproved storyboard text not the script approved and stamped by the BACC. The difference between the two scripts was one word: "unique". It was also the difference between approved and not approved. Looking to my account director for help on the matter, barely knowing where to start to fix the mess I had not created in my first TV production and believing this is what bosses are there for, he shouted at me, "Just fucking sort it!", leaving me in *Stress*. At the time I should have escalated the issue. I hope times have changed.

Questions 1 to 6, their answers and stories, will hopefully provide small levers to help increase agencies' control. Most importantly, agencies need to empathise; look at the whole situation from the marketer's perspective and deduce what their clients see, think, and feel about the situation. But the last two questions are judgements only agencies can make.

7. **Is the situation improvable? Am I able to affect change or influence others who can?**

The answers to the previous questions should help agencies answer this one. But the big question here is, "Does anybody else involved have an interest in changing things, too?" and "If not, could they?" Unless agency folk have a shared interest in creating change with their colleagues, their efforts will likely fizzle out or simply fall on deaf ears.

If account management finds its account in the depths of *Stress*, they shouldn't expect or even aim to teleport it to the top right-hand corner of *Flow* in the next campaign. A stable base camp – where it feels slightly less stressful or at least like nobody is trying to kill each other – is a far better and more realistic initial ambition.

Don't make us bite off more than we can chew

Shortly after I took on my role in Ogilvy Moscow, one of my larger clients called me to complain. This client had a fearsome reputation for savaging and firing agencies. In her previous role only months before she had already fired Ogilvy. (My client services director had become so scarred by this client that when I asked him what to get the client for Christmas, he suggested running past their offices with a wheelbarrow full of raw meat and flinging it through the doors as we passed.)

Their complaint was primarily about an ad that the agency had presented – which, in all fairness, was bloody awful – but after telling me so in no uncertain terms, they proceeded to complain further:

"And another thing," they literally yelled on the conference call, *"You still aren't doing our below-the-line and point of sale materials; we have to go to another agency for that."*

I was surprised by this.

"Why on earth would you want us to do more work?" Silence and confusion. I explained, *"As far as I can see you pretty much hate us right now and wouldn't work with us if you had a choice. Let me try to get us to a place where you don't hate us first. Then we can talk about additional scope. Right now, if we did your other work, too, you'd probably just hate us twice as much."*

My point was indisputable. The client had to agree that it would serve neither them nor us well if we attempted to take on more work when they weren't yet satisfied with the work we already had.

It took three years to turn around this piece of business, but we did it – and mostly with small steps.

8. How far am I prepared to go to effect change?

This last question is arguably the most important. Having worked on many difficult accounts in various agencies and been able to turn them around, I can say with some confidence that the consistent ingredient in my own success stories[35] has been bloody-minded determination.

If the client's behaviours and processes have got their agency into *Stress*, then the agency team will feel like the client doesn't deserve their discretionary effort; they don't deserve to have the very best the agency can do. But if it's the client's behaviour we want to change, the agency is unlikely to achieve it unless their client appreciates them. And the client can't appreciate the agency if it's not doing its best. So, to break this downward spiral, the agency must over commit and over deliver *despite* their client's behaviour.

This advice can sound counterintuitive in view of our desire to avoid stress and preserve our own mental health. But in making the commitment to change we can reframe our responsibility so we feel we have more control. While working on an account day-to-day means that our responsibility is to the client and to the agency for fulfilling our role, when we commit to turning around a piece of business, we must do it for ourselves. In so doing, we won't resent the effort required or the higher value we create. And, if the going gets too tough, we can say with integrity that we've done all we can. Everybody will have different breaking points, and it's important we find out what works for us but not to go beyond that breaking point. There's good reason why multiple people have said to me, and indeed I have said to others, "It's *only advertising – nobody dies.*"

---

35 N.B. – there have been many failures, too. Not every bad client relationship is fixable, at least not by me.

> We can't just overcommit to changing a client/agency relationship, we must have a strategy by which to change it.

Critically, if we decide to commit to turning around a piece of business and moving from *Stress* to *Flow*, we must not just run at it, we must have a *strategy for change*.

Talk about the relationship

Extraordinary as it may sound, clients and agencies still rarely talk about their relationships. If agencies are frustrated or stressed with their client relationship, I have often found the same is true for the client. Relationship conversations clear the air, demonstrate to the client that the agency cares about the state of the relationship, and gives the agency permission to say how the agency is experiencing it.

Speaking truth to power

As part of the HTBAG company's agency selection process, I employ an Acid Test which is a meeting format I have designed to help shortlist agencies for a final pitch. As the name implies, it's like a chemistry meeting but tougher. In this meeting I sometimes ask the agency's leadership to provide an example of when they had spoken an uncomfortable truth to power, i.e., when did they have to stand up to a client, what risk were they taking, and why? When Melissa Robertson was CEO of NOW Advertising, she told us of a client of theirs who had been very demanding, instructive, and unappreciative in the way she treated the agency team. NOW people on the account felt very stressed and demotivated, such that the issue needed to be addressed no matter how uncomfortable it might be and regardless of the potential consequences. Melissa broached the subject with client, who was shocked and embarrassed at the agency team's response to her behaviour. Overnight, this client's behaviour became inclusive, less confrontational, and much more polite. The agency team was transformed, their enthusiasm grew, and the performance of the agency and the business improved. In the client's biannual agency performance reviews which followed, NOW regularly smashed performance records, routinely scoring 9 of out 10.

Client satisfaction surveys, whether their results are good or bad, can provide the opportunity for agencies to talk about their relationships with their client. Relationship management surveys like the *Tuning Up* diagnostic are even more useful and revealing, particularly if the views of the front-line people are different to the leadership.

Take the lead, get ahead, and organise them

There is an inertia, a debilitating weight we feel from being in *Stress* that impedes our attempts to leave the quadrant. The withdrawal of discretionary effort is normal, as is the withdrawal of normal effort for that matter, so self-motivated determination is necessary to break away from it.

Anticipating a client's needs requires additional and discretionary effort, but it is terribly useful. Clients for whom an agency might feel they are in *Stress* often have the agency feeling that because they are not in control themselves. When under pressure, the client falls behind and then transfers the stress and the pressure to the agency. But if the agency asserts itself and starts taking the lead on forward planning of the campaigns for example, it does one of two things:

a. It allows the agency to drive the campaign development process by asking for briefs, identifying stakeholders, preparing timetables, etc.

b. It absolves the agency of some responsibility if the client doesn't produce what the agency needed in a timely manner and prompts the need to change.

I must have asked as many as twenty clients for their annual marketing plan. Only one has ever been able to provide one.

We should note here, again, that this is not necessarily the fault or intention of the client. For example, agencies are forever getting frustrated with their clients in the autumn when they can't confirm budgets for the following year. It wasn't until I was a consultant that my first client explained they were waiting for their own marketing budgets to be signed off (why more clients don't explain this to their agencies and agencies rephrase their financial planning year remains a mystery.)

Make additional responsibility conditional

Anybody feeling they're in *Stress* may seek to mitigate it by off-loading some of their responsibility if they're unable to increase their own control of the situation. It may be due to the mentality that goes with working in a service-oriented business, but agency folk are particularly susceptible to such discretionary increases in responsibility. It's critical to remember that such increases in responsibility *are discretionary* and therefore agencies can negotiate the necessary controls commensurate to them. An extreme example makes the point.

It's always better to gamble sober

One of the more bizarre examples of discretionary responsibility happened a couple of years into my role as group managing director of Ogilvy Moscow. A client who had recently transferred in from another country to be marketing director of Russia called me at about 7.00am one Friday morning.

I already knew him to be a bit of a party animal, and anybody who has lived in Moscow will attest that the city is very accommodating of hedonists. From his gravelly voice and the time of day it was clear he had a hangover something close to the size of Jupiter, but he sounded deadly serious, scared even.

"David, I need your help. I've fucked up really badly and I desperately need your help. It's really important, I'm screwed."

This was not the best possible start to any conversation, least of all one with a client who I didn't know particularly well. A thousand different scenarios raced through my mind of what might have happened, none of them good, the best of which was that he was calling me from jail and needed help getting out. What followed was not one of the scenarios I could have reasonably anticipated.

"What's wrong?" I asked.
"I was out last night with our MD. I've really fucked up. I could lose my job over this. We drank a lot; I mean A LOT. And he told me that his biggest frustration about Russia is that it takes forever to get anything done, everything moves too slowly. Too much red tape."

"True," I replied. (For the uninitiated, Russia is a very low-trust society and makes Terry Gilliam's dystopian movie, Brazil, look like the portrayal of an efficient Utopia of minimal bureaucracy.)
"So ...?" I asked.
"So I got mouthy ... I bet him that I could buy a Yellow Porsche 911 for the company and have it in the car park at work by Monday."
Silence
"You're joking. Tell me you're joking..." I said solemnly.
"I'm not joking. This isn't a wind up. He took me really seriously. We shook on it and everything. It's definitely not a joke."

By coincidence, not long before I had bought my own car privately. My PA helped me with the administration. Insurance alone is a nightmare. It took three days to register ownership, during which time the car wasn't insured and had temporary registration, which required temporary paperwork. Number plates didn't come with the car; they needed to be organised, too.

It's definitely not normal for advertising agencies to buy sports cars on behalf of their clients because of a drunken bet. So, I needed to set out the conditions of the control I would need and the responsibility I would take before I could even consider helping him.

"Even if we could help you, how can I possibly justify buying you a Yellow Porsche?"

"We'll use it for an internal comms campaign prize across the business, don't worry about that, already agreed," he replied.

Thankfully, Ogilvy Russia's owner, Leonid, was well connected across all sorts of businesses, including performance-car dealers, as it happened. While Leonid set about seeing if such a car were even in the country, I went back to the client and laid out our terms. I explained the situation to him, and the client agreed to our conditions.

Incredibly, Leonid found a Yellow Porsche 911 for about €140,000 that could be delivered to the client's car park the next day. It was a winter month and snowing, so they would need to shelter it (their responsibility), and because it was uninsurable, we recommended that they assign an armed guard (their responsibility). The money would have to be returned to the agency by Tuesday latest (their responsibility).

The car was delivered. We saved the client's face and possibly his job, and the money was returned as promised. Plus, the client paid us to develop an internal comms campaign for their whole company in which the winner of employee of the month would get the car for weekend.[36]

If you can't avoid *Stress*, at least enjoy yourself

Saatchi & Saatchi is credited with coining the expression "Fun, Fame or Fortune", demanding that every client must provide at least one. Most agencies adopt the principal. "Fun" means an account that is a pleasure to work on. "Fame" is an account that will make the agency and the people working on the account famous, a reputation builder. "Fortune" is an account that is very profitable.

Scrutinising expenses for fun

When I started at Grey Advertising in 1995, I was working on NYNEX Cablecomms, one of the franchise winners for laying fibreoptic cable and providing TV and telephone services to UK homes. From the moment I arrived on day one, it was clear I had no control whatsoever. The Group Account Director with whom I had interviewed, met me and said I wouldn't be working for him; I'd be working for somebody else who I hadn't met. I was shown to the other person's office who, I was told, was in a client meeting, and I was asked to wait. Presently, he arrived, and I met the late and truly great Neil Jenner.

Neil was the Group Account Director responsible for new business. Neil had previously started his own agency which had recently been bought by Grey, and Neil had transferred in as part of the acquisition. He was a robust, grey-haired, important-looking man. Neil seemed kind. He said hello, introduced himself, and then presented me with a fax from the NYNEX client. It listed in some detail approximately 28 failures of the agency – past failures, current failures, and even forecast ones. Neil told me to read it

---

36 Of course, that didn't work because of insurance and employees of the company being spread out over at least 9 of Russia's 11 time zones, but you can't win 'em all.

and be ready to meet the client in twenty minutes when he would come back to get me and promptly left me alone again in his office. Needless to say, working on that account was hell – *Stress*. This was not "Fame". It had some "Fortune", so it definitely needed "Fun".

My immediate boss was Kate Standen, an account director who, in addition to her normal directorial duties, looked after us and kept us relatively sane with "Fun", often taking us out for lunch or dinner, each time casually telling me to pick up the bill and put it on my expenses. By the end of my first month I had racked up hundreds of pounds of these and other expenses and was quite nervous that they amounted to more than I had claimed previously in my entire career. Kate told me not to worry, that our boss Neil would sign it off – in fact, Kate promised Neil wouldn't even look at the form I had filled out and would sign it away.

I knocked on his office door and asked if he'd authorise my expenses.

"Have a seat, petal," Neil said.

This is not what I had been promised by Kate. If he didn't approve my expenses, I would be out-of-pocket by more than I could afford. Neil pored over the summary page and slowly flicked through the attached receipts. Finally sitting back and looking at me sternly, he said:

"You know, petal, it really does take the sting out of signing these things when I can see something here you bought for me."

Apparently, Neil had been in on the fun agenda, too. I don't think another month went by in the following five years I spent at Grey when I didn't buy Neil lunch on my expense account. Neil became a great mentor to me, and I learned a huge amount from our lunchtime conversations.

Starting out on the road to change

"The Journey of a Thousand Miles
Starts from beneath your feet."

Lao-Tzu c. 500 B.C. Tao Te Ching
A new English Version, Stephen Mitchell

So, how do we take the first step? To effect meaningful and sustainable change agencies must take more control of the campaign development process during the stages and in the areas that rely particularly on the agencies' expertise. But this new process would have to be designed and agreed in advance with the client, prompting the question: how?

1. Start with the business problem – have a clear understanding of what the objective is that the agency and the client share. Our common interest is our pole star.

2. Define the role of the creative work or media strategy/idea to solve the problem. Consider how different it might need to be from what the client and the agency may have done before.

3. If necessary, be ready to explain how the strategy or idea works and therefore how it should influence the brief and the process.[37]

4. Assuming the objective isn't a sausage, or anything else derived by formula, propose a process that doesn't produce the predictable and mediocre sausage but that identifies the best advertising effectively. (Chapter Nine of my first book, *How to Buy a Gorilla*, looks at this is in some detail).

I won't pretend that this is easy. Some agencies will prefer to segment their clients, identifying those who present opportunities for them to produce better strategies and ideas and those who don't and applying their best efforts and talent accordingly. Therefore, if the agency is the instigator of change, if the agency wants to take more control and responsibility to produce better work, they may need to convince internal agency stakeholders to apply their discretionary effort, too.

As I have stated before, though, agencies which establish a clear, shared interest in the results of the agency's work, i.e., increasing their responsibility commensurate with their increased control, will make their argument for more control all the more persuasive.

Commensurate with the increased control agencies want, they must consider how that either matches their current responsibilities or how they could increase their responsibility to match their new level of control.

---

37 *Lemon*, by Orlando Wood is a perfect place to start for creative work. IPA October 2019.

Chapter Seven Summary

The journey to achieving greater agency control starts with developing a more thorough understanding of their clients and their clients' own controls and responsibilities. Agencies trying to wrest control from clients will fail more often than those who do so through improving relationships, trust, and reasoning that increasing their control is in their clients' best interests.

It's unlikely that too much time can be spent thoroughly understanding one another between an agency and its client, who are often divided by their definitions of a common vocabulary of words such as "breakthrough" and "original".

Not all client business problems require world-beating creative ideas and the highest production values. Agencies must start with the client's business problem before determining the solution. Some business models are more risk averse than others; some have a portfolio of brands and others only one. These differences influence creative strategy.

Use a measured journey to move from *Stress* to *Flow:*

1. Why am I in *Stress?* Is it me or is it the nature of the account and the brand?

2. Am I missing any context or information?

3. Is high control a regulatory requirement?

4. Are the processes themselves determining control?

5. Is client behaviour driving high control?

6. Have the agency's own behaviours and processes forced them into Stress?

7. Is the situation improvable? Can the agency affect change or influence others who can?

8. How far is the agency prepared to go to effect change?

Regular and constructive dialogue about the client-agency relationship clears the air, demonstrates to clients that the agency cares about their relationships, and gives the agency licence to say how the agency experiences their client.

Taking the lead with clients – anticipating their needs rather than reacting to them – can allow the agency to drive campaign development and limit responsibility if clients don't plan in a timely manner and expect agencies to make up lost time.

Additional responsibilities from clients must be made conditional on the commensurate controls required.

Some accounts are always reactive, dynamic, and high-pressure. Recognise them as such and make sure the agency team enjoy themselves while remaining vigilant to burn out.

The process of changing the nature of a client/agency relationship is often extremely difficult. It needs bloody-minded determination to overcome inertia and resistance.

Chapter Eight
Tuning Up
for pitches

"Power in the client-agency relationship usually rests with the client. His power comes from the alternatives that he sees to hiring us."

Blair Enns, *The Win Without Pitching Manifesto* 2010

One of the most frightening and exciting events in marketing and advertising is pitching – the client's most popular method of selecting a new agency (or reappointing an existing one). Pitch processes are usually intense, short, and are hugely variable in their integrity, fairness, transparency, and effectiveness depending upon the integrity and fairness of the clients, agencies, and intermediaries. Pitches are a minefield of responsibility and control, not least because they involve multiple different stakeholders across departments and companies. Some clients also have a procurement function and/or choose to engage an intermediary, such as my own company, to help them design and run a process.

For agencies, the combination of the high responsibility to win (or not lose) an account, the management of multiple client stakeholders with multiple interests (sometimes divergent or even mutually exclusive if one stakeholder wants to save and the other wants to invest), and time pressure make for perfect *Stress* conditions.

Some may be curious why I chose to quote Blair Enns' *The Win Without Pitching Manifesto*, when the majority of my own business consists of running pitches for my clients. But Blair would probably agree that much of what is wrong about most pitch processes comes down to the allocation of responsibility and control between the parties. Blair's and my positions aren't always entirely reconcilable. On a case-by-case basis we recognise that between a) the responsibility of a client to demonstrate to their organisation that there has been appropriate scrutiny in their choice of an agency and b) an agency's desire not to produce copious amounts of work free of charge, it's not uncommon for the client's position to win over the agencies' when it ought not.

We would both agree on being dead against the abuse of control in a pitch. Some clients and even intermediaries can employ questionable and not always detectable practises which overplay control to the unfair detriment of pitch participants. Examples would include opaque processes, including too many agencies in the process, and the demand for showcase RFIs at the start of the process when the odds of winning are worst. The competitive nature of the agency market allows clients to overplay their control like this, but it is ably assisted by many agencies, ignorant of the control they have in a pitch situation. As I say to my clients and participating agencies alike, "*If agencies don't take part, then I can't run pitches.*" Hence, I run, fair, transparent processes which require the least investment from agencies at the start when there are a handful of agencies and most at the end when there are usually only three.

> Brands and intermediaries can't run pitches without agencies.
> Hence agencies have more control than they might think.

Agencies' responsibility in pitches is not just to win for the revenue and the reputation but also not to lose their stake of time, energy, money, motivation, and reputation. The cost equivalent of time lost on large-scale pitches can easily reach hundreds of thousands of pounds.

Some of the high-control dangers that push agencies into Stress

1. **The wild card position**
    Being invited to pitch as an outsider – not meeting the criteria of other contenders but included more speculatively. Client *Non-stick* Agencies *Stress*.

2. **Foregone conclusions**
    Some clients already know who they want to work with but must be seen to apply a selection process, inviting agencies they have no intention of working with to be paper tigers to one they already want. Client *Non-stick* Agencies *Stress*.

3. **Black hole commitments**

   Many agencies will happily enter a pitch process not knowing what the process is – how many other agencies are participating, who the decision-makers are, how many rounds of presentations there will be. Once they're invested in the process, agencies lose control and agree to more and more work for fear of losing their investment to date. Client *Non-stick*, Agencies *Stress*.

4. **Moving goalposts**

   Similarly, some clients will introduce new agencies to the process after it has begun. Agency leaders and their new-business folk often try desperately to include themselves in a process after it has started, and unless there is a consequence, it is too easy for clients to agree. Often, they'll impose an additional round of presentations – when the agencies are already invested.[38] But for agencies already in the competition, it's hard to say no. It's akin to being invited on a holiday without being told where we're going, how long we'll be away, and how much it will cost us, just the promise of a lovely time if we're successful.

   Client *Non-stick*, New Agency *Non-stick/Flow*, other agencies *Stress*.

5. **Unwelcome partners**

   It's not uncommon for clients to want to see an integrated response to their brief – such as from a creative and a media agency together, or a media agency and a content development agency – working together. If the client decides which agencies will work together, both agencies are reliant on one another for their performance, neither with control over the other. Hence, both agencies are immediately in *Stress*, having to respond to the pitch and figure out how to get themselves into *Flow* for their own cooperation with no great accountability to one another for their competence. In this circumstance, early *Tuning Up* is essential.

---

38 At the risk of being a hypocrite, I confess to having done this once myself. However, both agencies were given the right to refuse, and the client would have had to make a decision without knowing which agency had refused, and the brief for their presentations was very tight – limiting their further investment.

Bear in mind that the client's responsibility to find the best agency is on a different level to their responsibility to agencies participating in the competition; so, although agencies see such clients in *Non-stick*, they may see themselves in *Flow* or *Stress*.

All these practices reduce the control of the agency in new-business processes without diminishing their responsibility. *Stress*. Why agencies don't issue terms and conditions for their participation in pitches bewilders me still. The IPA and ISBA recently published the Pitch Positive Pledge, of which I am of course a signatory. It's a good start but it doesn't go far enough in my view.

Client, agency, and intermediary responsibilities

On an operational level, clients are responsible for choosing the agency they believe will provide them with the highest possible value. The investment stakes are staggeringly high (responsibility) for agencies, so the process (control) must be faultlessly fair. But in addition to the sin list above, marketers are often required to work with marketing procurement, who sometimes even run or lead the whole process, potentially creating a conflict of interest.

If the procurement definition of agency value has a different emphasis on how much the agency wants to be paid for its services, as opposed to how much return they expect to gain from the investment, then marketing and procurement can have divergent objectives. If procurement has control of the process, the outcome for marketing is *Stress*, too.

Figure 20 – Unaligned interests

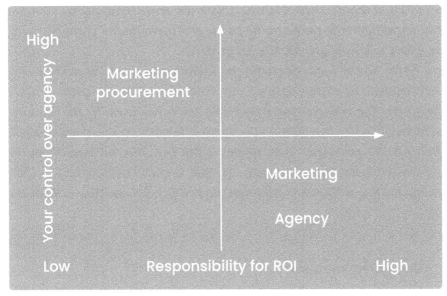

However, if marketing and procurement *Tune Up*, if they have shared, well-defined objectives, if these are shared with the agencies and the process is well managed, fair, and respectful of the agencies' investments, then all parties can be in *Flow*.

Figure 21 – Aligned interests

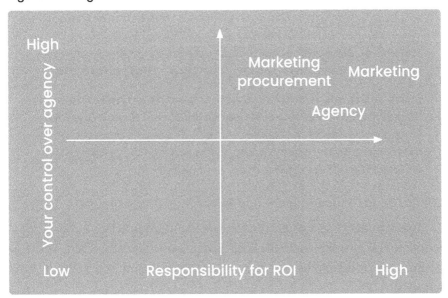

To the credit of those who developed The World Federation of Advertisers' 2020 report, *Project Spring*, this issue of potential conflict is now in the spotlight, but until incentives for procurement are changed, most interests will likely only be aligned on paper.

What is often unappreciated by clients and agencies alike is the real importance of the optimal outcome of a pitch competition. Too frequently the relative importance of a pitch is framed by the amount of money likely to be spent on the agency (fees) or on the client's behalf (billings). An advertiser that spends £10m per year on advertising is considered more important than one that spends £1m; a pitch brief for an agency fee of £50k is considered to be worth far less than one for an agency fee of £500k.

Unaligned Interests

Readers of my last book may recall my story of training marketing procurement at ISBA in 2011. At the beginning of a training session, I asked a room of about 10 marketing procurement delegates from major national and international brands two questions:

"Can you please raise your hand if you are personally incentivised to save money from your expenditure on marketing services?"

All hands went up.

"Could you please leave your hand up if your bonus is in any way contingent on the value of the marketing services you procure?"

Slowly but surely, every hand that had been raised and was being incentivised to take control in negotiations went down in the face of zero accountability. Non-stick. Unless marketing procurement is incentivised by the effectiveness of the services they procure, why wouldn't they always go for the lowest bidder?

Using budgets as a proxy for value is standard practice but is often a monumental mistake and belies the real responsibility involved. There is no linear relationship between marketing investment and value. It does not exist.

For example, some advertisers in the CPG sector consider packaging design to be a low-budget and therefore a low-value selection process for agencies, so they delegate the responsibility to more junior members of their team. I've even heard some advertising clients refer to packaging pitches as an opportunity for brand managers to "practice" running pitches. Design fees for packaging usually represent one of the lower investments in the marketing mix, but packaging is the ever-present representation of the brand and needs to work at the point of purchase. Otherwise, advertisers can spend tens of millions of pounds persuading their potential customers to buy their brand only to lose to a competitor with a better pack design at the point of purchase – on the shelf in a supermarket. Such pitches are run by clients in *Non-stick* – but only because such clients are unaware of the extent of their responsibility.

Market research companies are another good example of a sector that has increasingly been experiencing poorly run selection processes and heavy-handed negotiation from marketing procurement. Given marketers' reliance on accurate and well-interpreted research and intelligence for the effectiveness of their entire operation and investment, market research is probably the most important service to source well, even though its investment is far less than creative or media agencies. Like most services, paying less means buying less, whether it be recruitment of research subjects, field work, or time spent on analysis. Heavy-handed negotiation represents much higher risk for limited "savings". It's like competing in a trans-Saharan rally and buying a cheap, outdated map because it saves us a few quid.

Responsibility and control of the intermediary

Intermediaries have variable responsibility depending upon their business models. Their primary responsibility is of course to help a client find the best available agency to solve their business problem. Intermediaries are also responsible for making sure their pitch processes are fair and the investments made by all agencies involved are respected – not just out of decency but in their own interests, too. If agencies feel they have been treated unfairly or inappropriately they might refuse to work with the intermediary and thus limit the intermediary's ability to satisfy their primary responsibility: to find the best agencies for the clients.

Many of the larger intermediaries operate membership subscriptions for their agencies, increasing their control over them. The difference between them and others is like the difference between talent scouts and talent agents. One looks for what their clients need and the other sells clients the agencies they have from the pool of their members. Agencies are paying for representation – which is a clear division of responsibility for the intermediary between satisfying their members and their clients. Some clients are even unaware that the intermediaries' agencies have paid to have access to their pitches. Likewise, if agency members of intermediary clubs feel like they're not getting a fair crack of the whip for their membership fees, they may find themselves on pitches for which they might otherwise not have been selected and are unlikely to win. Intermediary – *Non-stick*, Agency – *Stress*.

The nature and degree of the different parties' responsibility is already complex before we consider what control they may have. To help focus on the principle of responsibility and corresponding control, it is probably helpful to summarise them primarily as:

Who	What
Client	Selecting the best available agency
Agency	Proving themselves to be the best available agency
Intermediary*	Designing and executing a process to find the best available agency

*N.B. – In the absence of an intermediary, these responsibilities pass to the client, with or without marketing procurement.

Client, agency, and intermediary controls

If the responsibilities in a pitch process appear complex, the mercurial and even volatile nature of control makes them look simple by comparison. The pitch process IS control, and the different approaches that can be employed make its consistency with each party's responsibility wildly variable, ranging from a harmonious, efficient well-oiled process to a train-wreck.

The ideal client delegates the design and management of the process to an intermediary with a clear brief for the desired outcome based on a specific business problem they want to solve. In contrast, the high-control client will want to determine the pitch process and even change it as they go along, such as adding extra selection criteria, changing the timings, adding or removing client stakeholders, and changing the scope of work.

Clients already have overall control in a pitch process, including granting access for meetings/discussions or information, the quality of the pitch brief, selection criteria, and so on. But they must be careful not to overplay that control at their own expense.

The agencies' highest control in a pitch is their choice to participate or not. Once they have agreed to take part, agencies' controls still include the resources they assign to it, how much they invest in the pitch, and the work they produce. But many agencies perceive pitches to impose more control in their processes than they actually do. Agencies often assume that if they haven't been told explicitly that they *can* do something then they assume they *can't* do it.

And agencies are generally poor at withdrawing from processes when they get the impression the odds are stacking against them or they aren't given the control to challenge the brief. Blair Enns has it right – again ...

We're liable. Like the frog,[39] we are the guilty party when we let the clients control the engagement and dictate to us how we will go about understanding his problem.

The Win Without Pitching Manifesto – Blair Enns

The reason I agree with Blair is that the purpose of the pitch process is to see the very best the agency can do. What makes my pitches more successful for my clients and agencies alike (to which even losing agencies attest) is the allocation of more control to agencies than most processes allow (flexibility of timings, client access, and so on). The sad irony of many pitch processes is that by limiting agencies' control, they limit their performance in a scenario that should be designed specifically to see them at their very best.

---

39 In a fable attributed to Aesop, a scorpion asks a frog to carry it over the river. The frog is concerned that the scorpion will sting him. The scorpion replies that they would both drown. So, the frog takes the scorpion, and the scorpion stings the frog, claiming, "I couldn't help it. It's in my nature."

> Too much control over agencies in pitch processes limits
> the very value the pitches are designed to showcase.

My clients understand at the outset that we have a duty to respect the agencies' investment and that once we have started off down the track, the process can only be changed with unanimous consent of all parties involved.

In a well-run, well-designed pitch process, the balance of control will change from one stage of the process to the next; something like this:

Figure 22 – Locus of control in the pitch process

	Client	Agency	Intermediary
Design and agree process	■		■
Invite agencies to participate		■	
Issue Request for information (RFI)	■		■
Access RFI	■		■
Shortlist for Acid Test	■		■
Acid Test meeting	■	■	■
Pitch shortlist	■		■
Pitch briefing	■		■
Tissue meeting and agenda		■	
Development of recommendations		■	
Pitch meeting and agenda, content	■	■	
Agency selection	■		■

■ Control over process or content

Given the stakes of new business are high both for clients (their dependence on the right agency) and agencies (the cost of pitching and the need for growth), it seems unconscionable that they could be compromised by an intermediary whose role is to guide the client with objective impartiality. Any scenario whereby an intermediary would derive any benefit beyond its client's fees would provide the means, opportunity, and motive to do the wrong thing – the intermediary would have high control but with split responsibility – *Non-stick*.

From time-to-time, agencies individually or collectively rail against poor pitch processes. And rightly so. In particular, many agencies resent the investment required in developing creative ideas to win business. A Canadian creative agency, Zulu Alpha Kilo, made a very entertaining video parodying clients asking for free creative work in pitches. In it we see our hapless hero playing the client, asking for a free coffee in a coffee bar, free breakfast in a diner, free personal training session with a personal trainer, free frame from a picture framer offering them preferred supplier status for coffee, breakfast, training, and framing in return. With genuinely amusing comic effect, our hero is turned down with varying degrees of impatience, incredulity, and anger by real business owners and professionals.

But there is no comparison between a) the risk of marketing investing in a poor advertising campaign upon which the whole marketing invest-ment might depend and b) a bad breakfast or poor cup of coffee. Of course, we pay for our coffee without a pitch, and if we don't like it, we don't have to buy it again. Coffee and breakfast purchases are low responsibility, low control, and low risk.

When the responsibility is that much weightier, as it is for purchasing the efforts of a team of people to deliver a fortune-changing marketing campaign, it can't be bought like a coffee or a breakfast. The increased responsibility requires increased control. The fact that some agencies still fail to grasp this is a big part of the problem. When I ran an agency, I, too, was blinkered by the responsibility I had to the agency and frustrated by the lack of control I perceived I had over new-business processes. Now I see the responsibility and controls of both sides very differently.

For the same reason training companies need to pitch, recruitment companies need to pitch, urban development companies need to pitch. It is a means of increasing the buyers' control to mitigate the risk of choice when the responsibility of that choice is so high.

That said, clients must assume more responsibility for the partici-pating agencies, not least because when they don't, the better agencies from which the clients would benefit more, won't participate in their selection processes.

Clients and agencies would do well to look at the different interme-diaries/pitch brokers through the lens of responsibility and control. It's clear to see that many of them have divided responsibilities because of their revenue models.

- Intermediaries charging agencies membership fees provide their clients access to only that part of the market – high control and split responsibility between member agencies and clients. *Non-stick.*

- Bigger agencies often pay higher intermediary membership fees, so there's a clear incentive for the intermediary to keep big agency members happier over their other less valuable members. *Non-stick.*

- Non-member agencies are routinely offered the opportunity to pitch through membership-based intermediaries in return for joining-up if they win, so their new-business victory is also a win for the inter-mediary. *Non-stick.*

The amount of control these intermediaries enjoy can be perilously far from the responsibility they ought to have to their clients. Such is the nature of conflicts of interest made clearer through the lens of respon-sibility and control.

Chapter Eight Summary

Pitches are a minefield of responsibility and control not least because they involve multiple different stakeholders across departments and companies.

The stakes involved and the one-sidedness of the selection process (clients doing the choosing once agencies agree to participate in a process) make pitch processes fertile ground for the abuse of control.

The competitive nature of the agency market allows clients and intermediaries to overplay their hands, but reputations last, and those that do must remember that they can't run pitch processes without agencies.

If the interests or responsibilities of marketers and marketing procurement are unaligned, it will likely have a detrimental value on the pitch outcome and long-term value of the agency service procured, in particular, if strategic and creative services are being bought on price then *caveat emptor,* and it's usually marketing that suffers.

Many intermediaries have conflicted responsibilities between their fee-paying members and their fee-paying clients. Clients using intermediaries should demand statements from them of all their pecuniary interests.

Agencies have more control than they might think but can be trapped by escalating investment in the process.

Given the responsibility level for the marketer and agency alike, *Tuning Up* with intermediaries and procurement is essential.

Part Three

Managing stress for ourselves

Looking at the Meikle Matrix for individuals, how responsibility and control manifest differently for different roles and how we can Tune Up our relationships for improved productivity and personal wellbeing.

Chapter Nine
Tuning Up for the individual

"One of the symptoms of an approaching nervous breakdown is the belief that one's work is terribly important."

Bertrand Russell, Philosopher 1872 - 1970

Self-determination is our birth right. If we allow another person to control what we do, or when or how we do it, it should be entirely at our discretion. At work we routinely cede such control and agree to be in certain places and do certain things on the basis that it is a sufficiently fair exchange for our wages. But, at any point we can change our minds – after all, that's what minds are for. We can constantly re-evaluate the exchange of money for ceding our control. It doesn't necessarily mean we can change things without having to face and deal with consequences of that action – the responsibility that goes with having free will (control) – but that is our decision to make.

It can be very easy to become wrapped up in a business and in a particular role, or with a specific employer. We make long-term business connections and friendships, we develop daily routines – we even move house according to our work – all of which increase our attachment to the employer.

Our lives revolve so much around what we do, it's usually the first thing that defines us as adults. When we're introduced to somebody new, it's 99 times out of 100 the first thing we ask: "What do you do?" followed by "Who do you work for?"

But we are not the sum total of our jobs.

Nor are we our employer's property. We have ultimate control over who we are and what we do. Of course, that's not to say anybody can do or be anything – or to deny that many people face disad-vantages that others do not – but there's a lot within the realms of possibility for most people, although some choices require a higher investment and commitment than others – retraining for a change in career, for example.

> We are much more than our jobs, we're not just human-shaped CVs.

In the advertising and marketing business it's not uncommon for our work to feel as if it's vital, although it's unlikely we hold other people's lives in the balance. Unlike a doctor or nurse or firefighter, if we don't show up or quit our job, nobody dies. But we're often made to feel loyal – even indispensable in our work. When we are cared for and compensated fairly for that commitment, it isn't a problem, but other times our employers can exploit that commitment. As we'll see later in this chapter, it's easy for our sense of responsibility to increase faster than our perceived or existential control.

It's natural to diminish our sense of responsibility when we cede control. Readers of my first book may recall my reference to a Dutch road traffic engineer, Hans Monderman, who developed a road safety concept called Shared Space. In a trial of his concept, Monderman decreased fatal accidents in the town of Drachten in Holland by removing all the traffic lights. As a result, drivers approaching a junction could no longer devolve responsibility for their safety to the traffic lights, so they slowed down and drove more carefully. As we learn to drive, we gradually develop an understanding of how things work and who has responsibility, such that when we're experienced drivers, we don't have the terror of responsibility the way most of us did when we first sat behind the steering wheel.

Driving self-driving cars

In the dawn of self-driving cars' potential to become commonplace, the insights of Monderman are seemingly being overlooked. The purpose of a self-driving car is to take control of the driving, but their owners are told that they must be ready to assume control at any moment and drive. So self-driving cars have control without responsibility – a *Non-stick* robot if you will. As we know, for every *Non-stick* there's a *Stress,* which must be the passive driver – who is ultimately responsible for the vehicle but is deferring control to it at the same time, a little like the stress of a driving instructor. Logically, doesn't the drivers' retention of responsibility for the car defeat the purpose of its autonomy? Whereas, on a human level, it feels like owners of driverless cars are being tempted to illegally devolve responsibility entirely to the car in order to derive the total benefit.

Personally, I would have thought some sort of taxi or train would be a better solution, whereby the driver devolves both control and responsibility and can have a drink or read a book.

Likewise, in a working situation, usually we will gradually feel more and more comfortable as the days go by that our own interests, and those of the company for which we are working, are aligned, or at least not conflicted.

But in the same way the fable states a frog can be boiled alive if put in cold water that is gradually heated.[40] in our work, we can often slip gradually from *Flow* to *Stress*. Social psychologists have understood this about people for decades.

It can be difficult to detect the source of stress when the causes are gradually decreasing control, the increasing weight of responsibility, or both. We've resigned ourselves to our circumstances as if they're beyond our control. Our tolerance is aided by the familiarity of our work and people around us, hope that our stressful circumstances will pass, and a sense of escalating commitment to our purpose. And it doesn't take long to get people to devolve responsibility for something they patently ought to take responsibility for at a higher level.

Take the legendary Milgram experiment as an example.

---

40 Apparently, this only works if you remove the sentient part of its brain, first leaving only involuntary functions – which doesn't seem very fair to me, but it serves as a useful metaphor.

Just following orders

The famous yet morally indefensible social psychology experiment by Stanley Milgram at Yale University in 1963 is a perfect examination of responsibility and control. For readers unfamiliar with the experiment, Milgram wanted to investigate the defence being made by those accused of genocide in the Nuremberg War Criminal trials. The common defence was, *"I was only following orders"*, which we could paraphrase according to our terms as, *"I was not in control so I am not responsible"*.

In the experiment, Milgram recruited male subjects through a newspaper ad asking for help in a Yale University study. Subjects were put into pairs and randomly labelled either the Teacher or the Learner. But the draw was fixed so that the volunteer was always the Teacher and the Learner was privy to the experiment.

The Learner had electrodes attached to his arms and was seated in a room adjacent to the Teacher where they could not be seen. The Teacher's room had what looked like a generator and a row of switches marked from 15 volts – a slight shock to 375 and 450 volts clearly labelled "Danger: Severe Shock" and "XXX", respectively.

The Learner was given a list of word pairs, and the Teacher tested him by giving him one word and asking for its partner from a multiple choice of four. The Teacher was told to administer a shock every time the Learner made a mistake and to increase the level of shock each time. The Teacher was also given a 45-volt shock which they thought was from the generator, but was in fact from a hidden battery, so they believed the authenticity of the machine.

The Learner would deliberately give mostly wrong answers. When the Teacher was hesitant as the voltage rose in 15-volt increments, they were given up to four standard prompts to continue:

1.   Please continue.

2.   The experiment requires you to continue.

3.   It is absolutely essential that you continue.

4.   You have no other choice but to continue.

At 300 volts the Teacher would hear banging on the walls from the actor playing the Learner. At 315 volts more frantic banging, but after that – silence.

As the voltage levels rose, the reactions from the Teacher also escalated – sweating, stuttering, lip-biting, questioning the researcher if they should continue. What Milgram repeatedly noted was that about 60% of people would go all the way up to 450 volts. About 90% were prepared to continue after hearing the pounding on the wall.

Other than possibly the odd psychopath caught in the recruitment process, most subjects felt the enormous stress of a mortal responsibility for the other subject whom they thought was a volunteer, just like them, and being under the strict control of the researcher - *Stress*. Nonetheless, they didn't take control – they just endured their circumstances against their better judgment.

Although I am sure we would all like to think we would escalate our control earlier to match the responsibility we felt and abandon the experiment, Milgram's results speak for themselves.

The point of re-examining this grotesque experiment is to reflect that it is easier than we would think to get sucked into the stress of huge responsibility without control. I would confidently speculate the experiment would have delivered vastly different results if the teacher had simply been instructed to administer 300 volts from the outset. I suspect the escalation is critical to the compliance of the teacher, even though it didn't take long. Similarly, if the subjects had been told they could leave at any time, the experiment would have failed – though of course they could.

The power of escalating commitment or escalating entrapment is nefariously and routinely used by blackmailers, child groomers, and confidence tricksters. People find themselves in compromised circum-stances in which they could never have imagined themselves but for the fact that it took many small steps to get there. Despite stories of frogs in hot water, we are all susceptible to this kind of entrapment if we are not sufficiently careful.

Thinking back to my own circumstances in the introduction to this book, if I had been told to fly to LA, work through the night several times in a week to try to make poor scripts work in the UK for the shoot that was starting the following week for advertising ideas that I hadn't seen, I would have either taken control – and replied with a colloquial expression, "Foxtrot Oscar" – or I would have absolved myself in advance for any responsibility for the outcome. Pressure creeps up on us, and over time it can get greater and greater and greater.

> Sometimes we have to stop and ask ourselves if our current circumstances would have been acceptable if they had been offered to us like that in the forst place – without any build up.

Tuning Up isn't only an exercise at the start of something; we must be ready to *Tune Up* at any time.

Organisations and businesses are imperfect. From time-to-time it is to be expected that work will be more stressful, and for short periods, under temporary circumstances, we can handle that. But stress is an insidious condition. The popular analogy is that stress is like holding a glass of water in an outstretched hand. For a minute it doesn't pose a problem, but when the minute becomes five minutes, or half an hour, or an hour, or a day, or a week, the glass becomes heavier and heavier until it is unbearable.

Our ultimate responsibility to ourselves means that we must be the arbiters of what is or is not too much. We must decide when to act, and we cannot necessarily rely on our employers to do it for us. This is not to suggest that all employers in advertising and marketing have grievous intent to exploit us regardless of our mental health. More and more employers are conscious of mental health, but a report by the Health and Safety Executive from March 2019 stated:

"The rate of self-reported work-related stress, depression or anxiety was broadly flat but has shown signs of increasing in recent years."

It's common not to try to fix things when we find ourselves deep in *Stress* – we don't want to make a fuss. But we should. It's neither a normal nor an acceptable practice for us – particularly in this industry where lives are not on the line – to make ourselves ill for its sake. So, we must try to fix it, or failing that, we must escalate the responsibility sufficiently so that we are back in control. First, we escalate the problem to our manager, who knowingly or not isn't fulfilling their duty of care for us. If the manager fails us, we escalate the issue to our employer, but if we are let down again, then we must escalate our responsibilities beyond our work – to ourselves.

There's a natural escalation matching the kind of control we have with our different levels of responsibilities.

Figure 23 – Levels of responsibility and control

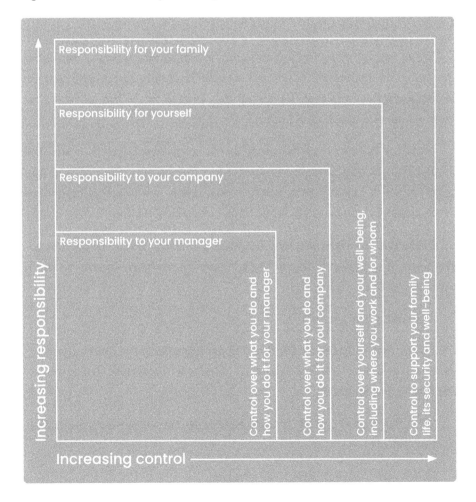

My friend and former colleague, Sue Higgs, now an executive creative director at Dentsu Creative London, published a blog not so long ago on LinkedIn of which these are extracts:

I was bullied out of my job at a large agency, a job I'd done for 10 years. This was 8 years ago, the guy who bullied me was let go only last year. They all knew his behaviour and he had form, yet the agency kept him mainly because he won Cannes Lions.

So 8 years ago, I chose to walk out of my job before I had a breakdown as it was really affecting my health, not really a choice to be honest but useful to feel I had one. It was probably the most frightening thing I'd done, I was/am a single mother with 3 lives that depended on me yet I knew I couldn't go under.

There was no 'conversation' then and it happened a year pre the Times Up, #Metoo movements. There was a really kind man in HR who told me to document it all and that the dossier that existed on the bad guy that was huge, yet no one would deal with it.

I still struggle to read the diary as it's so, so abusive and so sad and though I'm not that person anymore, I feel for the one who did, and still bears her scars. I was systematically broken down, side lined, gaslit, abused psychologically and isolated, made to feel worthless, the lot.

Every day he asked me why I bothered coming into work and he got more out of a junior than me. And I was/am a strong award-winning woman creative.

... So what is my point?

I know this still goes on. Workplaces are less tolerant of bullying behaviour and a lot less willing to turn a blind eye, hallelujah, behaviour is improving, but it's there.

Don't suffer in silence. It is scary especially when other lives depend on your livelihood.

Call it out. Use your voice. Tell someone.

It's bitterly ironic that the life in *Stress* diminishes our confidence, making it even more difficult to speak up when we need to most. And it was deeply regrettable to learn from the responses to Sue's blog that she was far from alone. While we must all act to stamp out bullying with a zero-tolerance approach, we must simultaneously try to identify people and encourage them to take control when they're in such dreadful circumstances.

However, it's important that companies distinguish clearly between bullying and accountability. While Sue's situation was personal and undoubtedly a case of bullying, anecdotally, there's an increasing tendency for some people to claim they're being bullied when they're being held accountable for performance and they've had both responsibility and control. Moreover, I've known an agency group CEO who, when asking difficult business questions of a member agency's CEO, was himself challenged by their HR director for being too challenging. When people have responsibility and commensurate control, it doesn't automatically mean they'll be good at everything they do all the time, or even that they're in the right job and are able to perform well in it. People in leadership positions with responsibility and control should expect to be asked difficult questions, that's part and parcel of their responsibility. How else can they continue to learn or be held accountable?

Getting out of hot water

When the stress becomes too much, our first course of action is to try to increase our control commensurate with our responsibility. It may not be a direct solution to the problem. As American comic Steven Wright – king of the one-liners – put it:

> "*My mechanic said to me, 'I couldn't repair your brakes, so I made your horn louder.*"

… we use whatever controls we have to solve the problem.

When we feel we have run out of ways to increase our control, we have three options:

1. **Quit and stay**

   Decrease our responsibility. Literally stop caring. We make the "w" sign with our hands, we mouth "whatever" to our controllers, and move ourselves to *Toil*. This situation isn't usually tolerable for a long time due to the sheer monotony of having neither control nor responsibility, but if we need the salary then it's a coping strategy to protect ourselves. We develop learned hopelessness and assume we'll fail to fulfil our responsibilities and wait until we're held accountable for our poor performance.

2. **Quit and go**

   If we find ourselves under an unsustainable amount of stress, we can decide the contract between employer and employee has been breached, as such that their hold over us is no longer valid and we can walk away. Ideally, we'd have the "fuck you" money from Chapter Two, but even if we don't, there's a point at which our own mental health is more important – even if, as was the case with Sue, we have dependents. As they say in aircraft emergencies, "*Please put on your own oxygen mask first before trying to assist others*". If the stress is sustainable for a while, we'll look for another position first.

3. **Taking the strain**

   Option three tends not to end well. We continue to accept responsibility, but we don't have the control required to fulfil it. Some people are resilient enough to manage *Stress* for a long time, even entire careers, but the impact of sustained stress can be horrendous. Stress is detrimental to physical and mental health, sapping energy, damaging relationships, causing accidents, and so on. Most of all, if we are unaware whether we can sustain prolonged periods in *Stress*, enduring it in order to find out could cause irreversible harm.

What's the worst that can happen?

The reason we can get trapped in *Stress*, whether in a job or in any other kind of relationship, is because we a) believe things will get better, b) don't have the control to change things, or c) are afraid of what might happen if we do. There's comfort in certainty – the "better the devil you know" mentality that makes us accept a status quo that we might have flatly rejected had it been presented to us from the outset. Too frequently we don't ask ourselves: "What's the worst that could happen?" if we take control back from our employers. Because nine times out of ten, the answer is "not much" or the likelihood of the worst-case scenario is so remote as to be ridiculous that we're trapped by it.

Financial dependence is one of the biggest and most common traps in our working lives. If we don't have independent means, then whenever we can, we should try to build some kind of financial parachute – significant savings upon which we can rely if our employer relinquishes ultimate control and lets us go, or if we want to take that control from them and leave their employ without another job to go to. This is an emergency fund, not one to be activated lightly or in the heat of a moment. And often, just the knowledge that it is there can make us *feel* more in control and better able to deal with challenging circumstances.

There is an underlying assumption that we cannot risk failing in our responsibilities in order to effect change. Any change represents risk, but it can be exhilarating and exciting instead of scary. To fall in love with somebody is to lose control, to cede the control over our happiness to somebody else. But it's a risk so worth taking that we have maxims for coping with the fallout of failed gambles – *"more fish in the sea"* and it being *"not the end of the world"*. Why can't the same excitement as we enjoy when we fall in love apply to other risks we take with our responsibilities? Not least when the upside of taking the risk is our own wellbeing.

In the brilliant, life-affirming Hal Ashby movie of 1971, *Harold and Maude*, a young Harold rebels against his wealthy, overbearing mother by repeatedly feigning his own suicide in increasingly bizarre, dramatic, and gory ways. His life is one of unending misery but for the satisfaction he derives from these morbid theatrics and a hobby of visiting strangers' funerals. Then Harold meets a 79-year-old character, Maude, played by the wonderful Ruth Gordon. Maude becomes Harold's inspiration, showing him how life is there to be lived, why to love, and why to risk. After Harold tells her of his suicidal theatrics, with passion and enthusiasm, Maude almost yells at Harold in her aging voice:

"A lot of people enjoy being dead. But they are not dead, really.
They're just backing away from life.
Reach out. Take a chance. Get hurt even.
But play as well as you can.
Go team, go!
Give me an L.
Give me an I.
Give me a V.
Give me an E.
L-I-V-E. LIVE!"
Maude winks at Harold
"... Otherwise, you got nothing to talk about in the locker room."

By way of a personal example, it's unlikely that anybody who knows or has met my mother would think she was much of a risk taker. Mum grew up in the United States in a town called Schenectady in up-state New York. It was the home of the General Electric Company, which was about all that made it famous (I was told once that Schenectady was voted the 7th most boring town in America. I can't find the source for that claim now; I can only assume it wasn't interesting enough to make it onto the Internet).

When we were talking at my brother's wedding in 1996, my mother said to me, *"Do you know that your brother and Fiona have been together as many years as your father and I were together for months before we got married? Eight."* A reckless choice by most of today's standards.

But that wasn't the risky bit.

My mother had attended Wells College in Aurora, New York, to read English, History, and German. One night her friends pressured her into going on a blind date, where she met my British father. Not only were they married eight months later, but my father's study visa was going to expire. The risk my mother took was to pack her worldly belongings into seven trunks, stick them and herself on a boat and sail to England (a country my mother had never previously visited and in which she knew nobody) for a life with my father. At the time, my father had no job or independent means; their only fallback was to live with his parents in their Prestwick bungalow for an indefinite period if he didn't find gainful employment.

My mother threw caution to the wind. She ceded control of her life, welfare, destiny – whatever we want to call it – she gambled everything based on having known my father for eight months. She travelled more than 3,000 miles away from her family and everybody she knew, in a world that was a lot bigger than the one we frequent fliers now know. Back then, the only contact was by letter. If people used the telephone, it was to say that somebody had died.

My point is that we must be careful not to go through life meticulously trying to equate our control with our responsibility. Otherwise, we'd never find out what might happen if we took a risk.[41]

As American journalist and author, Frank Scully, put it:

Why not go out on a limb? Isn't that where the fruit is?

When I was offered the role of Managing Director for Ogilvy Russia, I realised at the time that my only responsibility was to my mortgage for my London flat – I had no other ties, no partner, and most of my close friends had moved away from the city already. All I had was the opportunity to live abroad and a long-standing regret that I never did the French exchange at secondary school. I thought moving to Moscow might just scratch that itch. But I was nonetheless afraid.

When I was considering my options, my friend Murray asked me how I felt about the prospect of living in Russia. I replied that I was excited but filled with fear. Fear is a powerful controller. Fear of harm, fear of failure, fear of making a fool of ourselves. Murray laughed.

"FEAR *is actually an acronym*," he said with a broad smile. "It *stands for False Expectations Appearing Real.*" And he was right.

The false expectations that appear real are often what stop us from taking control and changing our circumstances. Often, we do nothing for fear that we won't be believed, or we might be seen as a troublemaker, or we could be fired, or have our reputation damaged.

---

41 It would be remiss not to note that my wife, Olga, took a similar risk when we married in 2005 after only 18 months together. In 2007, she, too, moved from her hometown of Moscow to the UK with everything she owned. But as a self-confessed control freak, she would admit to having taken as much control as humanly possible of everything she could since then.

That's not to say we should be gung-ho about confronting the people doing things that put us in Stress, but that too often the results of our inaction are far worse than the worst that could have happened by doing something.

Escape from Stress

It's not uncommon to find ourselves in the undesirable position of responsibility without control; the challenge can be to find the motivation and confidence to deal with it and then know what to do to increase our control.

Life in Stress tends to demotivate us, sap our energy, and drain our confidence, so the first step is to escalate our sense of responsibility, away from the employer/employee contract to the responsibility we have for ourselves, our sanity, and wellbeing. It is far easier to motivate ourselves on this level, but we can also seek encouragement from our friends and family. Don't fall into the trap of allowing stressful circumstances to make us feel inferior. As Eleanor Roosevelt said:

"*No one can make you feel inferior without your consent.*"

When we put our work life into perspective, compared to our responsibility to ourselves, it is easier to emotionally detach from it. After all, if we're in Stress, our employer has not fulfilled their duty of care in our employer/employee contract. This detachment from our work life helps us to be less emotional when confronting our circumstances with other people. When we are less emotional, we become less emphatic, more credible and reasoned in our thinking. Imagine a scenario where a boss frequently briefs too late on tasks and allows us insufficient time to do our job properly. Replying emotionally would be something like:

"*You always do this, I can't work like this. You never give me enough time.*"

Escalating responsibility to ourselves lets us to sound more objective.

"*I'll do my best with the time you've given me, but if you want to get the best from me then we'll need to work on our timings.*"

"*If you do this, then I'll do that*" is a construct of responsibility and control. "*If you don't give me enough time, then I can't be accountable for the outcome*" inextricably links responsibility and control. We don't have to say no, but we can make saying yes conditional.

Even if we feel calm, the things we say need to appear measured and in control. For example, arguing in absolutes is a common mistake: "*You always do x or never say y.*" We appear to be more credible and in control by saying, "*I find that often when this happens you do x*".

We must take our time to regroup and prepare. If the negotiation over *Tuning Up* is getting away from us or if it has been sprung on us without warning, we simply ask for time to think. Taking time is a means of taking control in a non-confrontational way by simply saying, "*Allow me a little time to prepare for this discussion*". The next trick is to use that time.

The response to our requests for change might be defensive and could include excuses about the importance of achieving an objective or that the circumstances are exceptional.

When this happens it's important that we remember that we have escalated our responsibility to being about us, about our wellbeing. In a job that's not about life or death, it's hard to find circumstances that justify compromising our wellbeing. We can explain that it's difficult for us to prioritise routinely unreasonable requests over our health. There isn't a trade-off to be had here. Work and health must not be mutually exclusive.

If these approaches fail then we can escalate by asking the other party how *they* think we feel. The questions can sound rhetorical so it's important to try to counter that with absolute sincerity. As an example, I once had lunch with a colleague and a client in a fancy Marco Pierre White Soho restaurant. The main courses arrived but one order was wrong. I didn't want to embarrass my client by making a terrible fuss, so I calmly pointed out the error and asked that it be remedied. The waiter said he would see what he could do and trotted off to the kitchen while we waited. Returning, he told us we would have to wait about 20 minutes for the right dish while they prepared it. So, I asked him to take all the main courses away because we wanted to eat together.

"I can, but we would then have to cook them all again and I will have to charge you for them all again."

"So how do you think we would feel about being charged again for all the dishes?"

"Not very happy." Silence and still no remedy was forthcoming.

"Is that an outcome you're prepared for?"

"No, I'm not." Again, a pause.

"So what do you suggest?"

Two minutes later he returned with the news that all our courses would be delivered in ten minutes' time and at no extra cost.

Asking somebody how they think we'd feel about their action or decision can be very powerful. It's useful to know whether they are knowingly doing something that will disappoint or hurt us.

When trying to gain control, it's most important that we don't lose more. Even at a point of complete powerlessness, just remaining calm and silent can get us closer to our goal. Silence can both imply we have more power than we do and allows the other person time to self-correct if they've been unreasonable. Silence can make people recognise their responsibility without spelling it out to them, or at least gives them time to recognise that responsibility for themselves. But we must be careful not to use silence as simply a passive aggressive lever.

Invest in yourself

Remember, too, that nobody can stop us getting smarter. When we're entering a negotiation with somebody we know to be difficult, we can research negotiating with difficult people. Such things improve our confidence and most likely our outcomes. But investing in ourselves also gives others more confidence to cede more control to us.

A very good friend of mine, Alex Fraser, was a creative director for one of London's most successful agencies. As one of the more approachable creative directors, he would sometimes be asked by account managers what they should do to become really good at their job. Alex would give the same answer to these aspiring account managers who asked him how they can succeed in their careers:

"If you want to be really good at your job, just read 5 books about advertising. It can be any 5 ... and you will probably be better read on the subject than most group account directors in London. I've got a bunch here you can borrow."

And he would point to a shelf full of advertising books above his desk.

As Chris Hirst, Global CEO for Havas Creative Network, put it in his excellent book *No Bullshit Leadership*[42]:

"I will travel anywhere in the world for the opportunity to understand or uncover something that may make me a better leader and coach. Once you view learning as part of your job, you'll be amazed at the breadth and variety of people who could teach you something new. I call this 'relentless learning'."

But, if you've reached Chapter Nine of this book, I'm likely preaching to the choir, so good for you, keep it up, and encourage others.

"The man who does not read has no advantage over the man who cannot read."

Mark Twain, Author 1835 - 1910

---

42 Christ Hirst, Profile Books, 2019

Chapter Nine Summary

Self-determination is our birth right. Working for a company is ceding control of our time in exchange for a salary and their duty of care for us.

While it's not unusual to cede control and responsibility to our employers in this way, ultimately, we have a greater responsibility to ourselves and our mental and physical wellbeing if our circumstances become stressful.

Stress and stressful circumstances don't always arrive suddenly. It's important to be vigilant and stay aware of our circumstances. Ask whether our circumstances would have been acceptable if they'd been proposed to us in the form they currently are.

In marketing and advertising it's almost inevitable that from time-to-time we'll experience stress. But when stress is normal, we must be the arbiter of what is or is not too much.

Remember that stress can diminish the confidence we need to escape it. Awareness of our situation, our responsibilities, and our controls can help us navigate a way out.

Our aversion to risk and the unknowable of what will happen if we were to reject our stressful circumstances outright will often keep us in *Stress* and make us fear trying to change them. So will financial dependency.

Sometimes the fear of what might happen is a false expectation of a worst case; it can stop us retaking control of our lives and fulfilling our responsibilities to ourselves.

Investing in ourselves, in our knowledge, skills, and personal development can be a means of gaining controls we need to move out of *Stress*. Read more and often.

Chapter Ten
Tuning Up for managers

"So much of what we call management consists
of making it difficult for people to work."

Peter Drucker, Management Consultant 1909 – 2005

The role of management is tricky and in ways different from the difficulties of leadership or the challenges facing individual workers in front-line roles. Managers have a range of responsibilities: to lead, coach, encourage, and develop people, but above all, they must deliver. Managers must execute functions and complete tasks to make things happen.

Under normal circumstances, people usually have the resources they require – people, time, equipment, and materials to fulfil the responsibilities of a managed team. In our imperfect world, abnormal situations are not uncommon, and under those circumstances our ability to meet our obligations become variable and the life of a manager becomes more difficult – control decreases while responsibility remains the same – *Stress*.

What we manage, the way we manage, and the way we allocate responsibility and control within our teams can have a significant impact on how well the team responds to these abnormal circumstances and how it affects us as managers.

The legacy management model is historically one of command and control over the people in the manager's team. Managers would rise through the ranks from lower positions, gradually demonstrating their ability and then their proficiency to execute increasingly complex or skilled tasks. Then they might receive some management training until they finally manage teams comprised of people filling the positions they once held themselves. In larger organisations, particularly the likes of franchise operations, this model would include voluminous instruction manuals directing team members in their day-to-day duties, supervised by the managers. In the event of an unfamiliar circumstance, front line workers would defer to their line manager who, in turn, might refer to a manual or just instruct the worker as to what course of action to take.

Normally, in this legacy model, workers have minimal responsibility and minimal control – *Toil*. Managers have greater responsibility and more control – *Flow*. But in the advertising and marketing business, there is seldom a "normal".

Unusual or abnormal is more normal than normal, if that makes sense. In most situations there are simply too many moving parts. Much of the process of developing and executing marketing campaigns depends upon the coordination of other people over whom "managers" do not have direct control, so management becomes quite a different skill set – one of influence rather than instruction.

The difference between serving coffee in a Starbucks and working in an advertising agency is the nature of the work each is producing. In a Starbucks there is a finite variability of tasks – making items on a set menu, following a cleaning regime, managing money, and serving customers according to a service policy. Everybody is controlled and the outcomes are therefore more predictable – and necessarily so. In an advertising agency, the problems that teams must solve usually offer unlimited possible solutions, so agencies are much more reliant on contributions initiated by the employees rather than the company.

But the command-and-control model is a legacy; it isn't written in stone that it's the most effective or efficient way to maximise value to customers. We only need to consider how people in the UK responded to Starbucks' insistence to have our name written on our cup and be read out when our order is ready.

According to *The Guardian Online* in 2019, a guy from Philadelphia gave his name in Starbucks as "Aziz" and his cup came back with "Isis" written on it. But arguably worse still, another Starbucks customer called "Ann-Louise" was handed her cup with her name written on it as "Anus". [43]

This excerpt from the Guardian demonstrates perfectly what happens

43 Guardian online, Starbucks: asking for customers' names builds resentment, not connection. 2 Sept 2019

when staff aren't allowed to think for themselves and sits in stark contrast to the success stories of companies like Timpson, the retail chain offering shoe repair and key cutting, amongst many other services.

We'd both be happier if I didn't help you

A personal example of this contrast starts when I lived in Notting Hill. On a few occasions I used the local branch of the national dry cleaners, Johnsons. I say "a few" because I wasn't happy with their work so I stopped using them. Years later, living in a village in Oxfordshire, I noticed my wife had used Johnsons. I asked her if she was happy with them – she said she was. So, when I wanted to get a jacket's sleeves taken up (design conventions around 'normal' human proportions would suggest I have the arms of an orangutan – whereas I just have the body shape), I took it to Johnsons. When I explained to lady in the shop what I needed, she said:

"We could do it for you, but I wouldn't recommend you use us – it's too complicated for the person we have at the moment. You should go to Stiches in the market square. I'm just scared we'd make a mess of it."

I was surprised but genuinely grateful for her honesty. Then I noticed that behind the counter there were copies of John Timpson's book *Key to Success*. Putting two and two together I asked, "Is this a Timpson company now?"

The woman in the shop looked up and visibly beamed at me. She actually shone.

"Yes!" she burst out and with more than a hint of pride. *"Do you know of him? He's brilliant. He bought us not long ago and it's been fantastic! I wouldn't have been allowed to do what I just did about your jacket before. I would have been fired by the previous owners. But do you know what Timpson tells us?"*

"No ..."

"He says, 'Just do what you think is right'. That's it! 'Just do what you think is right'."

This local branch of Johnsons now gets 100 percent of our custom for their services. Timpson does the opposite of command and control and gives total responsibility and total control.

John Timpson is a long-standing advocate of what he describes as Upside Down Management (see Figure 24 below). From Timpson's book of the same name:

"Originally, I saw Upside Down Management as a way of providing a better service by giving trust and freedom to the frontline, but now I know that everyone in the organisation should be trusted to do their job in the way they want. Managers can run their departments in their own way as long as they give the same freedom to all the members of their team. The principle even applies to me – I can't issue orders but I don't have to follow anyone else's rules. I might have to comply with the law but there is no need for me to follow 'best practice'. Like everyone else who works at Timpson, I do my job in my own way."

Figure 24 – Upside down management

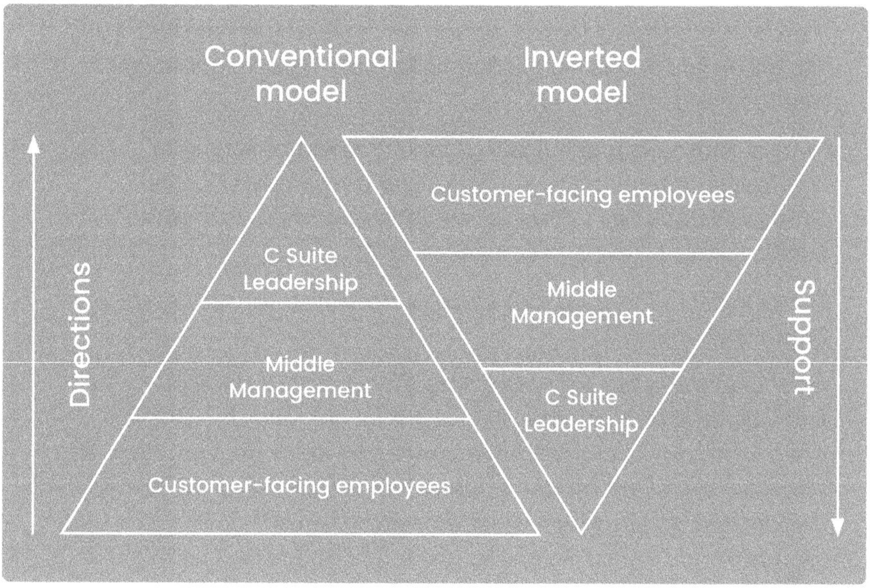

People who do the frontline job day after day are very likely to find better ways of doing things if we give them the freedom to do so. Management can spend a lot of their time far better if they watch and learn and reapply rather than command and control. Timpson goes a step further and *starts* by trusting the judgment of his employees. New managers in Timpson stores are immediately authorised to resolve any customer dispute up to £500 without recourse to another manager. £500 must be a high multiple of the average customer transaction and is certainly a very high threshold for compensation. The company is respecting the employee by giving them responsibility for customer satisfaction and control over dispute resolution. Far larger organisations, like energy utilities, will readily lose the far higher lifetime value of their customers because of poor or formulaic responses to their wrongdoings.

However, achieving this kind of empowerment and performance through delegation assumes that the receivers of the delegated responsibility and control understand it equally.

Timpson and Nordstrom, the luxury department chain store in the US that inspired John Timpson with their single rule for people of "*Use best judgement in all situations*", have the principles of delegated responsibility and control running through every fibre of their organisations.

Delegating effectively in management requires empathy for the person to whom we are delegating. Some people will be naturally more deferential than others, some may be suspicious that they might be being given enough rope to hang themselves. When delegating responsibility and control, managers cannot assume that what they say is heard the same way as it was intended. In a conservative, western setting, would it be an unfair assumption that a white, middleclass male with a privileged education might be readier to naturally assume responsibility and control when they are presented to him than somebody of equal intelligence, education, and ability whose life is not used to the trappings of institutionalised bias? As managers, we have to be aware of such potential differences.

It gets easier with practice, and some subordinates will get into step faster than others, but it's important to avoid a knowing-doing gap between what we've delegated and what they're ready to take on. I've found that giving people the control to say when and how they might want my further involvement helps. Saying, "*Would you like me to check in on you on this project, and if so, when?*" assures them that there is no trick, there is only a genuine desire for them to succeed, and that we're invested in making that happen.

> People we manage should have the control to say if and when
> they need our help and what kind of help they need.

Problems with unlimited possible solutions

When a large proportion of a role is solving complex problems or strategic/creative problems which have unlimited possible solutions, the role of management includes quality oversight.

A disadvantage of the top-down management style under these circumstances is that productivity can become bottle-necked by the manager. Likewise, solutions are limited to those deemed suitable by the manager. When those managed are instead briefed for the results their mangers want, they are free to innovate and may bring different and better ways of doing things.

Better solutions often come from the frontline

I once noticed a nurse in hospital getting rid of the bubbles in an IV tube by wrapping the tube around her index fingers, forcing the bubble to rise quickly. It was remarkable to me only because it achieved what other nurses were trying to do many times a day in the same hospital – but in a fraction of the time. At the time I asked the nurse why everybody didn't do what she was doing. She replied it was standard practice where she was from in New Zealand; she'd tried to tell hospital management, but nothing had happened – so she'd just continued to do it herself.

So, when does a manager let go and when should they intervene? The simple answer is: intervene when it matters and coach when it doesn't.

I was on the receiving end of just this way of managing when I started at Grey Advertising in London in 1995. My account director, Kate Standen, used to drive me a little crazy.[44] These were in the early days of email; in fact, it was still only relatively recently that people had computers on their desks at all, so decisions made in meetings and phone calls with

_____
44 I never told you this at the time. Sorry, Kate.

clients were being captured in contact reports. I would write one or two such reports daily and distribute them to the client – and internally where they were largely ignored by everybody as far as I could tell – well, everybody except Kate. With alarming regularity, the paper copy that had gone to Kate's in-tray would arrive back on my desk with Kate's distinctive handwriting in red biro all over it. The first time it happened, I apologised and explained it had already been sent out. "No *problem*," she replied, happily.

But it happened again and again. I asked several times if she wanted to see the contact reports before I sent them. "No, *it's not necessary*," she'd say. At the time, I was both frustrated and utterly bewildered; why did Kate constantly need to correct me after the fact? What was the point? It was only when the red ink became scarcer that I realised she had been coaching me to write better reports. Had Kate's quality control been applied in advance, the work would have been bottle-necked, wastefully using up her resource as manager, and I would have been absolved of responsibility for my work. Instead, by allowing me to send something out that was not up to her standard but was acceptable, Kate made it my responsibility to improve it. I had the control, Kate just pushed me to be more responsible.

Is that the best you can do?

There's an anecdote about Henry Kissinger and Winston Lord, a US diplomat which presents an interesting case of responsibility and control. Winston Lord was Kissinger's speechwriter, probably not the easiest of roles considering Kissinger was a speechwriter himself, and a harsh critic.

Lord prepared and submitted a speech for Kissinger's approval one evening. The feedback written on it from Kissinger the next morning was, *"Is this the best you can do?"* Lord then tweaked, revised, and resubmitted a second version a few days later. The following day, Kissinger called Lord into his office and again asked, *"Are you sure this is the best you can do?"* Lord replied, *"Well, I really thought so. I'll try one more time."* Reportedly, this cycle went on several more times, the same question came from Kissinger each time: *"Is this the best you can do?"*

Finally, Lord returned yet another draft of his speech to Kissinger's office, and when asked the same question, Lord apparently lost it. Furiously, he replied, *"Henry! I've beaten my brains out – this is the ninth draft! I know it's the best I can do; I can't possibly improve one more word!"*

Kissinger then looked at Lord and nonchalantly said, *"Well, in that case, now I'll read it."*

As funny as the Kissinger story might be, there's a vital difference to note between Henry Kissinger's and Kate Standen's MO. By any objective measure, Kissinger behaved like an asshole. Most managers don't have the time to waste by asking for draft after draft of unread work. Without specific feedback, acting this way is setting up the person being managed to fail. It's passive aggression.

Kissinger wasn't giving somebody freedom and responsibility; he was taking control from them by withholding the information (feedback) they needed to do their job well and more efficiently. Kissinger took his place in *Non-stick* and put Lord in *Stress*. Luckily, Lord was diligent enough to persist. If managers play the *"If you don't know what's wrong, I'm not going to tell you"* game, then the response of the person being managed will usually go one of two ways: a) *"Well, screw you, then, I'm not going to be responsible for your disappointment"* – *Toil* or b) frantically running around trying to change their behaviour in the hope that it will satisfy the complainant – *Stress*. Managers cannot rule out option a – which is a perfectly understandable reaction.

Double-loop learning

In managing others, it's important we remember one of the other poignant insights from Buckingham's *"First Break All the Rules"*, which was this: the golden rule of management:

"Manage others how you yourself would like to be managed."

... which is based on various religious quotations, such as from Luke 6:31 of *The Bible*:

"Do to others as you would have them do to you."

... and is also complete nonsense.

We might use it as a fall-back rule of thumb if we don't know well the person we're managing – that should get us to a basic level of decency. But logic alone is enough to suggest that it's supremely arrogant to think everybody is the same as us, that everybody responds to management, direction, instruction, encouragement the same way we do; that their priorities and their interests are the same as ours. As Buckingham put it:

"This thinking is well intentioned but overly simplistic, reminiscent perhaps of the four-year-old who proudly presents his mother a red truck for her birthday because that is the present he wants."

Particularly in the advertising and marketing business, many managers I've encountered have found it unfathomable that the people they manage might not have the same ambitions as they have for themselves. It is completely reasonable for people to derive satisfaction from simply doing a good job. Not everybody wants to increase their responsibility and the control with which to fulfil it. Many wise people work to live – and to be happy with their lot.

The result of applying the flawed golden rule can be huge frustration from managers, making them act like assholes all day, bewildered by other people's lack of ambition. But as the character Raylan Givens, a cool and stoic Deputy US Marshall in the TV series by FX: *Justified*, said:

"If you run into an asshole in the morning, you ran into an asshole. If you run into assholes all day, you're the asshole."

As a manager, the responsibility not to run into assholes all day may well be ours if we don't set out first to understand what makes our colleagues tick and then change our behaviours and management style of them accordingly.

Good managers will count their own behaviour as a variable, which they can control and change to achieve a desired result or response from an individual or team; something Chris Argyris called double loop learning in Chapter 6 of *Teaching Smart People to Learn* from his book – *On Organisational Learning*.[45]

---

45 Blackwell, 1992

"First, people define learning too narrowly as mere 'problem solving', so they focus on identifying and correcting errors in the external environment. Solving problems is important. But if learning is to persist, managers and employees must also look inward. They need to reflect critically on their own behaviour, identify the ways they often inadvertently contribute to the organisation's problems, and then change how they act. In particular, they must learn how the very way they go about defining and solving problems can be a source of problems in its own right.

I have coined the terms "single-loop" and "double-loop" learning to capture this crucial distinction. To give a simple analogy: a thermostat that automatically turns on the heat whenever the temperature in a room drops below 68 degrees is a good example of single- loop learning. A thermostat could ask, "Why am I set at 68 degrees?" and then explore whether or not some other temperature might more economically achieve the goal of heating the room would be engaging in double-loop learning."

In the shadow of the Covid-19 lockdown in the UK, I have already read pages and pages of speculation saying that the way we work will never be the same again. Probably it won't. But the bigger question is: how will we determine the new ways of working? When new processes and procedures are mandated, they are more often resisted than when they are co-created by leadership, management, and workers. By sharing the responsibility to design and embed new ways of working, organisations will not only harness their people's ideas and experience, but the mutual investment will make the process far more likely to be adhered to.

In 2011, Cali Ressler and Jody Thompson published the subtly titled book *Why Work Sucks and How to Fix It: The Results-Only Revolution*. A book that is far better than its title might suggest, it promotes the idea of the ROWE, the Results-Only Work Environment.

ROWE companies allow their employees to come and go as they please, attend meetings in person or dial in, not attend meetings at all (no meetings are obligatory), start and finish their working days as they wish – as long as they perform their jobs well, with high control and high responsibility. The results were:

1. Productivity went up
2. Employee engagement went up
3. Employee satisfaction went up
4. Absences from work went down

John Aylward, a friend and former colleague of mine, was director of marketing strategy at The GAP in San Francisco in 2011 when they introduced a Results-Only Work Environment. John recalls:

"It was genuinely transformational. We had been a culture of meeting addicts, hamstrung by our obsession with sitting around tables for status meetings and check-ins, seeking affirmation and building consensus rather than the action-oriented, fast-paced test-and-learn culture you want in a retail environment.

ROWE had two distinct benefits immediately after we launched. As soon as people didn't have to be in the office for 8 hours a day, status meetings just disappeared – people took more control of their calendars and focused on what they were responsible for delivering. About a third of meetings disappeared. In addition, clarity about goals with line managers made everyone much more focused and efficient in delivering real results.

At the same time, ROWE encouraged a much better work-life balance. Meetings could be taken from home or from the park. I could walk my dog and dial-in instead of sitting in a room. When I had to return home to London for a family emergency, I stayed for a couple of months and continued working rather than taking leave or even quitting, taking a lot of pressure off an already personally stressful time."

We don't have to have the answer. We don't have to know what the "new normal" will be. It doesn't matter as much as we think it does. The "new normal" might be that there's no such thing anymore. In much the same way as marketing businesses and agencies went consumer centric, organisations can go much more employee centric – creating the circumstances and flexibility that offers the most satisfaction and thereby the most productivity. And in creative industries like advertising and media, where motivated people solve creative problems better, this could only be a positive evolution.

"My way or the highway" managers

The poorest managers are the inflexible ones, the *"my way or the highway"* types – a kind of *"do unto others"* on steroids. It's a zero-sum management game whereby the manager either wins or the employee loses. Paradoxically, such managers can also be among the company's highest performers, but that does not mean a) that their attitude and approach to management is the reason they're a high performer or b) that they shouldn't be scrutinised for their behaviour.

High performance doesn't absolve managers of their responsibilities beyond achieving targets. The way they manage can also have indirect but nonetheless hugely detrimental effects on the larger organisation. Often, the more managers are lauded and praised for their performance the easier they can identify with the ivory towers of *Non-stick*.

Dictatorial management behaviour is about making life easier for the manager – or at least they think it is. If people are treated the same way, then managers don't have to remember how different people like to be treated differently – so managing them is easier and a lot more efficient. However, this imposes the managers' control over those they manage and thereby risks diminishing their reports' performance by limiting the scope within which workers can add value. Instructive management stops workers taking responsibility.

The imposition of control from managers on the managed also ignores the reservoir of information and experience within the team itself. Workers will also find ways to resist unnecessarily imposed control. They will listen to their managers tell them about "their way", they'll attend training, and they'll smile and nod – even when they see the new ways are patently unworkable or less efficient. But as soon as they go back to work and their manager's back is turned, they'll ignore them. This common response of workers is called "consent and evade". It's one of the main reasons organisational change projects so frequently fail.

The result of consent and evade is chaos and conflict. Managers get more and more frustrated by their people for not doing things the way they were supposed to because the managers had not considered themselves as a variable in the process of effecting change. They become intolerant and unaware of their own shortcomings, focusing instead on their inability to make somebody else act differently.

Richard Sutton's inspired book *The No Asshole Rule*[46] covers the topic superbly. It began life as an article for the *Harvard Business Review*. Several readers wrote to him to say that the rule was the centrepiece of their leadership style. Sutton's favourite reader's letter was from Roderick C. Hare, CEO of Mission Ridge capital:

"For most of my professional career, I have been telling anyone who would listen that I can work with just about every type of person, with one glaring exception – assholes. In fact, I have always used that very word. As much as I believe in tolerance and fairness, I have never lost a wink of sleep about being unapologetically intolerant of anyone who refuses to show respect for those around them."

It takes very little time for a poor manager to do real damage to a business, particularly in advertising agencies. It's not uncommon to see a new department head appointed and then fired[47] within a year or two in the wake of ruptured talent and lost clients.

Giving managers control

When, as an agency leader, I built a team of managers, I was highly conscious that they were all very different people in very different roles and with different lives and priorities – and they rightly had different needs and expectations of me. One needed little or no management, support, or anything at all in fact – he was very experienced, very capable, and my role was to support as *he* wanted or help him solve problems that affected the rest of the agency. Often, I found he was very helpful supporting me. My HR director, Vika Yakushkina, was the youngest on the management team. Amid a dearth of HR talent in Moscow, I had found somebody extremely capable, clever, and enthusiastic. I gave her more responsibility and control than she had possibly considered when she came for an initial interview to be a recruiter. Vika needed little more than reassurance in the early days and then to be pointed in the right direction and left to her own devices.

---

46 Sphere publishing UK 2007
47 "Fired" will often be reported as leaving the company of their own volition to "pursue other projects" and/or "spend more time with the family".

To the best of my memory, this is one of the first exchanges Vika and I had shortly after she accepted the role:

"So, have you got everything you need?" I asked.
"Well, mostly yes, but also no. I need about $10,000."

Up to that moment, I had believed that HR directors' overheads were the same as most people in an ad agency office – desk, laptop, phone, office. I hadn't accounted for $10,000 in my unwritten plan.

"What for?" I asked calmly.
"I need to build a recruitment and talent database. I need to build and keep records of the talent we have, the other talent our people know, and the other talent we meet."
"Oh," I said thoughtfully, pausing for a little thought. "And these things don't exist already?"
"Shitty ones do."

This felt like a real test of my conviction. I was convinced I had made a terrific hire, but Buckingham's test came immediately to mind. Question 2 of his list of 12 (see Chapter Two):

"Do I have the materials and equipment I need to do my work right?"

Within her first year, Vika had commissioned and built a sophisticated talent database that was the envy of the rest of Ogilvy's European network. The database itself provided a means of improving her control over a complex and chaotic marketplace of talent.

"It doesn't make sense to hire smart people and then tell them what to do; we hire smart people so they can tell us what to do."

Steve Jobs, Chairman and CEO Apple, 1955–2011

When we find the right talent, our role in management should be to get out of the way to provide the responsibility and control they want and need and then to be there to support as and when required. This principle has been borne out in the management of frontline staff, too. It's exactly what the agency owner, Leonid, had done for me and what I did in turn for the rest of the management.

Provide the shitstorm umbrella

One of the indirect consequences of using email as a primary work tool for the last 25 years is that it provides an almost forensic level of account-ability if something goes wrong. Agency team members with little experience can be directly exposed to clients for mistakes they make and vice versa. The unwitting perpetrator can find themselves exposed to a level of accountability for which they may not be prepared or deserve.

A critical role for management is to step in when the shit hits the fan and provide what Paul Harvey (see Chapter Three) perfectly described as a "shitstorm umbrella". When it starts raining down from client to agency, agency to client, or leadership to frontline, management must step in with their umbrellas and protect their team. Without it, the team will feel less safe to take initiatives, to innovate, to improvise in crises – all the things that can create the greatest value.

Allowing people to learn from their mistakes by creating a freedom-to-fail environment encourages initiative and innovation and demands additional responsibility from the manager. When an employee makes a mistake with all good intention, the consequence – the responsibility – should not be theirs alone. In creating that freedom to fail, management bears the responsibility for failure and therefore to protect the members of their team from the consequences. Were this not the case, then management could blithely promote a disingenuous freedom-to-fail environment, take all the positive results and then hang their people out to dry if something goes wrong.

It may be painfully clear which team member is at fault and why, but it remains solely the manager's duty to deal with whatever must subsequently follow.

Likewise, when it comes to disciplinary matters, only the manager has the responsibility to decide what to do. Neither party in a business-to-business relationship should attempt to run or interfere with another's team. Where misbehaviour might suggest that somebody should be fired, the manager is the one with the most complete information to make that determination and, although it might seem the natural outcome, it may not be the best course of action.

Managing our people on our terms

In the late 90s, a colleague of mine, let's call him Tom, got into very hot water over his behaviour toward a client at a party. Tom had had a very bad day with another client, *Stress,* had far too much to drink, and lost all sense of responsibility for his actions – *Non-stick.* To this day, I don't know what Tom said or did. But the following day, the client's manager, who was a vicious character at the best of times, took no time in demanding Tom's immediate dismissal. Tom's boss was Neil Jenner – a group director in the agency. Neil assured the client that Tom would be dealt with appropriately.

Neil called Tom into his office. I sat next to Tom in the open-plan office and the look on Tom's face clearly indicated that he fully expected to lose his job. Everything was quiet. There was no shouting, not even a mildly raised voice. A significant time later, Tom left Neil's office, face completely ashen, and went quickly to his desk and started working frantically, looking very worried but 100% focused.

I asked Tom what had happened. It transpired that he had received a very calm, balanced, reasonable but almighty dressing down – nothing he didn't deserve, he said, and then he had been asked to do a short-term project for Neil. I remember it was a Thursday.

"Neil asked me to do a complete market review and competitive analysis of ice cream in the UK and six other countries across Europe."

"Is that it?" I asked, thinking he'd got off quite lightly by my estimation.

"By Monday," Said Tom.

If it were to be done well, it was a staggering amount of work. Bear in mind, these were days before the internet went to every office desk. There was no Chat GPT, Google, Yahoo, etc.; the job required "proper research". Tom worked harder than I've ever seen anybody work in an advertising agency. He cancelled all his plans for the weekend and worked solidly from that moment until Monday when he presented his work to Neil. Tom looked broken.

Tom's punishment for his behaviour had been to feel what life is like in the farthest corner of *Stress.* However, he had complete control over everything but time – though he'd taken control of that to some degree by living in the office for the weekend. Tom's choice was to either suffer in *Stress* and do a bad job or take control using his own bloody-minded determination and get as far into *Flow* as possible.

Tuesday morning when Tom arrived at work, still tired and tail still squarely between his legs, he saw a memo (no email, remember?) in his in-tray. It was from Neil to Nigel Sharrocks, our Managing Director, and Roger Edwards, the agency Chairman. The memo described the herculean task Tom had been given, that Neil had not expected anybody could have achieved it to any reasonable degree of competence, but that Tom had not only done it but done it brilliantly, intelligently, and comprehensively right through the weekend. As Tom read it, he smiled, and holding back tears, he handed it to me.

Inside a week, Neil's *Tuning Up* management of Tom had seen him go from extreme *Stress* (bad client meeting) to *Non-stick* (bad behaviour) to *Stress* again (going to be fired), and then from *Stress* (the task) to *Flow* by trying really hard with this punishing project. But his punishment had given him unsupervised control in the way he did it and total responsibility for it – Tom saw for himself what he was capable of in *Flow*.

Conflict resolution – disagree, then commit

It's not unusual for areas of conflict to arise amid members of management, and while there's nothing wrong with good, healthy argument, there's a lot to consider about conflict resolution through the lens of responsibility and control. Many people can find conflict quite difficult. Although I relish a good debate, the stakes get higher when the two conflicted parties don't have a shared interest in the outcome. I'm far more at ease participating in an argument with somebody with whom I have a shared interest than I am with someone who doesn't. For the sake of preserving an ongoing relationship, we are all probably happier to compromise or capitulate when there's a shared interest than when there isn't.

However, often compromise can also be a course of abdication of responsibility by both parties. "*Let's meet in the middle*" is an arbitrary resolution. Why is the middle the right answer? Does it so often happen that a precise split is the optimal outcome? More likely it represents an outcome deemed fair rather than optimal. Instead, we should look at "if then" scenarios. *"If we do it your way (you have control), then you will have responsibility for the outcome."* And of course, the opposite is true. Whether consciously done or not, meeting in the middle is often a means of devolving responsibility. If the result of the compromise is suboptimal or even a failure, both get to claim it wasn't what they wanted; an argument made popular in the UK in recent years by the Brexit-voting public.

> "Meeting in the middle" is an arbitrary way of avoiding conflict and a means of devolving responsibility.

Taking a vote as a means of dispute resolution is a strategy frequently employed by those who would seek expedient resolution over agreeing a right or even most-right answer. But it also devolves responsibility between voters on the winning side and indeed all voters because "we agreed to have a vote". It is usually initiated by the likely victor, which to me is reason enough not to employ it. Business isn't democratic. Not all votes should be equal.

Should everyone on the board get a vote?

By way of example, in 2008, I was invited to be a patients' representative on the board of a London Hospital Network. This large committee comprised doctors, surgeons, and anaesthetists, a head of nursing, a head of IT, an estate manager, and a couple of other operational roles to a total of about 20. My role there was largely to observe and to offer the point of view of a member of the public if called upon to do so. However, I felt it my responsibility to assert some influence over the running of the meeting when a question being debated about a clinical issue was resolved to be put to a vote. I was both astonished and angry and said:

"I'm sorry to interrupt proceedings, but do I understand correctly that you want to resolve this issue by putting it to a vote of those around this table?"

The responses were both surprised and bemused that I'd interrupted at all, but they confirmed that this was exactly what they intended to do. I continued:

"In which case, I have a couple of questions for you. First, when did this board become a democracy, and where in its terms of reference does it state that one member one vote is a means of dispute resolution? Second, and with all due respect to the people gathered here who are not medically trained or qualified, why on earth would they have an equal say on an issue that is an entirely clinical question?"

To their credit, the chair of the meeting immediately understood my challenge, and rather than suggesting I mind my own business, they asked what I proposed they do instead. I replied,

"Argue. Bring forward new information. Consult other people, other hospitals. Don't just compromise or put it to a vote because it's easier; it's your responsibility to find the right answer, not the quickest one, isn't it?"

> Businesses and organisations are not democracies, not everybody should get a vote and votes are not all equal.

But to concede an argument when a debate has taken its course is not to devolve responsibility. There is control in the act of conceding. Again, from Richard Sutton's No Asshole Rule:

... enforcing a no asshole rule doesn't mean turning your organisation into a paradise for conflict-averse wimps ...

*The University of Michigan's Karl Weick advises, "Fight as if you are right; listen as if you are wrong." That is what Intel tries to teach through initial lectures, role playing, and, most essential, the ways in which managers and leaders fight. They teach people **how** to fight and **when** to fight. Their motto is "disagree and then commit".*

Crucially, within the ethos of constructive conflict, members of the same team have a shared interest. Their collective responsibility is for the betterment of the organisation and must supersede their egos. At a lower level it allows people to have an initial investment in their argument (responsibility) and to wrestle control (argument, debate, constructive conflict) but concede battles happily in the achievement of the shared goal.

"There is no limit to what can be accomplished if it doesn't matter who gets the credit."

Ralph Waldo Emerson - American Philosopher 1803 - 1882

Chapter Ten Summary

Managers are both givers and receivers of control but have broad ranging responsibilities to lead, coach, encourage, and develop people, but most of all to deliver their team's work.

In our imperfect world it is not uncommon for managers to have insufficient controls to precisely match their responsibilities. How managers manage, the way they manage and allocate responsibility and control in their teams, impacts how well they respond to day-to-day demands and these sometimes-imperfect conditions.

In the legacy management model, workers have minimal responsibility and minimal control – *Toil*. Managers have more responsibility and more control – *Flow*. This was always better suited to more limited value creation in production lines or limited-scope customer service and even so has been surpassed by "upside down management".

Upside Down Management sees the maximum possible responsibility and the maximum possible control allocated to the front-line people who are responsible for customer satisfaction and value creation.

The most effective managers will consider their own behaviour and their own modus operandi as variables – things that they can change to improve the value of the people for whom they are responsible.

The Results Only Work Environment (ROWE) represents a proven model for transference of responsibility and control to people and has repeatedly been shown to improve their engagement, productivity, and satisfaction and reduce absences.

Inflexible managers ("it's my way or the highway" types) position themselves in *Non-stick,* often forcing their delegates into *Stress.*

Good managers assume responsibility when things go wrong and provide their teams with "Shitstorm Umbrellas".

Managing multiple teams or disputes within large teams isn't a matter of representative democracy. Argument and debate focused on the shared responsibility of the group should be encouraged and enables a team to disagree and then commit.

Chapter Eleven
Tuning Up for leaders

"If your actions create a legacy that inspires others to dream more, learn more, do more, and become more, then you are an excellent leader."

Dolly Parton, singer, actress, author, businesswoman

I can't pretend to know everything there is to know about such a broad-reaching subject as leadership. There are many better books by other people on the subject. But I have experienced the responsibility and control of a leadership position in an agency, and I have applied the principles of the Meikle Matrix to good effect. My intention is to share those principles here in the hope that it can equally benefit other leaders.

Letting go of management

Before looking in more detail at what leadership is through the Meikle Matrix, it will be useful to examine what it isn't.

One of the biggest challenges for new leaders is to know when and how to stop being a manager. That doesn't mean never acting as a manager – leaders usually still have a team of managers to manage – but more to have the confidence in the team they build around them to delegate operational responsibility and control. In so doing, effective leaders free themselves to fulfil a more strategic role, thus leaving the operational parts of their previous position to others. Leaders will be there to support and advise of course, but they must let go, too, and more so than their managers have to let go to their own teams.

One trap that can draw leaders back to wanting to retake management control (and with it, knowingly or not, retaking management responsibility) is seeing other people operate differently to them. It's an almost universal truth of the human condition that we all believe the way we have always done things is the best way. Whether it is or not, purely by virtue of our having invested years in doing something one way, the belief persists. We tend to hold onto these beliefs for everything from running a company to the best way to fry an egg.

Leaders will often find their managers make judgements that they themselves wouldn't make. Their managers deal with problems in ways the leaders wouldn't themselves – and their managers may even do things better. That's not to say that many of the things their managers may do differently are wrong, they may just be different, and often the differences don't matter that much, if at all. But such is our investment in our own ways of doing things that leaders can quickly fall into the trap of imposing "their way" on their managers.

Make no mistake, when a leader sees somebody in management doing something wrong that matters, it is the leader's job to deal with it. But many things which can be tempting to the leader to control are not important enough or do not have a material consequence. In these situations, the key talent of the leader is to let go. Leaders will improve the value, the satisfaction, and the productivity of their managers if they leave them alone or, in some instances, encourage them to be left alone. We can call this act of not-doing negative capability.

Seemingly paradoxically, letting go does not mean losing touch. The best leaders will have a good understanding of what's going on in their organisations.

"Keep up the good work, whatever it is, whoever you are."

Responsibilities of leadership

One of the first responsibilities of leadership is to determine where the organisation is going, why it's going there, and how it's going to get there. Many leaders will compromise this responsibility by setting vague, intangible coordinates for the destination (so they can't tell if they've got there or not), matched with a strategy of "trying harder" to get there. Leaders with a clear vision and purpose, one to which every employee can contribute, will have more *Flow* employees, making for a more productive and successful organisation.

Providing employees with an authentic sense of purpose engenders a sense of responsibility in them, already moving them to the right-hand side of the Meikle Matrix into *Flow* or *Stress*. Then all they require is the appropriate control to match and they will have the conditions for peak performance.

It has been said that in the late sixties John F Kennedy was touring NASA after he had vowed the US would put a man on the moon before the end of the decade. On his tour, Kennedy met a janitor carrying a broom down a corridor. Kennedy casually asked the janitor what he did for NASA, to which he replied,

"I'm helping put a man on the moon."

Whether true or not, it's obvious who would derive more satisfaction from their work and apply themselves better to it between a) somebody whose job it is to keep floors clean and b) somebody whose job it is help put a man on the moon by keeping the floors clean. Combine that sense of purpose with the control to do our job properly and we have a work-force from top to bottom working in *Flow*.

> Combine a sense of purpose with the control to do our jobs properly and we have a workforce in *Flow* from top to bottom.

Creating the environment for success

As leaders, if we look after our people, they will reciprocate. It really is as simple as that. Looking after them has many facets when we use the lens of responsibility and control. In advertising more than marketing, a lot of what we might call "the basics" that help people at every level are often either not in place, not available, or unused – such as job descriptions.

If we look again at Marcus Buckingham's 12 questions (see Chapter Two) that indicate a strong workplace, number one on his list is "Do I *know what is expected of me at work?*" Agencies, in particular in my experience, are often poor at being specific about what is expected of different people in different roles, relying on some sort of osmosis or learning on the job. Yes, the roles in agencies are often varied and hard to define, but even to make that clear in a job description sets the expectation of employees to take control, take responsibility, and move into areas or do things with which they may not be entirely familiar. Importantly, an employee under these circumstances also needs to be assured of the company's duty of care, underlining that taking control and responsibility in unfamiliar areas does not just mean going out on a limb when circumstances might dictate.

Looking after our people shouldn't stop at fulfilling a duty of care to the lowest common denominator; it shouldn't be seen as an obligation but as an investment. It isn't always going to be clear how our investment is repaid, but it will be in many ways, through loyalty, discretionary effort, employer brand reputation, and day-to-day motivation. It's not only nice to be nice but it's also very good for business.

Aimee Luther is the Managing Director of a relatively young agency – The Liberty Guild. Whereas many agencies claim to be different, The Liberty Guild is established on a different model. From their website:

"We're not a "different kind of agency". We're not an agency. We're a Guild. An invitation-only curated association of the finest communication practitioners in the world. Every member is either an international-award-winner or outstanding in emerging fields. We deliver the very best strategic and creative solutions to Fortune 500 businesses on an 'on demand' basis."

The business recruits differently, uses office space differently, and it has a different approach to the way people in The Guild work:

"We're a Guild. An 'association of craftspeople grouped together for mutual aid and in pursuit of a common goal'. So, we nurture the talent and

ask them to nurture one another, enabling them to cultivate their passions, their side gigs, and their lives. Bringing balance. Because when they flourish, we all flourish, and our collective creativity is transformative."

One of the implications of this model is that The Liberty Guild has a large pool of essentially freelance talent for whom this balance represents the freedom to work more flexibly in terms of hours and geography. Other freelancers typically fight for themselves as sole traders with only themselves to look out for and nobody else looking out for them. But when the Covid-19 pandemic hit, one of the first things Aimee did was to ensure all the talent in the Guild had access to free private clinical psychotherapy during lockdown with HelloSelf, knowing that their mental health and stress may be headed quickly on a downward trajectory.

Mental health first aid

Hearts & Science Media agency is part of the Omnicom Media Group (OMG). Hearts & Science's Chief Experience Officer, Amy Matthews, is the UK co-chair of OMG Minds, the group's committee on mental health. Amy is also a Mental Health First-Aider, having completed a 2-day course by Mental Health First Aid England (MHFA).

"Everyone has mental health, as much as physical health. We all sit on continuums of both. Being able to spot when someone is struggling and providing support for our employees if they need it is fundamental to our duty of care as an employer.

In the workplace, mental health issues often manifest and can be confused with performance issues. Conversations about performance or mental health can be hard to start; people often worry about saying the wrong thing. However, they are crucial – more open conversations are key to working through and resolving mental health issues. This is where the MHFA's training has been invaluable, helping us learn how to spot the signs and giving us a clear framework to open conversations and provide further support."

Environments instilling accountability in leadership are important, too. Complaints procedures and whistle-blowing policies are essential to guarantee that people at every level will be heard. This is crucial when people find themselves in crisis, which – time and again – is caused by responsibility without control – *Stress*. Our responsibility as leaders is to provide our employees with the safe means to escalate issues and the procedures to get them from *Stress* to *Flow*.

At 35 years old, I was almost the youngest member of the management team I had built for Ogilvy Russia. I had needed to hire people older and far more experienced than me. It was clear that interviewing them was as much about them finding out about me as it was me about them. So, I provided some reassurance that I knew what I was doing by offering all members of the management team access to the agency's owner, Leonid, if a disagreement with me resulted in an impasse. Leonid was barely involved in the day-to-day business, but he remained available to me and the management team, and my accountability to the team was one of the reasons he made himself available to them, too.

The agency was growing fast at the time, the Russian economy was booming, but we were growing far faster than the market. Change was constant. Managing the business was like running down a hill, trying to ensure our feet kept up with our bodies. Some people and management needed little encouragement, whereas others needed reassurance to take initiative when it was needed. Creating an environment for success meant being available to support those who needed reassurance or guidance, having time to encourage and reward initiative, avoiding blamestorming if things went wrong, and constantly being clear about where responsibility and control lay.

My HR director, Vika, who I mentioned in the last chapter, provided an additional control for me to manage that environment by playing the role of my eyes and ears on the ground. Russian culture is highly deferential, with a strong sense of "us and them" between employees and management, and codes of silence when there are issues or mistakes. Vika and I could discuss how best to address problems or conflicts among people, and she was instrumental in helping people realise that they could count on fairness and impartiality if they were being mistreated by colleagues or management.

The times when I felt I could contribute most were ironically when I had least to do. Leaders who are in back-to-back meetings all day aren't available for walk-ins, but we managed to create a walk-in culture of openness such that support and advice was readily available in most instances. Time was one of the most effective controls I had, and I built a management team that afforded that to me.

A leader's responsibility for others' performance

The optimal functioning of the management team and the whole company can depend upon the adequate performance of certain individuals. Control freaks can create unworkable bottlenecks, damning themselves and the rest of the company to a life in *Stress*. Mavericks can often be found in *Flow* but have a tendency to slide into *Non-stick*. Mavericks are often popular in creative businesses – the quirky and cool creative director for example – but when they spend more than a few seconds in *Non-stick*, the leader needs to act. The consequence of anybody taking up residence in *Non-stick* is that at least one other person or a group of people is condemned to *Stress*.

In agencies there is often a reticence to deal with the ivory tower inhabitants of *Non-stick*, because *Non-stickers* usually believe they've earned the right to be there. *Non-stickers* will consider themselves either indispensable – or close enough to it – or forgiven for often unreasonable or petulant behaviour.

As a leader, there are two different routes we can take to deal with the *Non-sticker*. First, we can coach and encourage them to move to *Flow* – to take responsibility. Under any circumstances I can think of, this would be a sensible first step. Should that fail, we have two choices, first to manage the *Non-sticker* ourselves, to protect the rest of the team or certain individuals from falling into *Stress* by default, or to manage the *Non-sticker* out of the business. Pandering to a *Non-sticker*, managing their ego, and at the same time constantly firefighting to keep others out of *Stress* is not the best use of a leader's time. The good of the company must come before the needs of the *Non-stick* individual.

The damages caused by *Non-stickers* may not be apparent, but to name a few:

1. Good *Flowers* won't stick around or tolerate *Non-stickers* – they'll quit

2. We're left with companies of *Stressers*, leading to poorer productivity

3. The employer brand reputation is damaged, making it harder to replace the good people

To be blunt, most *Non-stickers* are thoroughbred assholes and need to go if they won't take the responsibility commensurate with their control.

It's all a work in progress

"Just because you are CEO, don't think you have landed. You must continually increase your learning, the way you think, and the way you approach the organization."

Indra Nooyi, former CEO PepsiCo

As leaders, to think we're the finished article is to assume that the future will be unchanged, and if 2020 taught us anything, we know that's not the case. We may have achieved a personal target, but that would be our personal responsibility, not our responsibility to the company. Rather than sliding into *Non-stick*, where we rest on our laurels, we must either redefine our goals and set about achieving them - or get out.

The best leaders will take the responsibility of continuous improvement both for themselves and for their organisations. I was once asked to assist in the performance appraisal of an exceptional leader as an external consultant. Their organisation's performance was outstanding – without question – as was their own performance. But when we reached the part of the appraisal about learning, they said there were no more training courses they could take; nothing their industry had to offer that they didn't already know. I suggested, *"Then perhaps you could learn from another industry and bring that learning into this one?"*

To suggest that we have nothing more to learn is so supremely arrogant and patently impossible that the appraisee immediately regretted what she'd said and reconsidered.

> Any leader who believes they are the finished article has, in so doing, perfectly demonstarted they are almost certainly not.

There's always more to learn, and by doing so we are increasing our knowledge and skills (control) so that we can increase our responsibility to do and achieve better.

Marketing leaders

On the face of it, leadership positions ought to naturally reside in *Flow*. As leaders we *should* have full control and ultimate responsibility because it is implied by the position, but it's not that straightforward. There are some more fortunate marketing leaders who have made it to *Flow*. For them, the job is to stay there and coach their management teams to get there and manage that way, too. But there are many leaders for whom there are still either constant battles for control that they must win to spend some time in, or stay in, *Flow*.

Marketing leaders can provide a good example of such a struggle. In any organisation of significant size, the lead marketer is not the same person as the company leader, to whom they report more often than not. In larger organisations, CMOs will most likely report to a management board, while often not being a member of it. Without a voice on the board for such a key organisational function as marketing, CMOs can therefore feel high responsibility without commensurate control – *Stress*.

As a leader, as head of a key department and its contribution, questions over subjects such as strategy, budget, and investment should be matters of asserting control rather than negotiating for it with their superiors. Marketing leaders should have earned their stripes with enough experience and judgement that afford them the trust of those to whom they report. Much of the time this is indeed the case, but how an organisation decides to respond to external influences, such as financial downturns or other unexpected crises, will show the true measure of their trust in the marketing leader.

Put another way, if a board of directors appoints a CMO, should we not question the board's competence to recruit if they cannot thereafter trust that CMO's judgement over their own?

Ironically, too often boards promise CMOs scope for bravery, change, and the sunlit uplands of total responsibility and control only to reel that control back in when they catch first sight of what real change looks like or in the face of the unexpected. We can derive two lessons from this recurrent behaviour.

The first is to predetermine the responsibility and control of the role. Much as I am critical of advertising agencies not defining their terms with their clients on taking a brief for descriptions, like "original" and "breakthrough", as a marketing leader, I would want to know the extent my authority (control) before accepting the role and its responsibilities.

The second is, regardless of whether that authority is granted, the way marketing leaders persuade their boards of their new ideas would benefit from the same kind of investment made by their agencies in presenting ideas. To think we don't need a proper presentation of ideas is bewildering. One-to-one relationships between marketing leaders and CEOs might be able to achieve higher levels of trust and efficiency such that the legendary "one pager" of strategy being sufficient for green lights, but most CEOs haven't been marketers themselves and the rest of the board almost certainly haven't. One of the key controls that marketing leaders need, therefore, is sufficient access to their stakeholders to allow them to make their cases for change or marketing investment properly. If the time isn't afforded in the board meetings to do this, then trying to have stakeholder meetings before, though laborious, would make the process better in the long run.

Cuts to marketing budgets are a common cause of stress and conflict.[48] When marketing leaders are forced to do things that they believe are wrong or simply not as good as they could be, there is a cascade effect as the instruction goes down the tiers of marketing to its agencies.

To elaborate:

Action 1) First instance, the board or CEO instructs the marketing leader to act contrary to the marketer's intention.

Outcome 1) The marketing leader has remained responsible for marketing performance but lost control – *Stress.*

---

48 We should note an exception here, which is a reality check for marketers and agency folk alike. In many businesses, not least the larger, publicly owned ones, rightly or wrongly, cash is king. Therefore, when the business experiences unforeseen dips in revenue, the cash must be found somewhere. While it can be the logical case that it shouldn't come from marketing investments, because it costs the company return on that investment, there are few budgets as sizable and flexible as marketing's.

Action 2) The marketing leader then must pass that mandate down to their department to execute the will of the board.

Outcome 2) In so doing, the marketing leader has reduced their team's control and forced their reports into *Stress*, too.

Action 3) In turn, the marketing department briefs their agencies.

Outcome 3) Which in turn loses control and moves to *Stress*.

At the end of the line, Action 4, which is also an outcome, involves either staying in *Stress* or abdicating responsibility through learned hopelessness that takes them to *Toil*. In this way, the toxicity of *Stress* creates a domino effect, forcing others in the work supply chain to become victims of it, too. And all the value and judgment of the marketing and agency teams diminishes from problem solvers – *Flow*, to stress puppies – *Stress*, to order takers – *Toil*.

Figure 25 – Domino effect in the Meikle Matrix

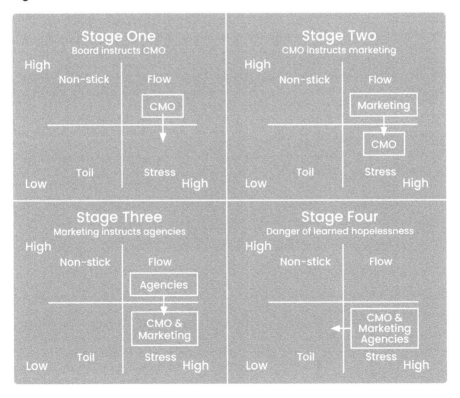

Leaders therefore must take responsibility for how they allocate responsibility and control to others to stop this domino effect of *Stress* diminishing their teams and their agencies' enthusiasm, productivity, and ultimately their value. The case study "Not music to my ears" in Chapter Five is a near perfect example of how this can happen. The stress caused to agencies is often the financial loss of budget cuts and finding themselves with a standing army.

Clients that take responsibility for the volatility of their budgets will agree minimum income guarantees with their agencies and have open conversations about the business imperatives than can force them to change course suddenly.

Agency leaders

In the high-energy and often chaotic world of agencies, promotion to leadership positions can be challenging. On the first day I assumed the role of Managing Director of Ogilvy Russia I was swamped by day-to-day operational issues that needed to be resolved and were being referred to me for decisions. In the afternoon there was literally a queue of people outside my office saying they needed answers or decisions. But as I got to grips with the company, with all good intention, I found myself problem solving and decision making, but the queue didn't go down, it grew. Again, a fan of the mixed metaphor, I'd spent my career plate spinning and firefighting – solving problems. Putting out fires can be rewarding and satisfying work; it makes us feel like we've done some good and accomplished something, like we're in control. But if I was to be effective in taking responsibility for the whole organisation, I also had to decide what NOT to do.

> Sometimes we have to let the plates fall to allow ourselves the bandwidth to create sustainable change.

I had heads of departments, but they weren't functioning as a management team and were often in the queue themselves, asking me to be arbiter of interdepartmental disputes. If I was to achieve meaningful change, I would need to delegate while knowing things would go wrong, so it felt that delegation itself was almost an act of wilful negligence of the responsibilities I had been fulfilling.

The key point here is that sacrifice is implicit in most organisational change. This has been illustrated time and again in sigmoid curves like the ones below (see Figure 26). The challenge for leaders is to recognise that the downward slope of the s-curve is not a dereliction of duty but more like the necessary sacrifice of a pawn to win the chess game. The manager's job is performance in the curve; the leader's job is the performance of multiple curves of change and innovation.

When Richard Morris took on the leadership of the media agency Initiative in 2017, he needed to navigate such a change and did so successfully by rebuilding a leadership team around a shared vision.

Growing Initiative

In 2017, UK media agency, Initiative, was a shadow of its former self. Once proudly listing General Motors, Tesco, and Unilever as clients, it had had a few difficult years. There was nothing wrong with its people, culture, or client service, it had just lost confidence and a competitive edge. Plus, new business was, as ever, fiercely contested, and helping clients grow through media and advertising is increasingly technical and complex.

Morris wrote:

"The opportunity to lead Initiative was one I couldn't miss. While some commentators were cynical, I saw the potential and I had the support of its parent, IPG.

I'd been in leadership roles for the previous five years, and hard-learned lessons during that time framed my approach to leading Initiative: vision, structure, trust, measurable goals, and a focus on people and clients.

We set a vision to grow our clients' brands by helping them take the initiative in culture. We believed the key to growth in a world of a million messages was brand relevance, and this required an intimate understanding of the cultures that bind groups of people together.

Internally, we set an ambition to double the size of the agency within three years. So, to deliver the vision and the ambition, we needed to restructure the agency around capabilities in strategy, insight, and analytics. This meant hiring new talent and reorientating the leadership team towards these skills.

A combination of old and new, each with clearly defined roles and responsibilities, we set about creating the conditions to make the leadership a high-performing team. Taking much from Patrick Lencioni's 'The Five Dysfunctions of Teams', we built a foundation of trust, allowing us to have conflict in the room without fear, sharpening our standards, our product, and our ambition. Crucially, we instilled belief in the wider agency that their leadership could attain the growth ambitions we had shared.

We gave people the freedom to succeed in ways they wanted to [control], guided by a few clear Key Performance Indicators (KPIs) [responsibilities]. Specifically, the KPIs were monthly people motivation, and quarterly client satisfaction measures. We believed a highly motivated agency would delight clients, which, in turn, would grow our business. This 'freedom in a framework' approach gave our leaders the latitude to take initiatives so long as they delighted their clients and motivated their people. We consistently achieved both KPIs. It wasn't always easy, but our commitment to these ideas, and our openness to feedback, pushed us forward to achieve what we set out to do.

We became one of the UK's fastest growing agencies, adding M&G, LEGO, Carlsberg, LV=, Converse, and Deliveroo to our client list. We won a Lion in Cannes and doubled the agency's size in revenue and headcount almost a year ahead of target."

Figure 26 – Sigmoid curves of change progressions

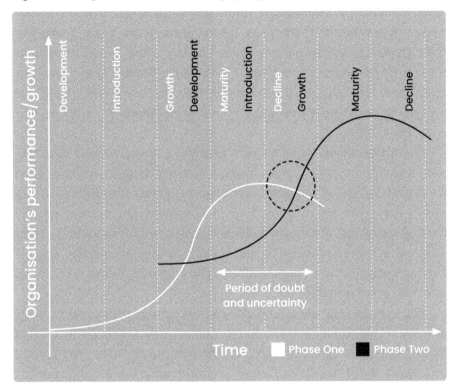

The Phase One curve represents the initial organisation; Phase Two represents the changed organisation. There is no limit to the number of phases, and leadership itself will change over the course of an organisation's life.

Leadership can be lonely, and no more so than at the point in which organisational performance seems to wane before Phase Two picks it up. This transition point will feel most like Stress. The burden of responsibility is not only in the company's performance declining but also in feeling the weight of its future performance not yet having been proven. There is much within the leader's control but more that feels like it isn't, particularly in not knowing how existing clients, prospective clients, and employees will respond to the changes.

Open and honest communication with these three groups of stakeholders is essential and must include the vision for the future and the purpose of the change. But, much like the cobbler's shoeless children, agencies have the intelligence and skills to manage their own businesses better than they often do. Agency leaders can apply strategy to their growth plans the same way they advise their clients to manage their own brands: map the agency market, identify those similarly sized agencies with similar service offerings, and run a full competitive analysis to identify their meaningful points of difference. In my experience, they seldom do.

As an intermediary, I find that genuine and meaningful differentiation in the creative agency market is something I routinely must do myself as part of the selection process. Rarely are differentiating agency propositions presented to me credibly and persuasively by creative agencies. Media agencies are easier to differentiate by their different business models, buying models, and proficiencies, but for any marketing services organisations, the employer brand is the most powerful point of difference.

The way leaders attract, retain, and develop talent should be their primary responsibility and within their control. By creating the place in which the best talent wants to work, the rest mostly looks after itself if we employ the principles of *Tuning Up*. Leaders can build a management team that releases them from the day-to-day operational responsibilities, and they therefore build a broader team of high-performing people capable of delivering the best possible value to their clients. Having gained the power and responsibility of a leadership position, the best thing to do is hand it all out to others.

The Master doesn't talk, he acts.
When his work is done,
The people say, "Amazing:
We did it, all by ourselves!"

Lao-Tzu c. 500 B.C. Tao Te Ching
A new English Version, Stephen Mitchell

Leaders who organise their people according to their needs, their proficiencies, their desires, and ambitions and with commensurate responsibility and control will build successful organisations of motivated and empowered teams of tremendous people.

Chapter Eleven Summary

The first step for new leaders is to recognise that their responsibilities may be elevated, but they must also let go of the management controls they are used to. Managers working for leaders will do things differently, and mostly they do not represent existential threats! Let go.

While the day-to-day controls of leaders will usually be far removed from the front line of work, effective leaders will stay close enough to the day-to-day operations and to observe responsibility and commensurate control at all levels first-hand.

It is the leader's responsibility to define the overriding responsibilities for the organisation – to define their purpose and reason for being. In this way, employees at every level can have a higher sense of responsibility and purpose – a requirement for *Flow*.

This responsibility, this higher sense of purpose, also provides the environment in which controls can be more confidently delegated.

Taking discretionary additional responsibility for the welfare of our organisation's people, looking out for those who may have fallen into *Stress,* and helping them find their way to *Flow* is not only morally the right thing to do, but it's also good for business.

Leaders have to be vigilant to spot *Non-stickers* because they are likely to leave *Stressers* in their wake. *Non-stickers* are also often damaging to the employer brand and staff morale – they are rarely worth their trouble and need to be either managed into *Flow* or out of the organisation.

Leaders can be in danger of sliding into *Non-stick* themselves and must have the humility to recognise they will never be the finished article and nor will their organisation.

Non-stick leadership forces the next level into *Stress,* which then cascades through management and supply chains, causing damage and/or increasing risk.

To mitigate the danger of slipping to *Non-stick,* leaders should build management teams of talented, challenging, and candid individuals who are unafraid to question them or challenge them.

Leaders must be capable of leading through the choppy periods of change, holding their nerve, and helping everyone else hold theirs. But those who organise their people according to their needs, abilities, proficiencies, desires, and ambitions and allocate the commensurate responsibility and control to them will build successful organisations of motivated and empowered teams of tremendous people.

Postscript

My mother is the middle of three sisters. The youngest, my late aunt Holly – and indisputably the joker of the three – once told my mother a story of two elderly women driving along a road one afternoon.

The first lady, Mavis, notices her friend Mabel just drove through a red light. Alarmed, but still calm, Mavis thought to herself,

It's probably a one-off, maybe it only just turned red. I'll let it go.

Shortly afterwards, Mabel drove straight through a second red light. This time, it was definitely on red. Alarmed, but outwardly calm, Mavis thought to herself:

Wow, OK, that's really not good. But it was probably just an honest mistake and I don't want to upset Mabel, so I won't say anything for now.

Until, just then, they went through a third red.

"Mabel!" Mavis cried, "*Did you not see we've just gone through THREE red lights in a row?*"

Mabel turned to Mavis.

"Oh ..." she calmly replied, "*... am I driving?*"

So, what has *Tuning Up* got to do with Mabel and my aunt Holly's indefensibly politically incorrect joke? Quite simply, and whether we know it or not, *we're all driving*. And it can be surprisingly easy to forget what control we have.

The ideas in *Tuning Up* were born from an insight derived from extreme stress, which is the direct result of having insufficient control to match our responsibilities. I am yet to find a single circumstance where this does not hold true. Most cases that might seem anomalous either haven't properly identified the responsibility or the control.

We might have ceded control to somebody else to whom we have become a passenger, but we can almost always take that control back. To stretch the metaphor, we might have taken responsibility to drive somebody else, but if they're a distracting or unpleasant passenger, we can decrease that responsibility. It won't always be the case; there will be times when we will be stressed and times when we will have the freedom of *Non-stick*, but most of the time we should have responsibility and control in commensurate measure, putting us in *Flow* – or in *Toil* when we simply have to do our chores. Instigating and managing our movement between these quadrants can be essential to our mental health and to help us perform at our best.

If we can't adjust our responsibility and control on one level, we can escalate or deescalate them until they match. Often this won't be done for us so, crucially, if we find ourselves at work in a perpetual state of responsibility without control that we cannot escape, then we need to seek help. Nobody deserves to be miserable in their work, nobody deserves to feel despondent and unhappy or stressed all the time, yet throughout my career, I have seen very many I would describe as exactly that. Satisfaction or even happiness and work are not mutually exclusive, and stress and misery are not rites of passage through which we must travel to progress in our careers.

When we consider complex operations that run efficiently and smoothly, everybody in them knows exactly who is in control of what and who is responsible for what. Some are precise and prescriptive to repeat procedures at speed, such as Formula One pit crews – others must deal with unpredictability, like surgical theatre staff, but in each of these scenarios, on a team level, there is a clear shared interest. This shared interest is the responsibility of the team – the controls are then distributed according to individual roles and proficiencies. Other organisations can have more fluid structures, but to be effective they will also have cultures, principles, values, and behaviours designed to get them all into *Flow*; but they aren't always the only influences to affect us, so we must keep our responsibility and control antennae handy, even when things are going well, and always be ready to *Tune Up* if necessary.

There may be times when the interests of the team and our own interests are not aligned. Sometimes, it's only for a short or specific period when priorities might change for a team or organization; other times, we'll see that they are irreconcilable. If they are irreconcilable, it's time to escalate and take responsibility for ourselves and the control to match.

It's wise not to rush to use the Meikle Matrix, but to think it through and take some time. Particularly in long-standing and established relationships with which we may have been struggling for a time, if we suddenly step outside the relationship and examine it and scrutinise it with the other party, instead of just working within it, it can be too much of a rug-pull. This is about improving relationships, not breaking them.

There may be times, too, when the Meikle Matrix won't work – when more control can't be negotiated. However, such circumstances are rare, and even understanding when we're in such circumstances can make them easier to handle. Sometimes, we have no choice but to try to pitch a tent in a hurricane, and if we do, all we can do is to try hard and do our best.

Managing an epiphany (if you have one)

Stress can be the canary in the coalmine that indicates the need to *Tune Up*. But when we first recognise the stress we might be under, a natural response might be anger and/or righteous indignation. We must be careful not to respond harshly and righteously, as this is surely the route to assholedom – not least because we have to be careful that we're not trading on any wrong assumptions. There can often be more to it than meets the eye about why we find ourselves in *Stress*, and when we haven't been in *Stress* for long, this is even more the case. Remember Hanlon's Razor – it's unlikely we've been put into *Stress* out of spite or malice.

We must try to be objective and look at our position from all angles. Challenge ourselves and any assumptions we're making about the control we have or think we don't have.

We must be clear about what we want to achieve. It should be about getting to *Flow*, not about winning or satisfying some need for revenge against injustice.

We must check for the cascade of stress. It might be that the person or people putting us in *Stress* are in *Stress* themselves. How can we help them help us?

Remember, we almost always have a choice, and crucially – when we find ourselves without the controls commensurate with our responsibility – we can sometimes negotiate our controls up or our responsibilities down. Or we can escalate the level to one where we have control and choose to be responsible for ourselves first.

And we can protect ourselves by choosing what we can be responsible for by managing our "fucks budget", i.e., the number and calibre of fucks we have to give – just without being an asshole about it.

> We must not fight every battle and must not expect
> to win every battle we choose to fight.

Next, the tips to help us thrive

Thriving is about finding our *Flow*. Getting into the place where we can perform to our best and finding that place for others. That's when work doesn't feel like something we want to avoid but something we want to embrace and enjoy, and the same goes for those around us.

Use *Tuning Up* and the Meikle Matrix constructively, forgive what might seem like sins of the past; this is about the future. Start with what those in the relationship have in common. What is our shared interest, our common objective or endeavour, upon which we can build mutual understanding of our responsibility and control?

We must allow others time to self-correct if we can. Try to lead them to find the right answer themselves rather than forcing answers on to them. If we can co-create new ways of working then it will build longer lasting and stronger relationships.

When we're fixing a situation and we get what we want, we must remain humble and just enjoy the *Flow*. It can be difficult for somebody to learn that they held more control than they ought or to have it made clear that they're a control freak. They'll come to terms with that learning experience their own way and most likely won't benefit from us rubbing it in.

Finally, once we've overcome the causes of *Stress* and found ourselves in *Flow*, we must help the next people find theirs, too.

Acknowledgements

Now I understand the concept of the "difficult second album". But assisted as I was by the Covid-19 lockdown and thereby an imposed sabbatical of sorts, it was thankfully quicker to write *Tuning Up* than I had feared – although painful at times, nonetheless. Much like my first book, *Tuning Up* wasn't only contributed to by those people involved directly in its development and production, but also and significantly by those from whom I have learnt so much along the way that brought me to this point. Of all of them, my greatest thanks must go to an anonymous doctor who worked for BUPA in 2001 in Canary Wharf and changed my outlook on stress forever and unwittingly provided the keystone thought for *Tuning Up*.

Second, I must express my gratitude to my first-round readers and advisors, none of whom have anything to do with advertising or marketing. My mother (the single research subject in the *can-I-explain-this-to-my-mum* test and an excellent proofreader), my brother Andrew Meikle for an experienced and wise management perspective, and especially to Ezra Meikle, (performing the does-a-recent-1st-in-English-graduate-representing-an-entire-generation-get-it? test). Your patience, enthusiasm, encouragement, and contributions were invaluable. Ez, you're a super star, thank you.

Though they have been recognised before, contributors to the development of the Meikle Matrix model must also be sincerely thanked again, in particular Rory Sutherland, Nick Ford, and my good friend Antonis Kocheilas.

My second-round readers, tyre-kickers, and reviewers whose wisdom and support I gratefully received and who have not been mentioned already: Jenny Biggam, Robin Bonn, Kate Broughton, Jamie Elliott, Dame Annette King, DBE, Diana Tickell, and Garrett O'Reilly.

Also, other authors who have contributed directly and indirectly: Marcus Buckingham, Mihaly Csikszentmihalyi, Alain De Botton, Carsten de Dreu, Blair Enns, Jed Hallam, Chris Hirst, Sarah Knight, Charlie Mackesy, Adam Morgan, Dan Pink, Cali Ressler, Luke Sullivan, Richard Sutton, John Timpson, Jody Thompson.

My gratitude for quotes, soundbites, stories, case studies, contributions, book recommendations, and general enthusiasm: John Aylward, Alberto Brandolini, Paul Burns, Rob Colbourn, Ed Commander, Edward L. Deci, Murray Douglas, Sam Drake, Holly Enderlin, Jamison Firestone, Alex Fraser, Michael Frankenburg, Ricky Gervais, Jon Goulding, Roderick C. Hare, Paul Harvey, Ben Hayes, Sue Higgs, Neil Jenner, Tom Lewis, Gustav Lundblad, Aimee Luther, Vicky Madden, Pete Markey, Amy Matthews, Craig Mazin, Daniel Meikle, David Metherell, Mel McMillan, Martin Moran, Richard Morris, Jonathan Newton, Indra Nooyi, Eaon Pritchard, Susi Raymakers, Melissa Robertson, Jack Rooney, Phil Rumbol, Nick Schon, Kate Standen, Andrew Stephens, Jonathan Stirling, Harvey Tate, Claire Van den Bosch, Robin Wight, Alice Wu, Vika Yakushkina and of course Leonid Shutov, whose faith in me to run his business in Moscow provided my greatest case study for the principles herein and an almost endless source of dinner party stories.

I must thank my friend Fan Carter for suggesting I use a writing strategy (a means of *controlling* yourself, your environment, and your schedule to ensure it is conducive to your *responsibility* to write. During the lockdown, that meant writing in the morning and gardening in the afternoon). Fan's sage advice made my difficult second album far less difficult.

Most of all, I must thank my lockdown companions who endured my physical company and often absent mind while writing this during the Covid-19 lockdown and beyond – my wife Olga and my son Daniel. Without their support, faith, and patience, I would not have been able to write *Tuning Up*.

Acknowledgements

www.ingramcontent.com/pod-product-compliance
Ingram Content Group UK Ltd.
Pitfield, Milton Keynes, MK11 3LW, UK
UKHW020044130325

456179UK00005B/19

* 9 7 8 1 7 3 9 4 6 3 7 1 7 *